Becoming Indigenous

Becoming Indigenous

Governing Imaginaries
in the Anthropocene

David Chandler and Julian Reid

ROWMAN & LITTLEFIELD
INTERNATIONAL
London • New York

Published by Rowman & Littlefield International, Ltd.
6 Tinworth Street, London, SE11 5AL, UK
www.rowmaninternational.com

Rowman & Littlefield International Ltd. is an affiliate of Rowman & Littlefield
4501 Forbes Boulevard, Suite 200, Lanham, Maryland 20706, USA
With additional offices in Boulder, New York, Toronto (Canada), and Plymouth (UK)
www.rowman.com

British Library Cataloguing in Publication Data
A catalogue record for this book is available from the British Library

ISBN: HB 978-1-78660-571-9
PB 978-1-78660-572-6

Library of Congress Cataloging-in-Publication Data Available

ISBN: 978-1-78660-571-9 (cloth : alk. paper)
ISBN: 978-1-78660-572-6 (pbk. : alk. paper)
ISBN: 978-1-78660-573-3 (electronic)

∞™ The paper used in this publication meets the minimum requirements of
American National Standard for Information Sciences—Permanence of Paper
for Printed Library Materials, ANSI/NISO Z39.48-1992.

Contents

Acknowledgements

This book would not have been possible without the many discussions we've had with various colleagues and the support of several institutions in the field.

David Chandler would like to thank coauthor, Julian Reid, University of Lapland, for the invitation to take part in the Kone Foundation/Finnish Academy project *Indigeneity in Waiting* (2016–2020), which enabled a range of international workshop and conference presentations; Marjo Lindroth and Heidi Sinevaara-Niskanen, University of Lapland, who were a vital influence, especially in the early stages, with their workshop at the Centre for the Study of Democracy, University of Westminster, in February 2016; Paulina Tambakaki, University of Westminster, for insights, suggestions and support throughout the writing process; and Olivia Rutazibwa, University of Portsmouth, Pol Bargués-Pedreny, Barcelona Centre for International Affairs, Angela Last, University of Leicester, and Doerthe Rosenow, Oxford Brookes University, for their inspiring work in bringing decolonial thought into relation with the Anthropocene.

Julian Reid would like to thank his colleagues at the University of Lapland, especially Marjo Lindroth and Heidi Sinevaara-Niskanen with whom he has collaborated on the project, *Indigeneity in Waiting* (2016–2020). Great thanks are owed to the Kone Foundation and the Finnish Academy for funding this particular research project and from which these ideas grew. Samuli Hurri and the Problematizations research team and their seminar series in the Faculty of Law at the University of Lapland have also been a great source of support toward the end of the book-writing process. The students he has taught and learnt from in master's courses in the International Relations program at the University of Lapland, *The Postcolonial Politics of Indigeneity* and *The International Relations of the Anthropocene*, have also provided much provocation to thought.

Opportunities to present these ideas in their early formulation at various other institutions were gratefully received and acted upon. Thanks to Michael Basseler at the University of Giessen in Germany for the invitation to keynote the Indigeneities conference in 2016, and to Magdalena Kmak for the invite to keynote the ETMU conference at the Åbo Akademi University in Turku, Finland, in 2018. Special thanks are owed to colleagues at Virginia Tech in the United States where Julian Reid spent time in 2017 as a research fellow. In particular, Jim Bohland at the Global Forum in Virginia Tech was a very warm and generous host as well as interlocutor. Geoffrey Whitehall at Acadia University in Canada was also a wonderful host in 2016 when testing out the thesis there. Other places where the ideas in this book were tried out include the University of Helsinki in Finland, Hamburg University in Germany, and the University of Copenhagen in Denmark. Thanks to those colleagues who engaged me there.

Most of all, Julian would like to thank Kirsi whose love and support means so much, and Miro and Kosma whose being is every day a source of such great inspiration. To Lumi, whose arrival as the book reached its completion, he gives all his thanks, for making the future fuller than could otherwise be imagined.

Early versions of some of the ideas presented here can be found in journals and book publications including the following:

David Chandler, 'The Transvaluation of Critique in the Anthropocene', *Global Society* 33:1 (2019).
David Chandler, 'Resilience and the End(s) of the Politics of Adaptation', *Resilience: International Politics, Practices and Discourses* 7:3 (2019).
David Chandler and Julian Reid, '"Being in Being": Contesting the Ontopolitics of Indigeneity Today', *The European Legacy* 23:3 (2018).
Julian Reid, 'Narrating Indigeneity in the Arctic: The Script of Disaster Resilience versus The Poetics of Autonomy' in Nikolas Selheim, Yuliya Zaika and Ilan Kelman (eds.), *Arctic Triumph: Northern Innovation and Persistence* (Springer, 2019).
Julian Reid, 'The Cliché of Resilience: Governing Indigeneity in the Arctic', *Arena Journal* 51/52 (2018).

Preface

This book is a stand-alone text but the problems it addresses and the arguments it makes are linked directly to those which we developed in our book, *The Neoliberal Subject: Resilience, Adaptation and Vulnerability* (Rowman & Littlefield, 2016). This book can be read as a development of the themes of *The Neoliberal Subject*, which provides the basics of the theoretical framework for approaching neoliberalism as a regime of power and its contemporary dependence on discourses of resilience and adaptation. It is this framing that we deploy in this book to problematize discourses on indigeneity, a field of research which was not tackled in *The Neoliberal Subject* and which itself indicates a shift in the neoliberal framings of crisis and self-responsibility.

The reader of both these texts will notice that the structure of this second book is different to the first, which centred on a discussion between the two of us, seeking to clarify an approach to contemporary liberal imaginaries of the human and its governance. In this second book we believe we have taken the analysis further and the result is a more synthetic approach. This, we hope, combines the different elements of our critique of neoliberalism and approach to the limits and potentials of the modern in the development of our joint theorization of the human project.

Chapter 1

Introduction

Becoming Indigenous

The arguments of different indigenous people based on spiritual relationships to the universe, to the landscape and to stones, rocks, insects and other things, seen and unseen, have been difficult arguments for Western systems of knowledge to deal with or accept. These arguments give a partial indication of the different world views and alternative ways of coming to know, and of being, which still endure within the indigenous world. . . . It is one of the few parts of ourselves which the West cannot decipher, cannot understand and cannot control . . . yet.

—(Linda Tuhiwai Smith, 1999)[1]

INTRODUCTION

This book is a critical engagement with the demand that we 'become indigenous' in order to cope with and adapt to the new conditions of the Anthropocene. In the chapters that follow we seek to establish a ground for this engagement through highlighting new approaches which construct what we analyse as the 'ontopolitics of indigeneity'. In our reading, indigeneity is increasingly becoming a crucial marker for imagining new modes of living and governing in our contemporary condition of climate crises and economic uncertainty. Indigeneity, as a form of ontopolitical imaginary, is not about fixed, essentialising or racialising definitions or understandings but rather is constructed as a speculative way of knowing and being: a way of knowing and being which is seen to be necessary if humanity is to survive and cope with the catastrophe of the Anthropocene. 'Becoming indigenous' is thereby not a matter of choice or of altruism; it is not, in itself, even directly a matter of solidarity with the struggles of indigenous peoples and communities. Becoming indigenous is a project of governing the imaginary of what it means to be an agent or actor in a world, which is held to demand new forms of adaptivity, resourcefulness and resilience.

A key concern for this project is the charting of the transformation of discourses of indigenous ways of being and knowing in the contemporary period of the Anthropocene. We very consciously and directly link these two aspects—the re-evaluation of indigenous knowledge and what is declared to be a new planetary epoch—because they share a new ontopolitical imaginary: a new set of grounding assumptions, which reshape and redistribute our perspectives on what knowledge is and how governance can operate. Key to both is the assertion that the culture/nature divide, so central to the modern episteme, no longer holds in the Anthropocene. Thus knowledge can no longer be understood as deriving from an objective understanding of a singular and universal external world, open to direction and control through the sciences of natural laws and processes. At the same time, governance can no longer operate on the assumption that policy areas can be separated and seen to work in linear and reductive terms of cause and effect.

To be clear, this book is a critique of Western academic and policy discourses that advocate the need to 'become indigenous'. We think that this demand is problematic, and this book is our attempt to explicate the growing consensus around it. Something is suspect. There is something strangely reassuring and unchallenging about the call to become indigenous. We can remember very different discourses of indigeneity: discourses of concern and of care, of trauma, of disease and dispossession, of the need to redress historic injustices, to overcome colonial dependencies, to demand opportunities for fuller participation and better social outcomes for indigenous peoples. These discourses were unsettling for Western readers. Also unsettling and controversial were discourses on the need for different research methods when dealing with indigenous concerns and for respect for alternative approaches to epistemology (see for example the path-breaking work of Linda Tuhiwai Smith, *Decolonizing Methodologies*, first published in 1999 [2012]). When Smith's work was published twenty years ago there was no close relationship between the Western academy and indigenous peoples; 'research' was 'one of the dirtiest words in the indigenous world's vocabulary . . . a process that exploits indigenous peoples, their culture, their knowledge and their resources' (Smith, 2012: xi). Today all this appears to have changed.

Today, if there is a problem, it is the one that Zoe Todd has raised on a number of occasions (Davis and Todd, 2017; Todd, 2015, 2016): indigenous thought has been appropriated by the Western academy, but in the process homogenised and inserted into Euro-Western academic discourses of resilience, the Anthropocene, actor network theory and object-oriented and speculative thinking, with hardly any concern for engaging contemporary indigenous scholars and thinkers (2016). The Western academy seemingly cannot get enough of indigenous thinking and approaches. However, as Todd argues, even if there is a nod to indigenous intellectual and political influences or vague mentions of collaboration, indigenous people are rarely considered 'as thinkers in their own right' rather than 'just disembodied representatives of an amorphous Indigeneity that serves European intellectual or political purposes' and very few indigenous voices are allowed to enter the academy (2016).

There is, she rightly argues, a huge disconnect between the use of indigenous approaches and any apparent concern or even interest in the real struggles of indigenous peoples and the ongoing reality of exclusion and the denial of rights. The hypocrisy would in any other circumstances surely be remarkable:

> to turn around and use Indigenous cosmologies and knowledge systems in a so-called new intellectual 'turn', all the while ignoring the contemporary realities of Indigenous peoples vis-à-vis colonial nation-states, or the many Indigenous thinkers who are themselves writing about these issues? And is it intellectually or ethically responsible or honest to pretend that European bodies do not still oppress Indigenous ones throughout the world? (Todd, 2016: 15–16)

We cannot but agree. In short, we suspect that the rise to prominence of what are seen to be 'indigenous' forms of thinking and acting has less to do with a progressive struggle of resistance to hegemonic forms of oppression and exploitation than with a new consensus on the need to adapt to perceived natural limits and constraints beyond human control. For us, the new forms of governing purporting to support, encourage and to draw from indigenous thought and practice are far too closely linked to contemporary philosophical and political trends in academic thought that equally seek to downplay the powers of human agency and the importance of political forms of subjectivity for transformative struggles and strategies. While leading international and domestic political institutions repeat mantras of resilience and adaptation, suborning human agency to the whims of market forces and 'natural' disasters, articulating the seeming stranglehold of neoliberal thinking (Chandler and Reid, 2016), leading critical academic voices, from feminist and scientifically informed theorists like Donna Haraway and Anna Tsing to popular social and political philosophers like Bruno Latour and Timothy Morton, seek to diminish the human and celebrate non-human agency instead.

This introductory chapter seeks to lay out the broad perspective of this book in four sections. Each section seeks to clarify key conceptions, which will be further developed in the book. The following section analyses the recolonisation of indigeneity in critical Western thought, based on the assumption that the Anthropocene removes the distinction between coloniser and colonised. The second section considers the limited nature of the critique of modernity informed by the assumption that new speculative and imaginary approaches are required rather than struggles grounded in modern territorial politics. The third section engages with the grounding of a demand to 'return' to indigeneity in ontopolitical assumptions which contrapose colonial modernity as whiteness with the futural analytics of indigeneity. The closing section introduces the chapters that follow.

THE (RE)COLONISATION OF INDIGENEITY

Indigenous knowledge is held out as attractive to Western academics and international institutions today, not on account of any precise content, but due to its proclaimed adaptivity and amenability to ever variable and changing conditions. As the United Nations Educational, Scientific and Cultural Organization states:

> The knowledge of indigenous peoples is not a static body of 'traditional' information. Indigenous peoples have always been confronted with environmental variability, unpredictability and change. Their knowledge is thus a dynamic system that is collectively and continuously re-visited, re-shaped and shared across a web of social actors. It maintains its adaptive capacity and vitality. (United Nations Educational, Scientific and Cultural Organization, 2017: 25)

The adaptive capacity of indigenous knowledge, often explicitly aligned with methods of coping with environmental crises and uncertainty, has seemingly captured the critical imaginations of philosophers as well as policy-makers (see Agrawal, 1995, 2002). So much so that Bruno Latour, one of the leading contemporary theorists of the Anthropocene, argues that humanity needs now to abandon modernity as a bad and worn-out idea and shift its investments to the project of becoming indigenous instead (2018: 102). The Anthropocene, framed in terms not just of catastrophic disruption to the Western way of life but the debunking of Western ideas, means that indigenous knowledge offers a crucial way forward. Those who thought they were modern have 'no choice but to become experts on the question of how to survive conquest, extermination [and] land grabs' (ibid.: 7). In which case, the Anthropocene can be seen as a great leveller, enabling settler colonial societies to return to or recover their capacity to access their own potential indigeneity and to learn how to cope with climate catastrophe from the very peoples they colonised. In order to enable this return, indigenous people become a necessary means to be put at the West's disposal. Four centuries of dispossession and oppression have meant that indigenous peoples now, at last, have something apart from land and resources of interest to policy advocates of Western power:

> Here is something that adds an unexpected meaning to the term 'postcolonial', as though there were a family resemblance between two feelings of loss: 'You have lost your territory? We have taken it from you? Well, you should know that we are in the process of losing it in turn. . . .' And thus, bizarrely, in the absence of a sense of fraternity that would be indecent, something like a new bond is displacing the classic conflict: 'How have you managed to resist and survive? It would be good if we too could learn this from you.' Following the questions comes a muffled, ironic response: 'Welcome to the club!' (Latour, 2018a: 7–8)

The ability to cope with the experience of loss and dispossession, and to learn humility from doing so, is now an asset desired by contemporary Western advocates. As Latour notes, this desire has nothing to do with 'a sense of fraternity' nor has it to do with any restorative move of righting past wrongs. It is the 'indigenous' knowledge of coping on the edge of crisis, of survival and adaptation, in the face of the threat of extinction, learnt by indigenous peoples on account of the violence of settler colonialism, which theorists like Latour now want to extract from them.[2] For Latour, what we are conceptualising as 'becoming indigenous' is phrased in the terminology of becoming 'Terrestrial' or becoming 'Earthbound', which he counterposes to the approach of 'Moderns' to knowledge and to policy governance (Latour, 1993, 2010, 2013). Indigenous knowledge, for Latour, is now available to give Western societies a 'second chance' (2018a: 106), beyond modernist governmental imaginaries of nationalism or globalism: 'For the Terrestrial is bound to the earth and to land, but it is also a way of worlding, in that it aligns with no borders, transcends all identities' (2018a: 54). Governance, in fact, is seen as breaking down into the crude binary of just two approaches: the modernist, white, Western one—based on the freedom of extraction within which governance is conceived in terms of command and control—responsible for causing environmental catastrophe[3]; and the new and necessary futuristic imaginary, alleged to be 'indigenous', and based upon a recognition of our dependency on nonhuman actors and relations, which can enable humanity to cope with and to survive our contemporary crisis.[4]

Key to the demand for indigenous knowledge, to ground and inform new approaches to governance, is the naming of this new geological era: the Anthropocene. The Anthropocene—a concept coined by Eugene Stormer in the

1980s and popularised by Paul Crutzen in the 2000s (Crutzen, 2002; Crutzen and Steffen, 2003; Crutzen and Stoermer, 2000)—refers to a new geological epoch[5] in which human activity is seen to have profound and irreparable effects on the environment.[6] This attention to a new epoch in which humanity appears to have impacted the earth in ways which mean that natural processes can no longer be separated from historical, social, economic and political effects has powerfully challenged the modernist understanding of the nature/culture divide, separating social and natural science, destabilising the assumptions of both.

We are told that nature can no longer be understood as operating on fixed or natural laws, while politics and culture can no longer be understood as operating in a separate sphere of autonomy and freedom. These assumptions, in both spheres, were central to modernist constructions of progress, which are now seen to no longer exist or to have always been problematic (Bonneuil and Fressoz, 2016; Clark, 2010; Haraway, 2015; Latour, 2014; Macfarlane, 2016; Proctor, 2013; Swyngedouw, 2011). Jeremy Davies (2016: 5) argues that 'The idea of the Anthropocene makes this state of being in between epochs the starting point for political thinking'. This starting point is, we are told, grounded on the fact that the Anthropocene, as our contemporary condition, forces a closure of modernist assumptions of progress. Like it or not, humanity needs to live within new nature-imposed boundaries. We are no longer separate from or dominant over our natural environment.

Thus, the division between agential 'man' and passive 'nature' is fundamentally challenged, with catastrophic events which seemed to be exceptional or highly improbable in the past becoming increasingly regular, even in the advanced West: 'in the era of global warming, nothing is really far away; there is no place where the orderly expectations of bourgeois life hold unchallenged sway' (Ghosh, 2016: 26). As Amitav Ghosh notes, expectations of normality, balance and order that defined the modern world view appear from today's vantage point to be a terrible error or hubris: as rationalism carried to the point of 'great derangement' (ibid.: 36). There is now a contemporary consensus that: 'There can be no more talk of a linear and inexorable progress' (Bonneuil and Fressoz, 2016: 21). Today human history cannot be understood as separate to geological history:

> The Anthropocene, as the reunion of human (historical) time and Earth (geological) time, between human agency and nonhuman agency, gives the lie to this—temporal, ontological, epistemological and institutional—great divide between nature and society. . . . It signals the return of the *Earth* into a *world* that Western industrial modernity on the whole represented to itself as above the earthly foundation. (Bonneuil and Fressoz, 2016: 32–33, emphasis in original)

Natural time is no longer somehow slow in comparison to the speed of human or cultural time. 'What is sure is that glaciers appear to slide quicker, ice to melt faster, species to disappear at a greater speed, than the slow, gigantic, majestic, inertial pace of politics, consciousness and sensibilities' (Latour, 2013: 129). Nature or the 'environment' is no longer to be seen as merely the 'background', but is itself a 'protagonist' upon the stage of action (Ghosh, 2016: 6). As Latour states, the positions are reversed, the background becomes foreground: 'what was until now a mere décor for human history is becoming the principal actor' (2013: 4). So much so that it could be said that the Anthropocene does not just overcome the culture/nature divide, 'it bypasses it entirely' (ibid.: 78):

> everything that was part of the background has now melted into the foreground. There is no environment any more, and thus no longer a need for environmentalism. We are post-natural for good. With the end of the political epistemology of the past that insured the presence of an indisputable outside arbiter—namely, Nature known by Science—*we are left without a land and without a body politic*. (Latour, 2013: 125, emphasis added)

We emphasise Latour's assertion that 'we are left without a land and without a body politic' to stress the grounding of the contemporary demand to 'become indigenous' in a claim to a universal condition of dispossession. Latour is not alone in arguing that, in the Anthropocene, we should realise that we are all now apparently 'indigenous' because we are all, apparently, dispossessed. It should be noted that this 'becoming indigenous' is based on an imaginary of loss, where the Anthropocene is seen as cutting humanity adrift from traditional frameworks of meaning and from territorial and historical belonging. These tropes of loss, already central to the critical theory of the Frankfurt School, in their disillusionment with modernist technical and bureaucratic modes of being (Adorno and Horkheimer, 1997) are magnified in contemporary critical sensitivities to the alienating speed of digital and technological change, causing 'the breakdown of inherited territorial immunities . . . heritages, cultures and social structures' (Stiegler, 2018: 111; see also Sloterdijk, 2013: 74–75).

According to Mario Blaser and Marisol de la Cadena: 'This is a new condition: now the colonisers are as threatened as the worlds they displaced and destroyed when they took over what they called terra nullis' (2018: 3). For Deborah Danowski and Eduardo Viveiros de Castro, the Anthropocene may be a new condition for Moderns or Europeans but it is not for indigenous people who 'have something to teach us when it comes to apocalypses, losses of world, demographic catastrophes, and ends of History' because 'for the native people of the Americas, the end of the world already happened—five centuries ago' with the arrival of European colonialism (2017: 104). Now, in the Anthropocene, we all need to face up to catastrophe and the loss of 'world'. No longer can we rely upon the certainties and fixed meanings provided by modernist constructions of the separation of humanity from nature. More than this, we are told that we need to face up to the fact that it was modernist approaches that caused the destruction we are facing:

> Let the reader imagine herself watching—or rather, acting in—a sci-fi B movie in which the Earth is taken over by an alien race pretending to be humans, whose goal is to dominate the planet and to extract all its resources, after having used its home planet to the full. . . . And now let the reader imagine that this *has already happened*, and that the alien race is, in fact 'we ourselves'. . . . suppose a small shift in sensibility has suddenly made that self-colonization visible to us. We would thus all be indigenous, that is Terrans, invaded by Europeans, that is Humans; all of us, of course, including Europeans, who were after all the first Terrans to be invaded. (Danowski and Viveiros de Castro 2017: 108)

This 'small shift in sensibility' for Danowski and Viveiros de Castro is 'a *becoming-indigenous*', in fact, 'a *rebecoming indigenous*', and is, they argue, not only 'perfectly possible—more than that it is actually taking place' as struggles against resource extractivism and for rights for the environment reveal (2017: 122). The ease with which it is possible to 'become indigenous' is also highlighted by Timothy Morton, the speculative realist and object-oriented ontology philosopher described by *The Guardian* newspaper as 'the philosopher prophet of the Anthropocene' (Blasdel, 2017). In his 2017 book *Humankind*, which he dedicates to the indigenous peoples–led movement to prevent the Dakota Access Pipeline, he signs up to the growing consensus arguing that Western people are less modern than is traditionally assumed. In fact, the claim to indigeneity does not necessarily involve colonial or any type of dispossession at all. We were all supposedly 'indigenous' before the great 'severing' of modernity provided 'a foundational, traumatic fissure' in the Moderns' existence, separating their understanding of themselves from that of their immersion in the natural world, as the Enlightenment severed human-nonhuman relations (2017: 16).

AN UNCRITICAL CRITIQUE

Why do these popular and widely cited Western academics argue that it is necessary for everyone to become indigenous? We believe that the simple answer is partially provided by Morton himself:

destructuring Western philosophy to include nonhumans in a meaningful way starts to look, from within culturalism, like appropriating non-Western cultures, and in particular the cultures of First Peoples, indigenous people . . . what this looks like to some is doing the unforgiveable, gauche, hippie thing of dressing up like a Native American . . . [object-oriented ontology] has been subjected precisely to this criticism, that it is appropriating indigenous cultures. . . . It is as if white Western thought is required to remain white, Western and patriarchal in order to provide an easy-to-identify target. (Morton, 2017: 11–12)

Contemporary critical and radical theorists stand widely accused of cultural appropriation of indigenous approaches and of excluding or downplaying the contributions of indigenous thought to contemporary understandings (Danowski and Viveiros de Castro, 2017; Davis and Todd, 2017; Todd, 2015). Thus it is partly out of defensiveness that Morton and other theorists seek to deny the specificity of the experience of indigenous dispossession and partly, we assume, the desire to advocate a new imaginary of governance, drawing upon alternative or 'non-modern' framings to articulate a 'second chance' for survival in the Anthropocene.

If Western publics are to become 'indigenous' and to be governed under the signs of resilience and adaptation, then, of course, a precondition is that the imagined gap between Moderns and the seemingly very different 'Earthbound' or 'Terran' modes of being is capable of being bridged.[7] It is little wonder that Morton is forced to brashly claim that 'humans never actually severed their indigeneity' (Morton, 2017: 118). Apparently the Anthropocene reveals that Western subjects were as much the victims of modernity, caught up in a 'Stockholm syndrome' imaginary, as those excluded from modernity (ibid.: 118). And, of course, with the help of the indigenous and their fellow-travellers and interpreters in the academy: 'It's not even difficult to find that indigeneity again' (ibid.: 118–19).

Thus, for the advocates of 'becoming indigenous', the debate, as much as there is one, about the Anthropocene could be seen to be shifting away from a discussion about the existence of the Anthropocene itself, and more about whether 'modernity' itself as a framework of knowing and governing ever actually existed. Latour has famously argued that 'We Have Never Been Modern' (1993), whereas for other theorists modernity is seriously challenged by the appearance of the Anthropocene or the 'intrusion of Gaia' (Morton, 2013: 19; Ghosh, 2016; Stengers, 2015). The key point is that the Anthropocene is understood to pose fundamentally different questions about how we can live without the certainties and signposts of modernity.

We believe that merely to accuse leading Western academics and theorists of opportunism and cultural appropriation would miss the underlying dynamic behind the demand to 'become indigenous' as a solution to the problems of the Anthropocene. If there is to be a flight from modernity, why should this lead to a 'return' to indigeneity? Perhaps it could be argued that the flight to indigeneity or the inculcation to become indigenous is a useful framing, enabling a substantial lowering of policy-horizons to merely surviving or coping in the present. What is particularly attractive about this framing of the rolling back of aspirations is that it can be legitimised and rationalised on the basis that retrenchment is actually a more 'authentic', more 'natural', more 'organic', more 'community'-oriented, more 'caring' approach, than the consumerist, extractivist, individualist, competitive approach of modernist demands for progress and ever higher living standards. All those promises of a better future, which were given lip service by elites when there was competition between the alternatives of Left and Right, are seemingly now off the table in the times of coping, crises and constraint of the Anthropocene.

It could be that the demand to become indigenous is also a useful framing to dismiss calls for dreams and images of the security and empowerment of the human and instead to demand community- and self-responsibility under the aegis of resilience. One thing that critical Anthropocene theorists seem to agree on is that there can be no technical fixes. Modernist aspirations to secure the human against the world are held to be precisely the problem that needs to be overcome (for example, Hamilton, 2017). It is precisely because the Anthropocene is ontopolitically constructed as a critique of modernist discourses of what it means for humans to achieve empowerment and security that there can be no 'faith in technofixes, whether secular or religious' (Haraway, 2015: 3). No pretence of geoengineering solutions 'which will ensure that it is possible to continue to extract and burn, without the temperature rising' (Stengers, 2015: 8).[8] And no possibility of fixed relations capable of regulation in the imaginary of 'spaceship Earth' (Latour, 2013: 66). The idea of a humanist or modernist solution, positing the idea of a 'good Anthropocene' (for example, Revkin, 2014) is anathema to those who seek to argue that the Anthropocene is 'after the world of modernity'. As Claire Colebrook states: 'Any "good" Anthropocene would be possible only by way of countless injustices' (2017: 18). Thus the modernist perspective is dismissed as the 'managerial variant' of the Anthropocene, where the concept could potentially be captured and 'become the official philosophy of a new technocratic and market-oriented geopower' (Bonneuil and Fressoz, 2016: xiii):

> Whereas it should mean a call to humility, the Anthropocene is summoned in support of a planetary hubris . . . [exemplified by] the Breakthrough Institute, an eco-modernist think-tank that celebrates the death of nature and preaches a 'good anthropocene', one in which advanced technology will save the planet . . . sentiments characteristic of early infancy, lie at the basis of such 'post-

nature' discourse, participating in the dream of total absorption of nature into the commercial technosphere of contemporary capitalism. (Bonneuil and Fressoz, 2016: 86)

While, for Bonneuil and Fressoz, eco-modernism smacks of 'early infancy', Clive Hamilton argues that this view of welcoming the Anthropocene epoch with imaginaries of geoengineering is 'reminiscent of Brian's song on the cross at the end of *Monty Python's Life of Brian*' (2015: 41; see also Hamilton, 2013). For others, such as Richard Grusin, the imaginary of the 'heroic agency of geoengineering' is merely another failed attempt to impose 'many of the same masculinist and human-centred solutions that have created the problems in the first place' (2017: ix). Simon Dalby (2017) asserts that any attempt to problem-solve in the manner of 'contemporary earth system science syntheses of the human transformation of the biosphere . . . [with its] assumption of separation as the starting point for governing a supposedly external realm is now simply untenable'.

In response to this closure and reversal of the dreams of modernisation, it seems that the future can only be secured on the basis of non-developmental approaches and indigenous knowledge can appear as crucial to enabling new possibilities, held to be inherent in existing communal forms of living and socio-technological forms of interconnectivity and networked community, building on new ways of making connections and seeing relationships (for example, Gibson-Graham and Roelvink, 2010). It is this need for a fluid awareness of relations in their specific and momentary context that has enabled the re-evaluation and transvaluation of indigenous ways of being and knowing. For Anthropocene epistemologies and ontologies, the actual existing reality contains much more possibility and potential than has been traditionally recognised by policy-makers and academics (for example, Grosz, 2011: 77, 183; Sharp, 2011). Thus the task is that of engaging more imaginatively, indeed speculatively, with the constantly emerging present, alert to the fact that these relationships need to become a matter of care, attention and opportunity.[9]

Perhaps emblematic of this shift is Anna Lowenhaupt Tsing's book, *The Mushroom at the End of the World: On the Possibility of Life in Capitalist Ruins* (2015). Her starting assumption is the end of the modernist dream of human progress, based on the division between humanity and nature: 'Without Man and Nature, all creatures can come back to life, and men and women can express themselves without the strictures of a parochially imagined rationality' (2015: vii). The importance of the book as an exemplar of the affirmation of the Anthropocene is that it self-consciously does not set out to be 'a critique of the dreams of modernization and progress', but rather to think past their end; to take up the 'imaginative challenge of living without those handrails, which once made us think we knew, collectively, where we were going' (ibid.: 2). The Anthropocene thus enables us to think 'after failure', 'after progress', 'after the end of the world'.

For Tsing, living with the end of modernist dreams of progress need not be a negative experience. Rather, we can come to realise that modernity itself was a barrier to living fuller lives. Our assumptions of progress, the idea that striving harder would lead to collective betterment, now seem no more emancipatory than religious promises of justice in the afterlife. Precarious and contingent life in modernity's 'ruins' can be empowering and creative, full of new possibilities which modernity foreclosed. As Tsing states: 'Progress is a forward march, drawing other kinds of time into its rhythms. Without that driving beat, we might notice other temporal patterns . . . agnostic about where we are going, we might look for what has been ignored because it never fit the time line of progress' (ibid.: 21). Her work, therefore, is constructed as a progressive work of enablement, allowing the reader to make the transition from mourning modernity to embracing its demise:

> I find myself surrounded by patchiness, that is, a mosaic of open-ended assemblages of entangled ways of life, with each further opening into a mosaic of temporal rhythms and spatial arcs. I argue that only an appreciation of current precarity as an earthwide condition allows us to notice this—the situation of the world. As long as authoritative analysis requires assumptions of growth, experts don't see the heterogeneity of space and time, even when it is obvious to ordinary participants and observers. . . . To appreciate the patchy unpredictability associated with our current condition, we need to reopen our imaginations. (Tsing, 2015: 4–5)

For the advocates of becoming indigenous, reopening our speculative imaginations enables the Anthropocene to be grasped as a world that is fuller, more lively and more entangled than the soulless, simplified and atomised world of modernity. As Quentin Meillassoux argues, the Anthropocene welcomes us to the 'great outdoors' (2008: 50), what speculatively exists rather than what exists in the stunted 'reality' of modernity. As Tsing suggests: 'Precarity means not being able to plan. But it also stimulates noticing, as one works with what is available' (2015: 278). In fact, the Anthropocene is serendipity itself, enabling us to develop just the sensitivities and new ways of speculative thinking and experimenting that we need to adapt to our new condition:

> What if, as I'm suggesting, precarity *is* the condition of our time—or, to put it another way, what if our time is ripe for sensing precarity? What if precarity, indeterminacy, and what we imagine as trivial are the centre of the systematicity we seek? (Tsing, 2015: 20)

Becoming indigenous recasts coping with precarity in a positive light. In the ruins of modernity there is more life than could possibly have been imagined by those subjects that were once convinced of their separation from the world. Our realisation that we can no longer go on in old, modernist ways enables us to appreciate indigenous thought and practices rather than fear the Anthropocene condition. Realising our precarious condition brings us back to the world: the Anthropocene is like an unseen force, imposing a new sociability and new set of sensitivities on the basis that we are no longer separate, no longer in control, no longer not interested in other actors and agencies with which we cohabit. The Anthropocene, for some theorists, is thereby less a world of doom and gloom and extinction than an invitation to speculatively explore other ways of being and knowing: in other words, to become indigenous.

In this approach of exploration and openness there is, of course, one out-look or approach that is unacceptable if we wish to become indigenous: the aspirational approach seeking to cash in on the promises of modernity. Governing discourses of progress and higher living standards are thus recast as craven consumptionism, dependent on the destruction of the environment and on the exclusion and degradation of non-Western modes of being. If becoming indigenous opens up new modes of being, in tune with natural constraints, then the problem is the recalcitrant, selfish and ignorant demands of the over-entitled and over-privileged denizens of the West: in other words, those who refuse the demand to 'become indigenous'. These destroyers of the world remain stuck in the narrow mind-set of modernity, putting their own needs and aspirations above all else. In the imaginary of this so-called indigenous or Earthbound alternative, attuned to the Anthropocene, the enemy becomes ontologised and a new form of ontopolitics emerges. As we discuss in the following section, the enemy of becoming indigenous is not corporatism, not colonialism, not even capitalism, or extractivism itself, but 'whiteness'. Just as indigeneity is a mode of being open to all enlightened enough to choose this second 'Enlightenment' after the closure of modernity, 'whiteness' is a mode of being or rather becoming, away from indigeneity, toward destruction and planetary barbarism.

THE NEW ONTOPOLITICAL DIVIDE

Ontopolitics is a key concept for this book, as the ontological assumptions of the Anthropocene are seen to necessitate new ways of being and new modes of knowledge and governance. Whereas for moderns, politics tended to mean transcending our existences as merely natural beings and achieving security from forces of nature, for the no-longer-modern beings of the Anthropocene the situation is reversed and it is the natural world itself that must shape and direct our politics by alerting us to the impossibilities of transcending our status as natural beings, dependent on the finite resources of the world which we inhabit. A new set of ontopolitical assumptions, as we have already seen, are beginning to inform contemporary social and political thought and are thus bringing indigenous ways of knowing and being from the margins to the centre of contemporary thinking.

As Jason Moore has illustrated, one of the key problems, for those who believe in material progress as the key to human betterment, has been that capitalism did not just exploit unpaid labour power but also the productive power of nonhuman labour. Thus, for Moore, it is not only that, as Marx noted, there is a tendency of the rate of profit to fall but there is also a tendency for the rate of 'ecological surplus' to fall,[10] with the depletion of energy and mineral resources (2015: 226). The drive to overcome boundaries to the appropriation of 'cheap nature' as well as 'cheap labour' gave capitalism a productive dynamic not based purely on the invisibility of human labour of unpaid reproduction (highlighted by feminist scholars, for example, Silvia Federici [2012] but also on the invisibility of nonhuman labour and resources (an invisibility which is now all too visible). What was seen to be the expansion of progress and human potential can be read as actually the extractive machine of capitalism ceaselessly seeking new untapped resources to exploit 'on the cheap'. This form of organising nature has now reached its limits, ironically because of the resistance of nonhuman 'nature' rather than a rebellion of humanity (see Read, 2017).

Perhaps an obvious analogy could be made with how the struggles of the warring kingdoms of Westeros, in the *Game of Thrones* television series, begin to pale into insignificance in comparison to the looming collective threat posed by the coming of winter and the White Walkers. Like the coming of winter, entry into the epoch of the Anthropocene is held to displace the modernist framework and context of political contestation. Modernist politics assumed that the 'is' of the world would look after itself, that is, that nature or the environment was just the backdrop or the stage for the great struggles between Left and Right. Today the positions seem to be reversed, as winter/ the Anthropocene is seen to push the politics of Left and Right from the foreground to the background (for Michel Serres, the 'subjective wars' between men are displaced by the consciousness of the 'objective war' being waged against nature [1995]).

This shift fundamentally alters the nature of politics and governance. Politics is no longer 'all about us', in the sense of what we might think a just or equitable world might be, and instead 'all about the world itself'. Stengers captures this nicely in her view that, while the problems of the Anthropocene may be caused by the coupling of the material processes of capitalism and geological forces of nature, the brutal intrusion of the planet or Gaia means that 'Struggling against Gaia makes no sense: it is a matter of learning to compose with her' (2015: 53). Stengers emphasises that '*there is no choice*' (ibid.: 58). This entails

> cutting the link . . . established [in the nineteenth century] between emancipation and what I would call an 'epic' version of materialism, a version that tends to substitute the tale of a conquest of nature by human labor for the fable of Man 'created to have dominion over the earth'. It is a seductive conceptual trick but one that bets on the earth available for this dominion or conquest. Naming Gaia is therefore to abandon the link between emancipation and epic conquest, indeed even between emancipation and most of the significations that, since the nine-teenth century, have been attached to what was baptized progress. (Stengers, 2015: 58)

As Amitav Ghosh asserts, the concept of human freedom that developed with the Enlightenment is held to disappear in the Anthropocene, as it is realised that humankind can never shed its dependence or transcend its constraints (2016: 119). For Bonneuil and Fressoz: 'the Anthropocene challenges the definition of freedom, long conceived in opposition to nature. . . . A freedom understood in this way sets human emancipation against nature, against the Earth as a whole' (2016: 40). Sara Nelson and Bruce Braun similarly argue that we are forced to accept that ideas of human autonomy and human freedom can no longer be credible today, 'if the Anthropocene represents the farcical realization of human autonomy in the form of planetary devastation' (2017: 233).

If the end of 'freedom' is to be recast as the demand for 'becoming indigenous', then freedom itself is recast as a privilege that is no longer justifiable: as a problem of 'whiteness'. Of course, whiteness is not an essentialist or racial category itself (although its ways of knowing and being are often essentialising and racialising). As Ruha Benjamin writes:

> Vampirically, white vitality feeds on black demise—from the extraction of (re)productive slave labor to build the nation's wealth to the ongoing erection of prison complexes to resuscitate rural economies—in these ways and many more, white life and black death are inextricable. (Benjamin, 2018: 41)

As Benjamin clearly states, what sounds like a fixed racial divide in fact seeks to 'denaturalise' white framings of race, not to make race disappear as a 'social construct' but to intensify the meanings associated with race, 'to denaturalise without dematerialising it, and to simultaneously attend to materiality without fixing race' (2018: 59). Whiteness, like indigeneity, thus becomes ontological: it's not about skin colour but something much deeper: a mode of being (see also Gabay, 2018: 9–22). In Donna Haraway's terms, it is a 'worlding practice premised on the commitment to endless growth and vastly unequal well being' (2018: 71–72). Whiteness has brought the world and the environment to its knees; whiteness is thereby nothing less than a genocidal mode of being:

> Its machine tools were and remain racially differentiated, human exceptionalist, heteronormative, biogenetic, compulsory family formation and reproduction. Middle-class white reproducing families: the American Dream. Expendable populations of colour everywhere: The American nightmare, including Population Bombs. (Haraway, 2018: 73)

As leading indigenous scholar and advocate Kim Tallbear argues: 'white bodies and white families in spaces of safety have been propagated in intimate co-constitution with the culling of black, red, and brown bodies and the wastelanding of their spaces' (Tallbear, 2018: 147). Paulla Ebron and Anna Tsing, in their review of feminist theory and the Anthropocene argue that the 'American Dream' of productivism and extractivism during the Cold War was based upon an ideology of 'whiteness as entitlement', enabling the imaginary of 'white families in protected enclaves' to export the environmental costs of their consumerism (2017: 671–72). In the new awareness that there is no 'outside'—no separation between humanity and the environment—then we all have to learn how to become indigenous: how to move beyond 'whiteness':

> To learn from the leadership of the Indigenous people, people of all backgrounds will have to adopt imaginative forms and social practices other than Cold War protected enclaves. To preserve even fragments of the Holocene ecologies that sustained life on earth for the last twelve thousand years, we will have to develop forms of kinship that limit Anthropocene aspirations. (Ebron and Tsing, 2017: 676)

Perhaps at the cutting edge of the curbing of 'white' unchecked privilege and of the demand to 'become indigenous' is the refashioning of population control as a practice of accepting and normalising 'natural' limits to the demands of production and consumption. For some contemporary radical feminist theorists 'becoming indigenous' is directly related to the re-education of 'whiteness' as entitlement, emphasised no more powerfully than in the critique of the traditional feminist demand for personal control over reproductive rights. White people stand accused of not doing responsible kin-making but irresponsibly making babies. Whiteness is thereby constructed as an atomised and alienated mode of being, which enables the world to be imagined from the standpoint of an autonomous individual subject with the world as merely its object or resource. Whiteness consumes and reproduces without any awareness or consciousness of limits, other than as barriers to be overcome. For Michelle Murphy:

> What reproductive justice politics can grapple with rich, white, settler colonial, heteronormative reproduction, of baby-making with expensive strollers assembled in supply chain capitalist webs, of fossil-fuel guzzling SUVs fed through pipelines, of oil turned into plastic toys destined for landfills and then microplastic gyres, of white property relations with empty rooms, of grocery stores stocked with the bright goods of multi-national corporations, and all the many forms of white possession and enablement? Reproduction here is not just the baby. Webs of relations and distributions of violence make possible the smooth life of abundant choice. (Murphy, 2018: 109)

Interestingly, when it comes to re-education for the Anthropocene, the solution to 'whiteness' is hardly ever 'blackness', as a mode of being, but nearly always indigeneity. Key to the displacement of blackness by indigeneity may be the fact that indigeneity can be constructed as existing outside and independently of contestations over inclusion and exclusion within modernist modes of being (Coulthard, 2014; Simpson, 2014, 2017). In contemporary constructions, indigeneity is often abstracted from specific struggles and contestations over rights and responsibilities and instead becomes an alternative way of being in and relating to the world, one which does not reproduce the problems of modernist anthropocentrism. Indeed, African American whiteness studies literatures are argued to be lacking this necessary vantage point and thereby also in need of 'becoming indigenous' (Moreton-Robinson, 2015: xix).

The ontopolitical imaginary of indigeneity is less concerned with contributing to existing struggles against white supremacy or other racialised structures, with discourses of equality or inclusion, or with liberal or modernist rights struggles, but with learning ways of becoming responsible and adaptive: ways of coping in the Anthropocene. It is therefore increasingly indigenous struggles and practices that are drawn upon as a way of articulating the ontopolitical imaginary of the Anthropocene. For example, for Donna Haraway: 'it is impossible to imagine serious opposition to today's Plantationocene and Capitalocene without aligning with the struggles and reworlding formations led by Indigenous peoples' (2018: 82). Indigeneity, as far as it is discursively treated with regard to new forms of governance, is not a naturalised or essentialised attribute of colour or ethnicity. Indigeneity is ontological: that is, indigeneity is much deeper than merely skin colour or

ethnicity but at the same time it is malleable in the way that racial essentialism is not. In the Anthropocene, as we have discussed previously, it is held
to be not only possible but, indeed, necessary, for everybody, including white
settler oppressors, to 'become indigenous'. We have not come across any
similar discursive framings regarding blackness.

A clue to how this could be possible is provided by Kim Tallbear, whose
work in this area has been exemplary. In her book *Native American DNA*
(2013) she traces how black populations as slave labour were expanded:
that one drop of black blood enabled the categorisation as black but that indigenous blood had no effect on categorisations of whiteness. As Tuck and
Yang note, blackness was *expansive* and indigeneity was *subtractive* (2012:
12). Indigenous people were assumed to be capable of becoming white in US
and Canadian constructions of nation-building. Colonial institutions 'that included residential schools, churches and missions were all designed to "save
the man and kill the Indian"' (Tallbear, 2018: 147). As Tallbear highlights:
'That is the odd nature of red as a race category in the United States. In ef-
forts to reduce numbers of Indigenous peoples and free up land for settlement,
red people were viewed as capable of being whitened' (2018: 147). Today
that process of racial ambiguity would appear to be operating in reverse. As
Tallbear notes (2013) in the United States, self-identification as indigenous
has risen 650 per cent between 1960 and 2000.

Bruno Latour, Timothy Morton and other leading theorists of the Anthropocene are not alone in their claim that 'becoming indigenous' is a return to
a more 'authentic' or 'grounded' form of being. The exact same narrative
had already been rehearsed in the US settler appropriation of indigeneity as a
similar 'second chance' move to innocence, as Tuck and Yang note, enabling
a national narrative that could 'reconcile settler guilt and complicity, and
rescue settler futurity' (2012: 3). They relate one highly relevant experience,
worth citing in full, for it highlights exactly the unease, which we have, regarding the demand to 'become indigenous':

> Recently in a symposium on the significance of Liberal Arts education in the
> United States, Eve [Tuck] presented an argument that Liberal Arts education
> has historically excluded any attention to or analysis of settler colonialism.
> This, Eve posited, makes Liberal Arts education complicit in the project of
> settler colonialism and, more so, has rendered the truer project of Liberal Arts
> education something like trying to make the settler indigenous to the land he
> occupies. The attendees were titillated by this idea, nodding and murmuring in
> approval and it was then that Eve realised that she was trying to say something
> incommensurable with what they expected her to say. She was completely
> misunderstood. Many in the audience heard this observation: that the work of
> Liberal Arts education is in part to teach settlers to be indigenous, as something

admirable, worthwhile, something wholesome, not as a problematic point of evidence about the reach of settler colonial erasure. (2012: 8)

While we are more than sympathetic to the goals of Tuck and Yang in problematising white desire to 'become indigenous', the 'easy adoption of decolonisation as a metaphor' and their highlighting of the dangers of 'the ways in which white people maintained and (re)produced white privilege in self-defined anti-racist settings' (2012: 9) our concern in the chapters that follow is to challenge the discursive framing at the heart of this process of the white (re)colonisation of indigeneity as a resource to buttress a retreat from human aspirations toward security, development and progress.

THE CONTENTS OF THIS BOOK

The six chapters and short conclusion that follow outline the problematic assimilation of an imaginary of indigeneity into Western discourses of knowledge and governance. Chapter 2, 'Dispossession', details how indigeneity is currently constructed as emanating not only from the experience of dispossession in the historical past, but as a way of being in the world grounded positively in dispossession, and which in being so offers itself as an antagonistic alternative to Western ways of being, grounded aggressively as they are in possessiveness, of land, of self and of others. In this chapter we argue that the opposite is actually true: that the present condition is one of being governed by regimes of power, the strategy of which depends on the production of dispossessed and non-possessive subjects. The task is to reject these discourses of entrapment and reclaim possession for ourselves. In doing so, much can yet be learned from minor traditions of thought and practice among indigenous peoples, both mythic and real, which, in contrast to today's dominant discourses on indigeneity, insist on the integral importance of possession as a foundation for political subjectivity. Whether indigenous or non-indigenous, the task is the same, we argue: to avoid being trapped by power, learn instead to hunt power, and cultivate the ultimate freedoms of autonomy and self-possession.

In 'Speculative Analytics', chapter 3, we engage with the development of what we are calling 'ontopolitical anthropology', the anthropological production of a certain imaginary of indigeneity, which rather than challenging the view of separate and distinct 'cultures' seeks to draw out from the ethnographic experience an alternative methodology able to reveal the speculative possibility of 'different worlds'. It focusses upon how discourses of the Anthropocene are seen to transform the temporality of indigenous analytics, articulating them as necessary for constructing alternative speculative futures and establishing indigenous knowledge in a 'symmetrical' framing, of equal standing to the modernist episteme. It closes by raising some problems with the approach of ontopolitical anthropology, in particular the way that it can be seen to reify or 'exoticise' indigenous thought and practices or, as we state, 'ontologise indigeneity'.

Chapter 4, 'Perseverance', outlines the problematic nature of current discourses on 'indigenous perseverance'. As an attribute, perseverance is asserted not only by indigenous peoples themselves but also by Western scholars of indigeneity. However, it is a colonial concept and perseverance has been attributed to indigenous peoples by Western observers since the very first colonial encounters with indigenous peoples by settlers dating back to the origins of the colonial project. Today the resurgence of the discourse on indigenous perseverance can only be understood in the context of a much wider valorisation of perseverance, among right-wing pyschologists concerned with convincing their readership that anybody can become a chief executive officer of a major corporation, as well as by leftists writing for the downtrodden 99 per cent who have already given up hope of being able to 'make it' under existing socioeconomic conditions and want to believe in another world beyond capitalism. It is also celebrated within radical political and social theory. It plays into epistemological shifts within critique that aim at dehumanising critique, promoting the ways of nonhuman living species, particularly plants, as the model on which to reshape human subjectivity. In this context we argue that the whole discourse of perseverance, whether in its application to indigenous peoples, or to other peoples, should be rejected.

We analyse the deployment of indigenous knowledge in pluriversal approaches in chapter 5, 'Pluriversal Politics', highlighting the influence of cybernetic constructions of embodied difference, underpinning some anthropological approaches, from which pluriversality draws. Drawing on analogous framings of object-oriented theorising, we argue that if 'becoming indigenous' involves the ontological imaginary of a 'pluriverse' of worlds side by side, without an external God's eye view, the problem becomes that of knowledge itself rather than that of a particular claim to reality. Drawing on the work of Eduardo Kohn, Anna Tsing and others, we highlight that if knowing cannot be separated from our embedded embodied being in the world, knowing can only be adaptive rather than representational. Knowledge rather than being liberating would then only serve to affirm and to reify that which already exists. The aspiration to dissolve the subject into its context—to reduce knowing to the self-awareness of our being—is therefore, we argue, a dangerous and problematic one.

In chapter 6, 'Resilience', we provide an overview of the problematic of resilience in the Anthropocene, where 'linear', 'top-down' or 'engineering' approaches to resilience are considered to be artificial or 'coercive', reproducing problems rather than mitigating them. It considers alternative cybernetic approaches, which often rely on the rolling out of ubiquitous computational technologies, like the Internet of Things, and the critique of these framings for their lack of agential possibilities. It then brings in an alternative resilience approach formulated around indigenous analytics and draws out the contradistinction between futural imaginaries and computational adaptation, which attempts to modulate around an equilibrium. The final section raises some problems with speculative imaginaries, suggesting that this approach to resilience can be seen to narrow rather than expand alternative possibilities.

Chapter 7, 'Governing Imaginaries', analyses indigenous arts and practices of the self as resources for the imagination and creation of alternatives to current discourses on the resilient self. Indigenous peoples are widely lauded today by Western anthropologists and policy-makers for the resilience that is supposedly innate to their cultures and senses of self. They are identified as exemplars that settler colonial societies must now learn from if they are to survive in the Anthropocene—this new era of supposedly unpreventable disasters and certain catastrophes. Against this dominant representation of indigenous resilience, the chapter will provide images of indigenous ways of being that depict them not simply as the resilient, willfully dispossessed, perseverant subjects of neoliberal lore, but power-savvy hunters of power, who know both how to trap and hunt power, as well as the risks of being trapped and hunted by power themselves. Inspired by the language of the Sámi, one indigenous people of the Arctic region, in which the word for trap (*giela*) is the same as the word for language (*giela*) itself, and by the great Sámi poet, Paulus Utsi, the chapter will demand that we learn to 'Ensnare the Language' of neoliberal resilience. Beyond that it will argue indigenous cultures are replete with images that express desire and belief in possibilities for human flourishing and security in the Anthropocene.

NOTES

1. From the second edition of *Decolonizing Methodologies* (2012: 78).

2. There is no clear definition of indigenous knowledge. This is not surprising considering that there are over seven thousand different indigenous languages and indigenous peoples inhabiting extremely diverse environments. What is believed to be shared is a collection of knowledge practices, a way of knowing itself, described

by First People's Worldwide (n.d.) as based upon the four principles: community, balance and harmony, learning from nature and sustainability and resilience.

3. As Claire Colebrook notes (2017: 16), discussion of the Anthropocene 'lends more weight to Walter Benjamin's claim that every document of civilization is a document of barbarism'.

4. As Dipesh Chakrabarty powerfully argues, this binary divide completely ignores the history of the non-Western and, in fact, anti-colonial demand for inclusion in modernity: 'where are the anti-colonial, late-modern and the late-modernising leaders of Asia and Africa—the Nehrus, the Nassers, the Sukarnos, the Nyereres, the Senghors, the Frantz Fanons—in this story?' (Chakrabarty, 2018: 273–74).

5. The previous understanding was that Earth was in the epoch of the Holocene, which began at the end of the last Ice Age, twelve thousand years ago. The Holocene is understood to be an epoch of relative temperature stability, which enabled the flourishing of human progress: the naming of the Anthropocene as a new epoch calls attention to how human impacts on the earth have brought this period of stability to an end. At the time of writing the International Commission on Stratigraphy had not reached a formal decision on the naming or dating of the Anthropocene as a new epoch.

6. Working Group on the Anthropocene, 2017. These impacts include the emissions of 'greenhouse' gases leading to global warming, the collapse of biodiversity including debate about whether we can speak of a 'sixth extinction', the acidification of the oceans and changes in biogeochemical cycles of water, nitrogen and phosphate. The earth system scientists of the Resilience Centre in Stockholm list nine planetary boundaries: stratospheric ozone depletion, loss of biosphere integrity (biodiversity loss and extinctions), chemical pollution and the release of novel entities, climate change, ocean acidification, freshwater consumption and the global hydrological cycle, land system change, nitrogen and phosphorus flows to the biosphere and oceans, and atmospheric aerosol loading. Four of these are currently operating beyond the safe operating space and two are not yet quantified (Stockholm Resilience Centre, 2017).

7. As Latour has consistently argued in his calls for 'diplomacy' and 'symmetry', perhaps most clearly alluded to in his praise and use of Richard White's historical work on the eighteenth-century colonial encounter, aptly titled *The Middle Ground* (2011); see Latour, 2018b.

8. See also Stengers (2017: 384): 'whatever the geoengineering method, it would require that we keep extracting and mobilizing the massive necessary resources, to keep on feeding the climate manipulating machine'.

9. In this regard, the implications of the Anthropocene accord closely with perspectives forwarded by a wide range of critical theorists associated with posthuman, new materialist and speculative realist approaches among others (for example, Barad, 2007; Bennett, 2010; Braidotti, 2013; Connolly, 2013; Coole and Frost, 2010; De-Landa, 2006; Harman, 2010).

10. Highlighted as a 'metabolic rift' by McKenzie Wark (2015: xiv): 'where one molecule after another is extracted by labor and technique to make things for humans, but the waste products don't return so that the cycle can renew itself'.

Chapter 2

Dispossession

INTRODUCTION

Becoming indigenous, as we outlined in the introductory chapter, is an increasingly dominant imaginary of the need to govern life through new modes of thought and practice. This book maps this dominant trend toward a particular reappropriation of indigeneity across a broad range of critical thought and charts its relation to neoliberal discourses on indigeneity whereby the virtues and capacities of indigenous peoples are extolled as ideals that the West ought to emulate (Rival, 2009; Wiebe, 2017: 149–51). The indigenous are celebrated in these discourses for their willful subordination to the world, their refusal to distinguish themselves as superior to other living species, or even living things from non-living things, and their capacities to live in a state of perpetual crisis by accepting the idea that no security from this world is possible. This is an image of the indigenous that scholars as well as powerful actors worldwide argue the West has much to learn from and which it must ultimately seek to embody.

This move of the West to embrace as well as produce a certain image of indigeneity, and by inference, indigenous peoples, undercuts some of the thrust of contemporary indigenous critique which has argued for an image of the indigenous as peoples whose ways of life and being are incommensurable with settler colonialism; peoples who in being the way that they are refuse to let go of being themselves (Simpson, 2014: 2). What if those ways, supposedly so distinct from Western ways of being, are now the very ways which Western regimes of governance find conducive to its project? How to make sense of what is taking place in this embrace? Is it an appropriation of knowledge in the manner that indigenous scholars warn against (Kuokkanen, 2007: xvii)? And if so, does it not undercut the very claim to marginality that the same scholars insist on as the necessary standpoint for indigenous inclusion within the academy (Kuokkanen, 2007: xviii)? Indeed what we see happening and what we point to in this book is a mode of appropriation which functions to mainstream certain currents within indigenous and non-indigenous thought and which demands subsequently a re-evaluation of the functions of indigeneity as a resource for resistance to dominant regimes of power.

It seems that it is not always easy to separate the demand for indigenous-centred forms of critique and the integration of indigenous study and advocacy into the academy from the appropriative movement of neoliberalism and the dominant mantras of the need for new strategies of resilience, adaptation and perseverance in our shared condition of the Anthropocene. It is true, of course, that many representatives of indigenous peoples, as well as many ethnographic observers and admirers of indigenous peoples in the West, identify resources in their knowledge and their ways of being which, in the idealised fashions with which they are described, hold out the possibility of healing our common relationship with the world (Kimmerer, 2013: x). Becoming indigenous is held out, quite literally (as we discussed in the introduction), as a process in which all can potentially engage in, and through which humanity in its entirety can set aside the ways of the colonist and learn anew how to live (Kimmerer, 2013: 207). Crucial in this process of becoming indigenous is the matter of human relationships to land and world. 'Becoming indigenous means living as if your children's future mattered, to take care of the land, as if our lives, both material and spiritual, depended on it' (Kimmerer, 2013: 9).

We argue by contrast that such a way of becoming indigenous does not provide an alternative to the dominant and all-powerful regime of subjectivity extolled by neoliberal regimes—regimes that dominate the human not least by seeking to regulate its relationships to the world. This is not intended as a critique of indigeneity as such, nor of drawing upon indigenous approaches or practices. Our point is that there is much in indigeneity and indigenous ways of life that gets left out of this discursive framing. In effect, the frame functions to discipline indigenous peoples as much as the Western populations who it is said must learn to live within it. Once we step outside this framing and engage with the many different realities of indigenous peoples, indigenous thinking and indigenous practices, we encounter forms of thought and practice which directly conflict with this disciplinary frame, and which can contribute to an alternative pathway, not just for indigenous peoples, but humans everywhere concerned with recovering the human imagination from its political debasement.

It would appear that there are many forms which resistance takes to Western attempts to appropriate a certain imaginary of indigeneity to the cause of environmental service and maintenance. As June Mary Rubis and Noah

Theriault note, there is often a refusal of indigenous peoples to 'play the part' they have been assigned (2019). As they state, Transnational Conservation non-governmental organisations recast 'as technical what are in fact intensely political interventions into Indigenous lands and lifeworlds' (2019: 7), which are 'premised on the notion that Indigenous communities are "natural partners" of conservation or can be made so through some combination of incentives, education, and disciplinary techniques' (2019: 6). In this sense, we seek to further an analytic of indigeneity that finds resonance with the work of Elizabeth Povinelli who has demonstrated how such refusals occur in the context of the ways in which liberal regimes seek to recognise indigenous difference (Povinelli, 2016: 82).

In this chapter we are concerned specifically with the discursive framing of indigenous peoples as dispossessed subjects. By this we mean not simply the ways in which indigenous peoples are recognised, increasingly, as having been dispossessed of their lands by settler colonial states and other regimes of power historically, but the ways in which their condition of dispossession is today valorised as a positive attribute of their ways of life. In contrast with the subject of Western modernity, it is claimed the indigenous have no interest in making the world they live in into their property. An indigenous approach to life and world starts from the principle, it is said, that *we belong to the world, the world does not belong to us* (Adese, 2014: 61). This is not just a normative claim. The task of becoming indigenous develops, it is supposed, from recognition of the truth that it is simply not possible to possess land in the ways that have been assumed in the West. The task is one of learning how to live with the land, in the understanding that we are possessed by it, rather than it belonging to us for our use and benefit. The conceit of the West, historically, and still today, it is maintained, is that of its belief in the ability to possess the land, subordinate it, and exploit it, as an object for human satisfaction.

Taking the logic of dispossession further, some argue that indigenous peoples have no concept of possession as such. In her recent book, *A Field Guide to Getting Lost*, the popular American writer Rebecca Solnit describes how in the language of the Wintu people of California there exists no account of the self as distinct from its other (2017: 17). Without an understanding of what is other the self has no understanding of possession, for only things that are other from the self can indeed be possessed. The self is the presupposition we make when we lay claim to possession. Linguistically this is evident in the many ways we make claim, in the English language at least, to possessing this or that. I say 'my arm, my leg, my body, my thoughts, my imagination, my friend, my house, my world, my land', and so on. In the language of the Wintu no such notion of 'my' this or that exists. As the anthropologist Dorothy Lee explains, this owes to the fact that 'the Wintu have a conception of the self which is markedly different to our own' (Lee, 1950: 538). For them the self is ontologically implicated in a world of things, which by dint of that prior implication it cannot possess but which may be said to possess it. This is an image of the self, availed to us by indigenous language and ways of being, as radically dispossessed, and itself an object of possession. For Solnit, this other way of being in the world and of experiencing the self is a source of wonder, attraction and potential emancipation, for the Western subject, which still errantly believes in its own autonomy from the world, and who is not the autonomous entity it sees itself as (Solnit, 2017: 17–25).

Against this emancipatory image of the dispossessed subject we will pose the figure of Don Juan, the Yaqui Indian, whose knowledge and intelligence is described in the ethnography of Carlos Castaneda. In the encounter between Castaneda and Don Juan what we see is precisely the mapping of a path toward becoming indigenous, but a path which projects itself toward a very different horizon than that being taken today. The world Don Juan teaches Castaneda about is not the ecological world of flora and fauna, knowledge about which has become strongly associated with indigenous peoples today, but the psychic world of the subject, and the faculties of will and practices of power through which the human can subdue it. Don Juan instructs his inquisitor indeed in how to 'stop that world' (1972: 15–243). There is nothing dispossessed in Don Juan. He seizes the world in order to stop it. Castaneda himself, the ethnographer, enters on a spiritual plane into his possession, entrapped by the old Indian (1972: 20). Don Juan instructs Castaneda, not in the knowledge of plants, but in techniques of the self, and especially in the arts by which one can avoid becoming possessed by others. The teachings of Don Juan are in other words a master class in the development of autonomy and freedom from others, and allow us to theorise indigeneity in conjunction with our own aspirations to theorise the human in its capacities to transcend its world and its relations to other people, and secure itself from that world and whatever it finds dangerous in it.

DISPOSSESSION

The concept of dispossession figures large in debates over indigenous peoples and the theorisation of their oppression. In terms of the will to combat liberalism and liberal theories and practices of the oppression of indigenous peoples this focus on the problem of dispossession is understandable. As is well detailed, liberal arguments dating back to the seventeenth century concerning the nature and right to property, especially arguments concerning the conditions for the exercise of the right to claim ownership of land, were fundamental for the colonial project and 'gigantic process of expropriation' by which indigenous peoples were subjected (Losurdo, 2016: 320; see also Lederman, 2016). Colonisers would not have been able to justify their projects without the underlying theories of property that served to legitimate the acts of dispossession of indigenous peoples.

Of all theories of property it is that of John Locke which has proved the most influential and powerful in legitimating colonial dispossessions of indigenous peoples. The central claim being that only peoples who mix their labour with the soil of the land on which they live, and not only improve, cultivate and develop it, but in doing so, subdue it, can claim the right to own it. As Locke put it,

> God, when he gave the World in common to all Mankind, commanded Man also to labour, and the Penury of his Condition required it of him. God and his Reason commanded him to subdue the Earth, *i.e.* improve it for the Benefit of Life, and therein lay out something upon it that was his own, his Labour. He that in Obedience to this Command of God, subdued, tilled and sowed any part of it, thereby annexed to it something that was his *Property*, which another had no Title to, nor could without Injury take from him. (2016: 18)

The distinction between those who subdue and develop the land and those who leave it 'to Nature without any improvement' such that it becomes 'uncultivated waste' (Locke, 2016: 20) has provided the basis for the dispossession of indigenous peoples of the right to land historically (Lederman, 2016). This distinction concerns not simply, of course, the relationships of peoples to particular lands, but their relationships to 'the Earth' and 'the World' as such, as evidenced in the quotation from Locke's *Second Treatise of Government* (2016). Is the people in question one which has subdued the world given to it by the Christian God and through its development of the soil become its master, or is it a people that lives ignorantly in subordination to the world, 'rich in Land' and yet 'poor in all the Comforts of Life', living off the land without improving it, and thus themselves forming part of the world which developed human beings can claim both mastery and ownership of (Locke, 2016: 22)? These are the questions which underlie the Lockean theory of property and which inevitably provided the basis not just for the dispossession of indigenous peoples of the lands on which they lived, as well as the denial of their right to land, but the racism which in turn legitimated the long history of continuing violence against them. No wonder, then, that the development of supposedly postliberal theories of political subjectivity is involving reflection upon the nature of dispossession itself.

It is utilised often by indigenous scholars and activists themselves (Barker, 2015; Coulthard, 2014; Moreton-Robinson, 2015; Pasternak, 2015; Simpson,

2014) to flag up the fact that indigenous peoples have 'not only been subjugated and oppressed by the West' but also 'divested of their lands, the territorial foundation of their societies, which in turn have become the territorial foundations for the creation of new, European-style, settler-colonial societies' (Nichols, 2017: 8–9). As such, dispossession has been construed as a specific kind of process, intrinsic to colonialism, and fundamental to the indigenous experience of the violence of the West. This way of approaching indigeneity and understanding the nature of indigenous subjugation under conditions of colonialism can easily be encountered in Western thought itself. Karl Polanyi, writing in the mid-twentieth century, described how 'the social and cultural system of native life' is shattered once 'the native' is dispossessed of the land on which he or she depends (2001: 187–88). Indeed Polanyi, though a nineteenth-century Viennese economic historian, shared much of the ontological worldview we are now taught to associate with indigenous peoples. 'Land', he argued, 'is an element of nature inextricably interwoven with man's institutions . . . it invests man's life with stability; it is the site of his habitation; it is a condition of his physical safety; it is the landscape and the seasons. We might as well be born without hands and feet as carrying on his life without land' (Polanyi, 2001: 187). He decried the economic and political rationalities that motivated the dispossession of indigenous lands by colonisers for much the same reasons as today, construing it as a 'death blow' to indigenous peoples (Polanyi, 2001: 302).

As a concept within modern political discourse, however, dispossession has a much wider history, originating in the seventeenth century, not just in Locke, but in the ideas of activists and thinkers concerned with challenging the institutions of landed aristocracy in Europe, and developing in the eighteenth century, most significantly in the work of Rousseau, who identified in dispossession and the establishment of property, the origin of all violence, as well as the wide range of forms which warfare, conflict and competition would gradually assume among humankind, and their attendant emotions, desires and states of perception.

> A black inclination to harm one another, a secret jealousy that is all the more dangerous as it often assumes the mask of benevolence in order to strike its blow in greater safety: in a word, competition and rivalry on the one hand, conflict of interests on the other, and always the hidden desire to profit at another's expense; all these evils are the first effect of property, and the inseparable train of nascent inequality. (Rousseau, 1997: 171)

By the nineteenth century it had become integral especially to anarchist claims concerning the illegitimacy of modern property, albeit articulated more often in terms of 'expropriation' (Nichols, 2017: 5). For Marx it played an absolutely essential role in understanding the historical development of capital and the downfall he predicted for it (1976: 928–30). 'The expropriation of the great mass of the people from the soil' formed the prehistory of capital, he argued, while the expropriation of exploitative capitalists by a revolting working class would shape its end (Marx, 1976: 928–29). Eventually, the expropriators are themselves to be expropriated by this one revolutionary class that seeks the abolition of capital through its dispossession, while other classes fight against capital only to save their existences (Marx, 1976: 929–30).

Marx himself often employed the German term *enteignung* only to shift in his later work to the Latin term 'expropriation'. When *Das Kapital* was translated into English, the terms of dispossession and expropriation were employed interchangeably, suggesting that there is little to choose between the two concepts (Nichols, 2017: 6). Today, for whatever reason, the concept of dispossession would seem to have become the more powerful, at the very least with reference to indigenous politics, but also considering wider trends in critical theory, exemplified by influential works employing the concept by leading thinkers such as David Harvey and Judith Butler (Butler and Athanasiou, 2013; Harvey, 2005: 178–79, 2013: 137–82; Nichols, 2017). Within this trend it is possible to detect differences concerning the politics of dispossession. There is a contrast at the very least between Butler who eschews possessiveness as such as a property and capacity for progressive visions of what political subjectivity might become, as well as aligning herself forthrightly with indigenous movements the world over, and Harvey who maintains a belief in the progressive potentials of processes of dispossession insofar as they can contribute to more universally socialist futures, as well as being cognizant of the ways in which indigenous movements sometimes function to prevent the realisation of such futures, as long as they 'refuse to abandon their own particularity' (Harvey, 2013: 179). Indeed, Harvey also notes how in the recent past indigenous movements have not only prevented projects for the realisation of socialism, but created a 'Trojan Horse' for offensives sponsored by the Central Intelligence Agency in promotion of neoliberal regimes, such as in Nicaragua in the 1980s where it took advantage of the resistance of Mesquito Indians to socialist development in order to wage war against the Sandinistas (Harvey, 2013: 165).

Regardless of these political differences, the concept of dispossession is argued to be of great relevance for understandings of the 'territorial acquisition logic of settler colonization' which has underpinned both liberal and socialist models of development emanating from the West (Nichols, 2017: 9). Glen Sean Coulthard writes,

A settler-colonial relationship is one characterized by a particular form of domination; that is it is a relationship where power—in this case, interrelated discursive and non-discursive facets of economic, gendered, racial, and state power—has been structured into a relatively secure or sedimented set of hierarchical social relations that continue to facilitate the *dispossession* of Indigenous peoples of their lands and self-determining authority. (Coulthard, 2014: 7)

Coulthard recognises the importance of the insights of Marx for our abilities to address the dispossessive natures of both colonialism and capitalism while also underscoring the distinctive nature of the experiences of indigenous peoples with regard to their exposures to these regimes of power. Rejecting Marx would be a mistake for indigenous peoples, he maintains, while arguing for the necessity of revising the Marxian framework in conversation with the critical thought and practices of indigenous peoples themselves (Coulthard, 2014: 8).

One crucial point for revision is that dispossession cannot be considered, as Marx suggested it might, a process confined to a particular historical period. It is indeed ongoing and alive today, Coulthard maintains (2014: 9). Secondly it cannot be considered, from an indigenous perspective at least, a necessary developmental stage in the process of capitalist expansion such that it provides the foundation for a subsequent developmental and progressive stage of socialism (Coulthard, 2014: 9–10). Indeed, Coulthard argues that Marx and Marxists have been mistaken in viewing colonialism as itself simply a feature of capitalism, and that it is necessary by contrast to focus on colonialism independently from capitalism, in order to comprehend the functions of dispossession from an indigenous perspective. The power relationship of a settler-state such as Canada to indigenous peoples has been fundamentally organised around the dispossession of their lands and not the extraction of their labour (Coulthard, 2014: 12–13). Crucially, as Coulthard also asserts, it is the dispossession of land and not the extraction of labour which continues to shape the dominant modes of indigenous resistance and critique (2014: 13). The theory and practice of indigenous resistance to colonialism has to be understood, he argues, as a struggle oriented around 'the question of land' (Coulthard, 2014: 13). As many other indigenous scholars have argued, as a historical process and technique of power it has particular relevance for indigenous peoples because so much of indigenous knowledge and culture emanates from their relations to land (Wildcat et al., 2014). Being dispossessed territorially has meant being dispossessed of the very knowledge on which indigenous cultures and ways of being are based. Thus the struggle against dispossession has to mean a struggle to foster systems of indigenous education premised on indigenous knowledge and intelligence emanating from the land (Wildcat et al., 2014: II). The indigenous subject strengthens itself, on account of the ability to recover its relation to the land. Its knowledge and intelligence grows the more and better it is able to recover that relation.

Anger at having been dispossessed of one's own land pervades the literatures of indigenous peoples. It is an anger that is directed at what the Aboriginal thinker Aileen Moreton-Robinson names the White Possessive: that subject whose sense of belonging, home and place in the world derives from the dispossession of 'the original owners of the land' (2015: 3), including indigenous peoples such as her own people, the Goenpul tribe, a part of the Quandamooka nation of Stradbroke Island in Queensland, Australia. Unlike other exponents of indigenous ways, however, Moreton-Robinson does not reject the concept of possession altogether. Her critique is concerned with distinguishing between indigenous and Western accounts of who is the land's rightful possessor. In this context, she sees not simply a conflict between two different parties, but a struggle that pitches two conflicting concepts of possession against each other. On the one hand that concept of the White Possessive who subscribes to a liberal account of possession compatible with 'the logic of capital' (2015: 3), and on the other an indigenous concept of possession, in its 'incommensurable difference', based as Moreton-Robinson asserts it to be, on 'an ontological relationship with land' (2015: 11). In claiming possession of the land, indigenous subjects also understand themselves, in what might seem like a paradox, as belonging to the land. For this is what having an ontological relationship to land entails. One is part of the land as much as the land is part of you, rather than being simply its transcendental possessor, in the supposedly non-ontological sense in which the White Possessive claims ownership.

Some ambiguity exists, then, as to whether the indigenous project implies an attempt to recover a prior relation of possession with land, on account of their being the rightful owners of the land, because they are 'ontologically' embedded in it, or whether it is a project based around the celebration of dispossession as such. The latter perspective is better expressed in the work of Jennifer Adese who distinguishes more simply and clearly between indigenous peoples who 'live with the land' instead of living in domination and exploitation of it as Westerners are said to do (Adese, 2014: 53). In the words of one Metis elder quoted by Adese, Adrian Hope, 'we belong to the land, the land does not belong to us' (Adese, 2014: 61). From the perspective of an indigenous community such as the Metis, it is simply not possible to possess land, irrespective of what Moreton-Robinson might say. The task is one of learning how to live with the land, in the understanding that we are possessed by it. The conceit of the West, historically, and still today, it is maintained in these indigenous approaches, is that of its belief in the ability to possess it.

The condition of being without possession of land, then, when seen from some influential indigenous perspectives, is not in itself to be decried. The problem is that of being dispossessed of the relation with the land, which founds indigenous subjectivity, knowledge and intelligence. To a certain extent this nuancing of the condition of dispossession, and loss of land, in indigenous critique, powerfully rearticulates the widely made assertion as to the 'theft' of indigenous lands by colonial powers. What has been stolen is not simply the land but a way of being in relation with land that is avowedly not based on possession of land as such, and for this reason loss of world might be a better operative conception than merely theft of property.

It is for this reason perhaps, also, that the colonial dispossession of indigenous peoples has rarely led to arguments merely for the return of those lands to indigenous peoples, but an articulation of the experience and condition of indigenous dispossession itself as a basis on which to theorise not only their subjectivity under conditions of colonialism, but political subjectivity on a universal scale. Such thinking is encountered forcefully in the work of Judith Butler and Athena Athanasiou, titled *Dispossession*, which engages in it explicitly (Butler and Athanasiou, 2013). Their project is to consider dispossession both as an act, 'as one way that subjects are radically de-instituted', and also as an attribute of the subject which offers a counter-movement to the forces of dispossession (Butler and Athanasiou, 2013: 28). In other words in addressing the histories and continuing realities of powers which dispossess indigenous peoples and others groups they want to contest it on these deeper terrains of its subject-formations. The problem they identify is that not simply of the right to dispossess but the assumption of possession at the heart of the liberal subject. The assumption of having transcended nature that was crucial to the distinction between colonising and colonised subjects. They want to avoid any avowal of a subject which 'possesses itself and its object world, and whose relations with others are defined by possession and its instrumentalities' in the development of struggles against regimes of power which serve to dispossess indigenous peoples (Butler and Athanasiou, 2013: 28). 'Prizing the forms of responsibility and resistance that emerge from a "dispossessed" subject' they underline their awareness that 'dispossession constitutes a form of suffering for those displaced and colonized' (Butler and Athanasiou, 2013: ix). For this reason, they express a gesture of solidarity toward those indigenous peoples who have been historically dispossessed of their lands accompanied by a normative gesture of constraint upon the indigenous, lest they seek recourse to the forms of possessive individualism Butler and Athanasiou otherwise identify with colonisers. 'How to become dispossessed of the sovereign self and enter into forms of collectivity that oppose forms of dispossession that systematically jettison populations from modes of collective belonging and justice' is thus their question (Butler and Athanasiou, 2013: xi).

Likewise it is the question of how to oppose forms of dispossession in ways that function doubly to produce dispossessed forms of subjectivity

(Goldstein, 2014; Porter, 2014). Too many social and political struggles against dispossession are thought to recuperate the same logic of possession that accounted for the original dispossession from which the struggles in question emerged. As Libby Porter expresses it, 'the social field of rights-based struggle becomes stuck in a mode that seeks parity only within the frame of liberal "possessive individualism". Rights under this conception are a bundle of things that can be possessed, held, alienated and exchanged, and express the positionality of a possessing unitary subject' (Porter, 2014: 394). The project of liberalism, taken to be that not simply of dispossessing peoples of their lands for liberal development, but of reconstituting those peoples as liberal, requires that they too partake in the logic of possession, becoming themselves, possessive subjects, claiming rights to property and procedures consistent with their liberalisation. This invitation, to become possessive, partake in the logic of possession, and emerge a fully fledged liberal subject, has to be refused. Indeed one could summarise the thrust of a wide range of critiques, deriving from postcolonial theorists and critical indigenous scholars, as expressing the urgency of this refusal, including preeminent authors such as Porter, Pasternak, Coulthard, Moreton-Robinson, Simpson and Nichols (Barker, 2015; Coulthard, 2014; Moreton-Robinson, 2015; Nichols, 2017; Pasternak, 2015; Porter, 2014; Simpson, 2014).

In many ways this critique lives in and off the shadow of Fanon, still. Since Fanon, at the very least, we have known that the invitation is not what it seems to be. One cannot move from colonised subject to liberal subject without conceding fully to one's subjugation to the colonial schema itself. The sustainability of colonial power depends on the capacity to transform the colonised population into subjects of imperial rule (Coulthard, 2007: 6). Liberation from colonial subjugation requires the colonial subject to wage war on that schema itself (Reid, 2006). Embracing the logic of possession cannot work, therefore, as a mode of resistance to liberal colonialism. It does not work to produce justice even in the most naive senses. In situations where peoples have been dispossessed of the lands on which they live, or as is often the case nowadays, displaced, from one place of abode to another, the ability to come into possession of another land, or other place, simply does not do justice to the loss experienced. 'There is no genuine space in compensation payment calculus to attend to the loss and grief of a neighbourhood abandoned, the bulldozing of a home, the erasing of memories or the shattering of lives' as Porter argues (Porter, 2014: 397).

Of course, as Porter admits, this critique does not quite apply in the context of indigenous claims. It is, as she expresses it succinctly, 'a different manifestation of a possessory calculus at work in the recognition politics around indigenous land rights, for clearly indigenous claims are intrinsically linked to particular spaces. The whole notion of indigenous property is that it is inalienable, and cannot be traded for another locale on the planet' (Porter, 2014: 397). The struggles of indigenous peoples, in Australia for example, to repossess their lands through the claiming of indigenous title rights is real and ongoing, and meeting with some success. The royalties being paid to title-owning indigenous people by mining companies in Australia has led to a growing Aboriginal middle class. Of course, success here is measured simply in terms of the socio-economic betterment of Aboriginal peoples under market conditions—their abilities to exploit their possessions through trade with other market actors, particularly resource-seeking extractive industries. A fact deeply problematic for anyone concerned with the deeper political problem of the growing entrenchment of liberalism and the underlying colonisation of the indigenous which such socio-economic success implies.

Similar problems and dynamics have been observed, in the Canadian context, by Shiri Pasternak, who describes the ways in which indigenous struggles against the legacies of colonialism, and in particular attempts to overhaul the Indian Act in Canada, involve indigenous groups in taking political positions, which only serve to entangle them further with neoliberal logics of possession (2015). The lack of private property rights on Indian reserves deprives indigenous groups of the abilities to access home mortgages, and therefore credit, which in turn excludes them from the market economy, it is argued by some representatives of indigenous communities in Canada (Pasternak, 2015: 179). In these terms, the struggle for indigenous enfranchisement asserts a logic of the right to possession which in turn serves to subject indigenous groups to neoliberal governance (Pasternak, 2015: 180). It is for these reasons that opposition to dispossession is believed to require a different mode of engagement: something other than a mere assertion of struggles for possession.

THE DISPOSSESSED SUBJECT

In Pasternak's view the struggle between collective and individual rights of possession is the key terrain on which larger struggles against settler colonialism is today taking place (Pasternak, 2015: 180). The struggle of indigenous groups to overcome the forms of poverty they have been subject to on account of historical strategies of colonialism has to avoid falling for the traps being set by neoliberal regimes that offer the promise of economic enfranchisement through the degradation of the very collectivities that constitute indigeneity. Colonialism is presented within the imaginaries of such promises as simply the denial of access to the market economy, and thus is it that neoliberalism is able to present itself as an anti-colonial force (Pasternak, 2015: 180).

The name Butler and Athanasiou give to this form of politics is 'performative'. Performativity describes the ways by which dispossessed subjects produce themselves as political subjects in the contexts of their conditions of dispossession without resorting to an assertion of a self-possessed and possessive subject (Butler and Athanasiou, 2013: 97–103). It is a politics which applies and can be found, they argue, among a remarkably wide variety of subject positions: indigenous peoples dispossessed of their land, but also refugees and the stateless, the *sans papiers*, migrant labourers, as well as sexual minorities such as the transgendered; 'dispossessed by regimes of gender and sexual normativity' (Butler and Athanasiou, 2013: 108). Regardless of the normative constraint against becoming possessive, these are groups the precarious conditions of which prevent, in actuality, much ability for the assertion of 'the logic of possession' (Butler and Athanasiou, 2013: 126). The performative emerges, they argue, 'precisely as the specific power of the precarious—unauthorized by existing legal regimes, abandoned by the law itself—to demand the end to their precarity' (Butler and Athanasiou, 2013: 121).

Butler and Athanasiou discuss a certain number of concrete instances of performativity; the singing of the national anthem of the United States in Spanish by illegal immigrants in the streets of Los Angeles in 2006 (2013: 141); the street demonstrations and self-immolations in Morocco and Tunisia in 2010 and 2011, which together contributed to the revolutions of the Arab Spring (2013: 144); hunger strikes (2013: 146); the marches of women across the deserts of Northern Mexico to protest rapes occurring there (2013: 147); the performance art of Regina Jose Galindo (2013: 169)—all of these are said to express instances of peoples dispossessing themselves in order to dispossess coercive powers (2013: 146). Other instances discussed and theorised by scholars of performativity include naked blogging, such as that of the Egyptian woman, Aliaa Magda Elmahdy, whose posting of naked pictures of herself is seen to have contributed not just to the Egyptian revolution of 2011, but to a reconfiguration of the body politic and a reimagining of the theatre of the political (Eileraas, 2014). The use of public nudity by the Femen movement, including their mobilisation against Islamic oppression and the 'international topless jihad day', is also discussed in this framework (Reestorff, 2014). We might also think, poignantly, of the acts of self-dispossession occurring on Mediterranean shores right now, by which peoples give over their homes to refugees dispossessed of their own homes and places by warring regimes in Syria and elsewhere.

What all such instances have in common, Butler and Athanasiou argue, is that 'rather than implying a transcendent euphoria of effective will or redemption', their performance 'pertains to the ordinary and extraordinary forces of endurance and survival' (2013: 181). This is not a politics which aims at the constitution of a subject of possession but one that (re-)produces its dispossession while seeking to displace, also, present regimes of dispossession through 'a labor of sensing, imagining, envisaging, and forging an alternative to the present' (2013: 193). An alternative grounded avowedly in the condition and subject of dispossession. How, indeed, to dispossess the dispossessed of any desire to become the possessor is the deeply ironic and paradoxical task they set themselves. In this sense, whatever the authors might discursively claim, their work is also an argument for dispossession in the negative sense they claim to oppose. It presupposes a politics that can only function through modes of dispossession performed upon peoples, and not simply in opposition to it. It is a politics which constructs a particular kind of body. A body which is obdurate, persistent, insistent on its continuous and collective thereness, organised without hierarchy, enacting its message, performatively, through the occupation of public space and the display of this body, individually as well as collectively, only. It is not a body that can ever or will ever master the space it occupies.

The argument, of course, is that this way of performing political subjectivity is necessary as a turn away from and against the liberal tradition of thinking and practicing political subjectivity, based as it supposedly has been on the assumption of a body which masters, possesses and improves the space it occupies. Instead we have to grasp the body as a thing which performs a poiesis in space, where poiesis is understood to be a double movement involving both desubjugation and self-making. This understanding of the body, or indeed 'the subject', as such derives from Butler's interpretation of Foucault's account of the subject whereby poiesis is said to be the central practice in and of subject formation. Poieis is central to the mode of existence of the subject, Butler argues, which must risk itself in making itself in order to desubjugate itself from particular regimes of truth (2002: 214). This is not a theory of the subject as transcendent or masterly or in possession of itself or others. In contrast, it posits the idea that there can be no formation of self or subject outside of subjugating modes of subjectivation. The subject is always, regardless of its capacities to make itself, orchestrated by power (Butler, 2002: 226).

In the work of Butler and others we can see that the indigenous subject is undergoing a transformation. No longer seen simply as a subject which calls for political solidarity in a struggle against colonial or neoliberal domination in order to assert its repossession of worlds of which it has been robbed, but one which performs a new understanding of politics and ontology through a way of being dispossessed held to challenge hegemonic ways of asserting possession. Here, it is not resistance but defeat itself that is celebrated (Blaser, 2013: 556).[1] The indigenous subject is not to be conceptualised in terms of what worlds it might stake a claim for but in terms of what it has been turned into by the very regimes that have exploited it.

POSSESSION AS POWER

As a concept possession has, of course, also spiritual connotations. We speak of he or she who is possessed, by spirits, by ideas, by passions or simply by forces, which move it this way or that. It is an embodied state that we associate with a range of ways of being. In the worlds of indigenous peoples there are many instances of shamans and sorcerers; figures who developed and employed practices of such possession to achieve this or that end. The world of the indigenous is not simply made up of plants, animals, nature, ecosystems, in the manner that is so often presupposed by indigenous critique. And the task with respect to the world is not simply that of learning how to accept our being possessed by that world. The world is there, in the words of Don Juan, the Yaqui Indian sorcerer, encountered by the great anthropologist, Carlos Castaneda, for example, 'to be stopped' (1972: 10–14).

Castaneda's study of Don Juan is controversial, on account of questions concerning the factual versus fictional nature of the ethnographic research on which it was based, but authoritative voices in the field of anthropology have credited it with being among the greatest works that discipline has produced on account precisely of the ways in which it deploys the imagination as method (Needham, 1978: 76). For us it is of great relevance for how it illustrates the conflict between different ways of becoming indigenous. When Castaneda seeks out Don Juan in Arizona it is in the interest of learning from him about plants (1972: 17–25). Castaneda is convinced Don Juan, as a holder of indigenous knowledge, knows a great deal about certain plants, which can be of relevance to his anthropological research. Don Juan dismisses this interest of his inquisitor, saying 'there is nothing to learn about plants, because there is nothing to say about them' (Castaneda, 1972: 23). In other words he denies Castaneda's desire to learn in the manner of learning that has become so fundamental to Western interests in indigenous knowledge today. There is a vast gulf between the model of subjectivity and form of knowledge imparted by Don Juan and that which today's self-appointed representatives of indigenous knowledge offer us. For Robin Wall Kimmerer, for example, the future of the species depends fundamentally on its abilities not just to learn about plants, but to learn from plants. Plants themselves are the holders of the deepest wisdom, she maintains, and can potentially teach us how to live. 'Their wisdom is apparent in the way that they live. They teach us by example. They've been on the earth far longer than we have been, and have had time to figure things out' (Kimmerer, 2013: 9).

Don Juan, like Wall Kimmerer, is interested in what can be known of this world, and how indeed one can learn to live, for such learning is indeed a project and an art. Yet when pressed by Castaneda on his knowledge of the plants of this world Don Juan rebuffs his interrogator. This is not to say that Don Juan rejects Castaneda. In contrast, he wants to engage his ethnographer on the subject of the world in a different way. The world Don Juan is interested in discussing is not the biological world of flora and fauna, knowledge about which has become so strongly associated with indigenous peoples, and questions about which he reacts to with 'despair and disbelief' (Castaneda, 1972: 43), but the psychic world of the subject, and the faculties of will and practices of power through which the human can subdue it. Don Juan will instruct his inquisitor indeed in how to stop that world (1972: 15–243). There is nothing dispossessed in Don Juan. He possesses the world, not the other way around. Castaneda himself, the ethnographer, enters into his possession, entrapped by the old Indian (1972: 20). Don Juan will instruct Castaneda, not in the knowledge of plants, but in techniques of the self, and especially in the arts by which one can avoid becoming possessed by others. The teachings of Don Juan are a master class in the development of autonomy and freedom from others.

The first lesson Don Juan gives Castaneda in this vein is in 'erasing personal history' (1972: 26–34). Don Juan describes how he, like so many indigenous peoples, had a 'terribly strong attachment' to his own history and to that of his Yaqui people (Castaneda, 1972: 28). Castaneda the ethnographer tries to pin him down. 'You are a Yaqui. You can't change that', he says (Castaneda, 1972: 28). 'Am I?' Don Juan replies. 'You don't know what I am . . . you will never know who or what I am, because I don't have a personal history' (Castaneda, 1972: 29). Don Juan's lesson in the erasure of one's history is deliberately aimed, as he explains, at avoiding being trapped by others, averting the danger of being pinned down, and caught in the discursive framings of others (Castaneda, 1972: 29). Questions about one's history are 'a bunch of crap' (Castaneda, 1972: 29). This is not a practice of the Yaqui people, it is a practice of Don Juan, in disregard of any specific ethnic identity and any affiliation to a people. Erasing our histories makes us 'free from the encumbering thoughts of other people' (Castaneda, 1972: 30). Instead of playing into the traps of identities and the discursive framings of others, Don Juan maintains it is best to 'build up a fog around yourself' and cultivate 'the ultimate freedom of being unknown' (Castaneda, 1972: 31).

CONCLUSION

The dominant form of constructing indigenous thought and practices, which we encounter today, is the claim that indigenous subjectivity is defined by a sense of the interconnectedness of the self to others. The life histories of indigenous peoples are said to 'show a moral ordering of sociality that emphasizes mutual support and concern for those with whom they are interconnected' (Moreton-Robinson, 2015: 15). Don Juan, by way of contrast to this dominant image of the indigenous subject, emphasises the importance of disconnection as life practice and as the basis of ethics. 'Your friends, those who have known you for a long time, you must leave them quickly', he advises Castaneda (1972: 42).

What Don Juan is really concerned with is truth: the search for it, and the ability of the subject to align itself with its own truths, and to act, without doubt or remorse. 'I have no doubts or remorse', he says, 'everything I do is my decision and my responsibility' because in this world 'there is no time for regrets or doubts. There is only time for decisions' (Castaneda, 1972: 56). For Don Juan the task is one of freeing the self from doubt and attaining the power of decision, which is the hallmark of sovereign subjectivity. This is the major source of inequality between Don Juan and Castaneda, not the knowledge of plants, which Castaneda seeks out the Indian for, but the powers of decision as well as perception, which distinguish Don Juan's relation to the world from that of the anthropologist. If Don Juan is to be the anthropologist's informant it will be as a source of information concerning how to achieve such a powerful relation to the world and become 'a hunter and a warrior' in distinction to 'the pimp' which is Castaneda—an impoverished subject who does not know how to fight his own battles but only those of other peoples (Castaneda, 1972: 74). 'Is hunting the way of the Yaqui Indians?' asks Castaneda. Don Juan replies in the negative (Castaneda, 1972: 72). It is pointless to try to reduce the ways of relating to the world Don Juan describes to his indigeneity. It is simply a superior way of being, one which creates its own 'world of precise acts and feelings and decisions' (Castaneda, 1972: 74).

NOTE

1. Blaser cites, to clarify, the phrase of Erich Fox Tree, who as a counterpoint to James Scott's 'everyday forms of resistance' argues that the focus should be 'everyday forms of existence' in reference to the everyday practices that preserve non-modern modes of existence but that are not intended as resistance but nevertheless, defy the modern ontology (2013: 556n22).

Chapter 3

Speculative Analytics

If we are now suborned to becoming indigenous then it is clear that indigeneity is futural rather than a mere product of the past. Although the demand is often posed as a return from or recalling of modernity, this should not be understood to construct indigenous ways of being as fixed or discrete products of some distinct time or space. Thus the Anthropocene does not merely call for a critique of modernity but also for the assertive or speculative demand for a non-modern way of thinking and being in the world: a demand for a new ontopolitics. Just as Bruno Latour argues 'We Have Never Been Modern' (1993), so we are told by ontopolitical anthropology that the indigenous 'were never pre-modern'. The idea of Western 'science' was just as false as the idea of indigenous 'culture'. As Elizabeth Povinelli argues, the reduction of indigenous analytics to a form of cultural belief was a crucial fiction of 'setter late liberalism' (2016: 33). Indigenous knowledge as it is contemporarily constructed in the Western academy is then not premodern but necessarily postmodern, or after modernity. As Deborah Danowski and Eduardo Viveiros de Castro argue, in relation to Amerindian collectives:

> their relatively simple technologies that are nonetheless open to high-intensity syncretic assemblages, are a 'figuration of the future', *not a remnant of the past*. Masters of technoprimitivist bricolage and politico-metaphysical metamorphosis, they are one of the possible chances, in fact, of a *subsistence of the future*. (Danowski and Viveiros de Castro, 2017: 123)

How indigenous knowledge could be transvalued, constructed into forms that become futural and post- rather than premodern, is the subject of this chapter. We seek to question the ease with which this process of transformation or transvaluation has occurred and highlight some problems with this form of recolonising indigeneity for Western consumption, both in terms of our understanding of indigeneity and in terms of critical theorising itself. In the following, we seek to unpack the process of how indigenous ways of knowing have become enrolled in the project of displacing Western or modern approaches to knowledge. In doing so, we draw upon anthropological insights offered by leading theorists, such as Philippe Descola, Eduardo Viveiros de Castro, Elisabeth Povinelli, Bruno Latour, Donna Haraway and Isabelle Stengers.

The chapter is organised in four sections. The first engages with the development of what we are calling 'ontopolitical anthropology', the anthropological production of a certain understanding of indigeneity, which rather than challenging the view of separate and distinct 'cultures' seeks to draw out from the ethnographic experience an alternative methodology able to reveal the speculative possibility of 'different worlds'. The second section focusses upon how discourses of the Anthropocene are seen to transform the temporality of indigenous analytics, articulating them as necessary for constructing alternative speculative futures. The following section engages more closely with debates within anthropology over indigenous analytics, which seek to establish indigenous knowledge in a 'symmetrical' framing, of equal standing to the modernist episteme (such as Descola, 2013a, 2013b; Holbraad and Pedersen, 2017; Viveiros de Castro, 2014). The final section raises some problems with the approach of ontopolitical anthropology, in particular the way that it can be seen to reify or 'exoticise' indigenous thought and practices or, as we state, 'ontologize indigeneity'.

ONTOPOLITICAL ANTHROPOLOGY

Discussions of indigenous knowledge as a new analytics for the Anthropocene need to be understood in the context of long-standing debates over anthropological method. Anthropology has a long and chequered history as a 'science' of human societal differences and has struggled to get away from its racial and colonial heritage (Lea, 2012). Modern anthropology has developed in distinct national 'schools', drawing on different social and philosophical traditions and divided between more universalist structural or functionalist approaches and more relativist approaches, stressing the distinctiveness of separate cultures. The former often operated through analogy with Western forms of organisational life, projecting a Western interpretation on to non-modern societies, problematically understood to be more 'primitive' or 'savage' versions of the West. These approaches were increasingly understood to be reductionist, always understanding other cultures on the basis of a single method of explanation (Descola, 2013b: 16) whether through rational choice, the use of behaviouralism or some other approach to natural or contextual constraints. The latter approaches, stressing cultural difference, which were often informed by poststructuralist positions, were also seen to be problematic, accused of relativising and 'exoticising' non-modern societies: seeking to understand them on their own terms, reducing cultural understandings to processes of language and cognition (see Agrawal, 1995).

One response to this dilemma of universalising cultural understandings or relativising them was the 'hybridisation' position, emphasising the porousness or adaptability of cultural boundaries. Culture was not a dead or static aspect but a way of being and becoming. Paying attention to the reality of indigenous communities meant seeing that they were entangled with many pressures, forces and demands of the world. Indigenous communities, like any others, were immersed in relations, which they were influenced by and also influenced, as Marshall Sahlins noted (back in 1999) when he talked about 'the indigenization of modernity' (1999: x):

> The struggle of non-Western peoples to create their own cultural versions of modernity undoes the received Western opposition of tradition vs. change, custom vs. rationality—and most notably its twentieth century version of tradition vs. development. (Sahlins, 1999: xi)

It is important to note that 'indigenous peoples' are a relatively recent construction, emerging from struggles for rights and recognition in the 1970s, primarily led by the American Indian Movement and the Canadian Indian Brotherhood (Smith, 2012: 7). Indigenous struggles in the 1980s became more overtly political as indigenous movements were able to gain national and even international political support for increased rights and recognition and for opposition to ongoing resource extraction, dispossession and displacement (Lindroth and Sinevaara-Niskanen, 2018: 1–25). Political theorists were therefore drawn to particularly focus on indigenous resistance to the nation-state (see, for example, Tully, 1995). As indigenous peoples became feted as important political actors in their own right, critical appropriations of these struggles moved beyond the classist peasant studies of the 1960s to 1980s to embrace more culturalist approaches that appreciated the distinctive epistemological and cosmological dimensions of indigenous political resistance. Nevertheless, this attention to cultures rejected the idea that cultures were somehow fixed or pristine or exotic:

> Cultures are . . . densely interdependent in their formation and identity. They exist in complex historical processes of interaction with other cultures. . . . Cultural

diversity is not a phenomenon of exotic and incommensurable others in distant
lands and at different stages of development . . . interaction and interdependency
of cultures is not a recent phenomenon; the cultures of the world have been
shaped and formed by interaction for a millennium. (Tully, 1995: 11)

As political theorist James Tully's work exemplifies, in the 1990s, Western
critical academics attempted to highlight the importance of cultural distinctions as a pluralising and disruptive force, keeping open the foundational
assumptions of modernist liberal constitutionalism (1995). The struggles of
indigenous groups and communities for rights and recognition in the 1980s
and 1990s led not to the idea of an alternative analytics after modernity but to
the idea of a plural and globalised world where cultures were living, changing and entangled sets of practices and experiences (see also Andersen, 2014;
Battiste, 2000; Simpson, 2014; Sissons, 2005). Thus Sahlins's view of the
'indigenization of modernity' sought to critique the binaries and hierarchies,
which informed the anthropological gaze and to problematise the attempt
to construct fixed differences and distinctions which categorised and essentialised indigenous societies.

Until the late 1990s the marginal position of indigenous peoples meant
that for most theorists, indigenous communities and indigenous thought were
constrained by settler-colonialism. As Linda Tuhiwai Smith stated (in 1999),
'Our colonial experience traps us in the project of modernity. There can be
no 'postmodern' for us until we have settled some business of the modern'
(Smith, 2012: 35). This is a far cry from contemporary interpretations and
translations of the power and potential of indigenous knowledge. In the 2000s
and 2010s an alternative response to the poststructuralist or relativist position
emerged, one that was informed by debates in continental philosophy and focussed on moving beyond deconstruction based upon interpretive framings of
meaning through symbolic interaction and language as representation. While
for culturalist approaches the emphasis was upon how the abstraction of language removed the reality of the world, as signs lost their signification and
meaning, the 'ontological' or 'ontopolitical' turn in anthropology sought to
ground the discipline in the use of ethnographic materials for the production
of alternative realities. It is here, in making this 'turn', that indigenous knowledge as futural method becomes central. In anthropology, this focus managed
to evade the discipline's difficulties with reducing the 'other' through either a
universalist or relativist approach: the other was to be no longer the object of
knowledge but the subject of a new metaphysics of knowing.

This shift of subject positions was enabled through the dismissal of the
modernist divide between plural and subjective 'culture' and universal and
objective 'nature'. Contemporary theorists claim that indigenous approaches

enable them to solve the problems of anthropological methods and to move beyond cultural frameworks of analysis in order to take alterity seriously. Literally, the demand of the ontopolitical turn in anthropology is to 'become indigenous': to take the appearance of the world as the starting point for alternative speculative futures. Indigenous knowledge then becomes the practice and method of anthropology, deriving from the ontopolitics of interpreting what the world itself, in its fluid multiplicity or the 'liveliness of life', might be enabling, as opposed to how it is constructed by the subject. Here, 'becoming indigenous', as a set of analytics, has as its goal not the understanding of indigenous groups or communities as 'cultures' but the application of indigenous ways of knowing to speculative knowledge-production per se. In this respect, ontopolitical anthropology puts indigenous knowledge on the same level as Western or modern ways of generating meaning (as we shall analyse later) as a symmetrically similar process but with different outcomes (Descola, 2013a; Latour, 2009, 2010; Viveiros de Castro, 2014).

To put our argument upfront, ontopolitical anthropology makes two essentialising moves. First, analytically there is the construction of a strict epistemological and ontological division between the 'indigenous' and the 'modern', or the indigenous and the colonial, one very much resembling Latour's division between the Human and the 'Earthbound' (2013). This is ontopolitical as there is an implicit connection between the epistemological distinctions (that is, the ways of knowing—a process of speculation based upon embodied experience versus an abstract process of causal rationalisation) and the ontological underpinnings (that is, what is to be known—a multiverse of speculative possibilities). Here the struggle is clear. If anything, it is a little reminiscent of the Cold War articulation of a clear divide—geographic, political and ideological—between the 'capitalist West' and the 'communist East'. Except this time the divide is between the modernist/colonial West and allegedly non-modern colonised/'indigenous communities'. This level of crudity in the spatial, ethnographic and epistemic mapping of the world is rarely overtly argued in the anthropological literature, and merely smuggled in through the exclusive focus on selected indigenous groups and, even then, only certain peripheral aspects, such as shamanic practices, held to hold the key to indigenous being, for their critical anthropological interlocutors (Bessire and Bond, 2014).[1]

The second move is the extraction of an analytic that can be generalised. The analytic is not exactly the same in every case but it can generally be directly mapped onto contemporary continental theorising, often claiming authority from readings of the work of Deleuze and Guattari, phenomenology and semiotics, or indirectly via posthumanism, actor-network theory, new materialism and object-oriented ontology. Ontopolitical anthropology is distinct as a practice in that its concern is the generation of an alternative analytics rather than an understanding of indigenous life and practices per se. While we might have some sympathy with speculative futurism undertaken as a philosophical practice, here we particularly seek to highlight the problematic conceit of ontopolitical anthropology, which seeks to ground this particular metaphysical analytic in a feigned solidarity with and concern for indigenous people and societies. The fact that some academics engaged in ontopolitical anthropology (or using the work derived from this) have longstanding commitments to indigenous struggles and see this work as enabling these claims does not detract from what we see as both the problematic nature of the underlying political philosophy nor the risk of exoticising or ontologising indigeneity itself.

We claim that the indigenous play a vital role for contemporary theorists, not so much as objects of study in their own right (old-fashioned anthropology) nor as a focus of political solidarity (old-fashioned politics) but rather as a vicarious stage army for critical scholars meeting the fashionable demand to develop non-modern approaches to knowledge production. For many critical theorists, feminists, posthumanists, new materialists, actor-network theorists and object-oriented ontologists, indigeneous thought (as produced through the lens of ontopolitical anthropology) plays a fundamental role in supplementing and legitimating their experiments in 'provincialising' the foundations of Western epistemology in the culture/nature divide. This role is one that is largely accidental, based on a particular reading and engagement, which constructs indigenous thought as non-Western or non-modern, insofar as it allocates agency to nonhuman actors. Before Donna Haraway's anthropological colleagues constructed the indigenous in this way, Japanese thought played a similar role in destabilising the grounds of Western methods and approaches (1989; see also Morita, in de la Cadena et al., 2015: 442)[2]; for other social and political theorists, this role of 'the other' had been regularly played by Confucian and other Oriental frameworks of thought (see, for example, Dallmayr, 2010). We suggest that the demand for ontopolitical anthropology (and its market in terms of article citations and book sales) is driven less by any interest in indigeneity than by the desire of critical theorists to give additional legitimacy to their speculative projects.

ANTHROPOLOGY AND THE ANTHROPOCENE

The failure of modernity—allegedly played out in the global warming, climate change, species extinction and ocean acidification of our contemporary world—was already beginning to be rehearsed in the field of anthropology in the late 1980s and 1990s. The failure of modernist frameworks (as discussed previously) to know or take seriously indigenous knowledge became the vector through which indigenous knowledge was to remake Western anthropology. While modernity was constructed as successful, the question posed by anthropologists was why indigenous cultures got things 'wrong'. As Descola notes:

> In ethnographic enquiries, the dualism of nature and culture that the observer carries with him thus effectively compels him to approach the system of objectification of reality which he studies as a more or less impoverished variant of that which is familiar to us, the local system ultimately proving to be incapable of completely objectifying our own reality. (Descola, 2013b: 57)

By the 2000s, this approach increasingly became displaced through a shift away from cultural frameworks of understanding. Now indigenous knowledge was used to show how earlier assumptions of Western anthropology got things 'wrong'. Through ontopolitical anthropology, indigenous knowledge became translated into Western self-knowledge. This translation is the ground upon which the injunction to 'become indigenous' is enabled and conditioned. The first thing that Western anthropologists were understood to have gotten wrong was their assumption that nature was objective or universal and that culture was subjective and multiple. The undoing of Western modernist assumptions of the divide between culture and nature, which (as analysed in the introduction) is increasingly commonplace in the Anthropocene, was first developed in the field of anthropology. In short, it could be said that whereas Columbus's 'discovery' of the Americas may have founded modernity, the anthropological 'discovery' of Amerindian 'perspectivism' and 'multi-naturalism' (Viveiros de Castro, 2014) has sounded the death-knell of modernity. Modernity then, it could be said, was not killed off by critical theorists or political struggle, nor by the Anthropocene and global warming, but by the discovery of 'indigenous knowledge' as the futural alternative to the modernist episteme.[3]

The Anthropocene (as we have said) is a great leveller. It would seem that the Anthropocene heralds the end of the modernist conceit that culture is subjective and plural and nature is objective, singular and universal. It was, of course, these very binaries that established the modern episteme, with its hierarchies, cuts and separations, as superior to the backward, non-modern cosmologies of the others of the West, including of course, the indigenous. Whereas other 'others' of the West were constructed as somewhere behind, but capable of catching up, the indigenous were understood in the colonial imaginary as distinctive, precisely because they lacked the modernist division between culture and nature. What in modernity was held to make indigeneity stand apart and to make indigenous knowledge distinctive from modernist knowledge, now, after modernity, was to put indigeneity and indigenous understandings at a high premium.

Those who were previously 'civilised' now needed to be 'uncivilised' and those earlier seen to be uncivilised would become the new civilisers. That is the injunction to 'become indigenous'. As Danowski and Viveiros de Castro state, indigenous cultures, like the Amerindians 'are part of that enormous minority of peoples who have never been modern, as they have never had a Nature that they either have lost or needed to liberate themselves from' (Danowski and Viveiros de Castro, 2017: 69). Indigenous 'animism' or 'anthropomorphism' is a perfect inversion of Western 'anthropocentrism': rather than humans being a special or superior species, being human-for-itself and not-human-for-another is a universal trait of life itself (ibid.: 72). If 'Humans' (with a capital 'H') led to the Anthropocene then perhaps inversing a modernist ontology will get us out of it. For Viveiros de Castro and Danowski it is possible that:

> the generally small populations and 'relatively weak' technologies of indigenous peoples and so many other sociopolitical minorities of the Earth could become a crucial advantage and resource in a post-catastrophic time, or, if one wishes, in a *permanently* diminished human world . . . *we*—the people of the (capitalist) Core, the overweight, mediatically controlled, psychopharmacologically stabilized automata of technologically 'advanced' societies . . . might be the ones who will have to *scale down* our precious ways of living. (Danowski and Viveiros de Castro, 2017: 95–96)

Even more importantly, they argue 'indigenous people have something to teach us when it comes to apocalypses, losses of world, demographic catastrophes, and ends of History . . . : for the native people of the Americas, *the end of the world already happened*—five centuries ago (Danowski and Viveiros de Castro, 2017: 104). In the genocidal colonisation of the Americas, those who survived were *humans without world* (ibid.: 105). The arrival of the Anthropocene means that: 'The enemy, in short, is "us"—we Humans' (Danowski and Viveiros de Castro, 2017: 111).

In arguing that the struggle against 'the Human' enrols Bruno Latour, Isabelle Stengers, Donna Haraway and Elizabeth Povinelli (Danowski and Viveiros de Castro, 2017: 111), they make it clear that the construction of this modern/indigenous binary involves the white Western academy as key interpreters of indigeneity as analytical method. This capacity for critical theorists to speak on behalf of the indigenous would not be possible without anthropology's ontopolitical turn, transforming indigenous knowledge into a method or set of analytics available to all. Armed with the understanding of indigeneity as method, these anthropologically informed theorists can then anoint themselves as the intellectual gurus, leading the struggles of the indigenous and of others, constructed as a collective resistance to the Anthropocene:

> The world 'without Man' of this Anthropocene lived in a mode of resistance would thus converge with the world 'made of people' of Amerindian cosmologies: Gaia's definitive transcendence becomes indistinguishable from the originary anthropogeomorphic immanence postulated by the 'people of Pachamama'. (Danowski and Viveiros de Castro, 2017: 112)

The conceptualisations of 'Gaia' of Latour and of Stengers and Donna Haraway's imaginary of the 'Chuthulucene' stand in as representations, 'indistinguishable' from the speculative analytics culled from ontopolitical anthropology. These radical critics, who seek to rein back innovation and technological development, are unlikely to be read as conservative or reactionary if they can succeed in foregrounding the need for an 'indigenous' alternative on the basis that the left's view of progress and freedom forgets the limits of the environment and its sustainability (as discussed in the introduction; see also Chakrabarty, 2015; Danowski and Viveiros de Castro, 2017: 116–17; Holbraad and Pedersen, 2017; Stengers, 2015). It also helps their cause if they are able to enrol their constructed indigenous stage army against those who still harbour illusions in the 'Human', with its dreams of 'progress'.

This is the key trope of 'becoming indigenous': indigeneity as the imaginary of a speculative future after modernity. It is important to emphasise that the Anthropocene plays a fundamentally important role in 'becoming indigenous' because these speculative analytics depend upon a speculative engagement with the present. If we still lived in modernity, then the struggles of real and differentiated indigenous and non-indigenous peoples would have to take centre stage, rather than the speculative analytics so beloved of critical theorists in the West. However, in the Anthropocene, the dice are loaded in favour of the Western academy's critical theorists and their indigenous imaginary because, or so we are informed, the 'Humans' 'have already lost the war; *their world is already over*' (Danowski and Viveiros de Castro, 2017: 119).

But all is not lost; there is a 'second chance'. While the modernist world of the Human may be over, 'there are many worlds in the World', and the Western academic interpreters of the indigenous, who have extrapolated their method and their analytics, will guide us to these other worlds 'to come', because 'we have a lot to learn from these minor peoples who resist in an impoverished world which is not even their own any more' (Danowski and Viveiros de Castro, 2017: 120). 'Becoming indigenous' is the slogan less of a resistance to modernity and the destruction it is seen to be wreaking upon the world, than of an imaginary future that is always immanent in its becoming:

> How can someone *desire backwardness* as their *future*? Maybe the scandal has a reason for being: maybe it is impossible historically to go back to being indigenous. But it is perfectly possible—more than that, this is actually taking place—to experience a *becoming-indigenous*, local and global, particular as well as general; a *ceaseless rebecoming-indigenous*. (Danowski and Viveiros de Castro, 2017: 122)

While Danowski and Viveiros de Castro refer to popular movements in Brazil, they also hint at the global struggles against the occupation of the Moderns 'in Africa, Australasia, Mongolia, in the backstreets and basements of Fortress Europe' (Danowski and Viveiros de Castro, 2017: 122). But, of course, in the Anthropocene, the war against the colonisation of the world by Moderns and Humans is not a matter of ethnic essentialism but of a political and ethical way of being, held to keep future possibilities open. Once indigeneity is a matter of methodology or analytical framing, we are all inculcated in the struggle and are required to take sides. The future lies with those who are aware that the modernist world is already over. As noted at the start of this chapter, indigeneity is '*not a remnant of the past*' (ibid.: 123): 'Masters of technoprimitivist bricolage and politico-metaphysical metamorphosis, they are one of the possible chances, in fact, of a *subsistence of the future*' (ibid.: 123).

INDIGENOUS ANALYTICS

Indigenous analytics are held to expand our world, not by adding one more cultural perspective, another way of seeing, but by providing a different world after 'the end of the world' (Morton, 2013). Eduardo Viveiros de Castro, already cited extensively previously, is widely seen as the 'father of anthropology's ontological turn' (Holbraad and Pedersen, 2017: 157) and his influential book *Cannibal Metaphysics* (2014) has been described as 'the first attempt by a "real" anthropologist at doing speculative philosophy on the basis of ethnographic materials' (Skafish, 2014: 10). It should be emphasised that Viveiros de Castro is not setting out an ontology, and to this extent there is often misunderstanding of the meaning of 'the ontological turn'. His is a speculative philosophy, which can much more usefully be understood as sharing the approach of speculative realism. The speculative realist position is well set out by Quentin Meillassoux, who argues that since Immanuel Kant's division of the world between the noumenal world (the world 'in itself', which is independent of us) and the phenomenal world (which is the world as we experience and perceive it) the modernist episteme has focussed upon knowledge as always a product of our relation to the world, as a correlation between the thinking subject and the world as it is apprehended by that subject, as it is given to thought. Meillassoux calls this 'correlationism': the fact that 'we only ever have access to the correlation between thinking and being, and never to either term considered apart from the other' (2008: 5).

'Correlationism', as a modernist episteme, is held to separate the subject from the world, making the world inaccessible. Man is in the world but trapped in consciousness and language 'as in a transparent cage', where 'Everything is outside, yet it is impossible to get out' (Meillassoux, 2008: 6). For Meillassoux, speculative thought enables an escape from this modernist cage, enabling critical theorists to take the world more seriously again, rather than merely focussing on the intersubjective construction of meanings. Taking the world more seriously means speculating on a reality that is independent of human thought and thereby opening up to 'a great outdoors' (ibid.: 50). This speculative framing posits being as the key to thought, rather than prioritising thought. As Elisabeth Povinelli argues, this inverses the modernist conception which always prioritises thought, the subject and life and denies agency to 'Nonlife' (2016: 176).[4] For Ray Brassier, along with Meillassoux one of the most influential speculative realists, speculative realism would allow being to dethrone the power of thought; instead, thought's limits would 'index the autonomy of the object in its capacity to turn thought into a thing' (2007: 229).

It is Viveiros de Castro who has brought Amerindian 'perspectivism' and 'multi-naturalism' to the centre of anthropological thinking on indigeneity as a performative example of the application of a speculative method. In Amerindian cosmology, different beings have fundamentally different perspectives on the world, but share the same forms of 'soul' or cognition. All types of being see themselves as humans and see other types of being according to their own affordances and ways of being, normally related to their relational status as predator or prey (Viveiros de Castro, 2014: 57). The practice of shamanism foregrounds this 'perspectivism' as the shaman can cross the barrier between species and become an interlocutor able to take on the perspective or point of view of other beings to understand their intentions or will (ibid.: 60–61, 152). It is this framing that enables Viveiros de Castro to translate Amerindian culture into the terminology of Deleuzian or vital materialist speculative philosophy. But, more importantly, this highlights that for ontopolitical anthropology, perspectivism is a method or set of analytics that seeks to go beyond 'correlationism'. Rather than being imprisoned in a 'transparent cage', 'perspectivism' enables the world to be grasped through speculative shifts of perspective to those of other beings, with other embodied ways of knowing.

Whereas in the modern ontology, scientific knowledge seeks to reduce objects or occurrences to objective outcomes of causal chains of interconnection, 'Amerindian epistemological convention follows the inverse principle, which is that an object is an insufficiently interpreted subject' (Viveiros de Castro, 2014: 62) Objects, to be known, have to become subjects, replete with individual intentionality and wills. The sphere of 'nature' as brute facts or mechanical causation is drastically reduced and the sphere of 'culture' or of subjectivity and agency becomes much greater. This increase in 'perspectives' should not be confused with epistemological relativism; Viveiros de Castro argues that this is an ontological perspectivism as perspectives are correct or true for different forms of being (ibid.: 70).[5]

It is the distinctions between ontological forms of being that make this form of perspectivism 'multinatural': 'different kinds of being see the same things differently' (Viveiros de Castro, 2014: 71). The difference is not in different forms of representation as the perspective is a product of the affordances of the body not of the mind. There is one way of knowing—or one culture—but each form of life knows its world differently. There is no thing 'in-itself' somehow outside these multiple perspectives (ibid.: 73). 'Every point of view is "total", and no point of view knows its like or equivalent' (ibid.: 157–58). Every 'thing' is thereby many things at once, in superposition, thus: 'The indigenous theory of perspectivism emerges from an implicit comparison between the ways the different modes of corporeality "naturally" experience the world as affective multiplicity' (ibid.: 87).

Viveiros de Castro presents a speculative method of using indigenous ethnographic materials to inverse the modernist episteme, thus bringing indigenous thought to the same level as modernist thought. But, of course, this framing is not merely derived from the indigenous themselves; the point is to extract speculative philosophy from them:

> The philosophy of Deleuze . . . is where I found the most appropriate machine for retransmitting the sonar frequency that I had picked up from Amerindian thought. Perspectivism and multinaturalism, which are, again, objects that have been resynthesized by anthropological discourse (indigenous theories, I dare say, do not present themselves in such conveniently pre-packaged fashion!), are the result of the encounter between a certain becoming-Deleuzian of Amerindian ethnology and a certain becoming-Indian of Deleuze and Guattari's thought—a becoming-Indian that decisively passes . . . through the chapter concerning becomings in *A Thousand Plateaus*. (Viveiros de Castro, 2014: 92–93)

The key point for ontopolitical anthropology is that indigenous analytics opens up the speculative potential of the world. As Viveiros de Castro argues, this shares much with the 'symmetric' epistemology of Bruno Latour:

'in which knowing is no longer a way of representing the unknown but of interacting with it, i.e., a way of creating rather than contemplating, reflecting, or communicating' (Viveiros de Castro, 2014: 105). This is not 'an interpretation' of Amerindian thought, but rather an 'experimentation' with it, beginning by 'affirming the equivalence, in principle, of anthropological and indigenous discourse' (ibid.: 188–89). This is creative for Viveiros de Castro, leaning on Latour, as: 'The task of knowledge is no longer to unify diversity through representation but, as Latour again puts it, of "multiplying the agents and agencies populating our world"' (ibid.: 105).

This approach, of 'symmetrical anthropology' (Descola, 2013b: 69), argues that indigenous knowledge speculatively brings new agents and actants into being in ways which could be understood as no different from the natural sciences: 'it locates Moderns and non-Moderns on the same plane and proposes to consider identically all the collectives within which the repartitions between beings and properties are at work' (Descola, 2013b: 71). Latour argues that there should be no distinction between the two methods and that both are equally valid (1993, 1996): 'All nature-cultures are similar in that they simultaneously construct humans, divinities and nonhumans' (1993: 106). As Descola puts it:

> In denying to modern dualism the structuring function that it had hitherto been granted, in emphasizing that, everywhere and always, humans enlist crowds of nonhumans in the fabric of communal life, symmetrical anthropology places on an equal footing Amazonian tribes and biological laboratories, pilgrimages to Our Lady and synchrotrons. (Descola, 2013b: 71)

While the position of treating indigenous knowledge as method can enable equating it with modernist knowledge it has also been used to provincialise modernist approaches further, particularly in the context of the Anthropocene. For these approaches, most notably, that of Descola, the modern episteme becomes just one of four ways of understanding the relationship between culture and nature (2013a). Or, even more directly, for Viveiros de Castro: 'If real philosophy abounds in imaginary savages, anthropological geophilosophy makes imaginary philosophy with real savages' (2014: 192). While the speculative nature of the philosophy is fairly straightforward, the idea of 'real savages' (no matter how 'playfully' it may be articulated) as the claimed basis for a particular brand of metaphysics—the ontopolitics of the Anthropocene—is problematic. As Bassire and Bond state, despite the claims of Viveiros de Castro, Latour and Descola to evade metaphysical or ontological claims about the nature of reality, essentialising regularly slips in with the association of certain ways of thinking with ethnic groups and communities (Bessire and Bond, 2014). This problem is highlighted by Brazilian anthropologist Alcida Rita Ramos, who argues that the crude binaries at work in perspectivist approaches, inspired by de Castro's work, are 'essentialist' and 'exoticizing', diminishing the intellectual value of indigenous thinking by making it a foil for projecting Western thought (2012):

> abdicating the central role of ethnographic research as a means to arrive at a deeper understanding of and respect for indigenous peoples . . . as a theory, perspectivism is, at best, indifferent to the historical and political predicament of indigenous life in the modern world. It may be fair to say that the more extensive and deeper ethnographic knowledge is, the less arrogant we become and the more clearly we perceive the folly of projecting our theoretical ambitions on indigenous peoples. (Ramos, 2012: 489)

ONTOLOGISING INDIGENEITY

The role of the speculative analytics of the 'indigenous' in much contemporary critical theory is to lend substance to the critical and speculative desire to 'challenge the coloniality of knowledge' itself (Rosenow, 2018: 9), which is a substantially different focus than the coloniality of real inequalities and injustices in the world. Indigenous knowledge is, in these framings, not about a method of struggle or about justifications for land rights and resources but very specifically about knowledge-production itself, or as Viveiros de Castro writes, 'conceptual self-determination'. It is a generalisable analytic or practice of knowledge production, specifically for the use of non-indigenous theorists.[6] Yet, for some, the price is too high to pay in terms of what we are calling the 'ontologisation' of indigeneity itself. As Descola himself notes, in relation to Tim Ingold's approach to the indigenous as illustrating an 'ontology of dwelling':

> While such a position is entirely legitimate as a philosophical profession of faith, it is hardly so on the anthropological plane which Ingold aims to occupy. It simply inverses the common ethnocentric prejudice: it is no longer the animism of archaic peoples that appears as an incomplete version or clumsy prefiguration of the true objectification of reality as Moderns establish it, but it is rather this very objectification that appears as a monstrous outgrowth dissimulating the truth of the primordial experience of the world, of which the hunter-gatherers assisted by phenomenology, give us a better account. (2013b: 66)

The critical injunction to become indigenous should be understood as an injunction to take up a particular way of being in the world: to have a particular ethic of being, a particular form of critical stance. At the close of (critical anthropologists) Martin Holbraad and Morten Pedersen's recent book *The Ontological Turn* (2017) this is articulated well. Becoming indigenous can thus be understood to be an open-ended critical project, where the world itself becomes the critical subject or agency and the critical theorist or activist is not attempting to impose themselves upon the world but rather to become a facilitator or enabler in speculatively letting the world speak back to power, hegemony and limits. The task of critique then is 'not unlike an artist probing and sensing her way through the bundle of forces that the affordance of her materials enable or even compels her to release" (2017: 292). The task of critical anthropology is to 'intensely abstract conceptual scaling or "sculpting" that works by eliciting certain dynamics and potentials present "within things" into intensified versions of these things themselves' (ibid.). The task of critique is to make the world more 'alive', more real and intense (see also Puig de la Bellacasa, 2017).

Indigenous knowledge as method or as analytic becomes a tool to be universalised for a new 'post-critical' ethic of care. As Holbraad and Perdersen accurately observe, becoming indigenous thus becomes an alternative to earlier ethics of critique. It is a far cry from the old left doctrinaires who proclaimed that they had divined a single and absolute truth of the world that they would disseminate and implement through the party. It is also very different to the post-Marxist left's critique through deconstruction, attempting to reveal the hegemonic forces behind truth claims and to remove the grounds of certainty (see Bargués-Pedreny, 2019). The construction of indigenous knowledge as critique seeks to articulate constructive or positive alternatives through drawing them out from the world itself. The problem, of course, is that these self-aggrandising claims of critical theorists and activists 'representing' or 'giving voice' to the world, the environment or mountains and rivers can easily sound like the height of white or colonial hubris.

The construction of indigenous knowledge as an analytic available for export to Western critical activists and theorists therefore becomes vital for the viability of these (otherwise deeply problematic) claims. We call the production of indigenous knowledge in these terms 'ontopolitical' as it grounds a new ethic of politics, not in the needs and desires of the political subject but allegedly in the world itself or rather in its speculative affordances. In alleging that 'post-critique' works on the basis of the 'conceptual affordances present in a body of ethnographic materials', Holbraad and Pedersen argue that indigenous analytics 'imply a peculiarly non- or anti-normative stance' (2017: 294). Rather than 'a means to externally defined political ends' they claim that this approach is 'a political end in its own right' (ibid.: 295). This is because indigenous analytics of bringing the world to life on its own terms and intensifying these is 'oriented towards the production of difference, or "alterity", as such' (ibid.: 296). Here the critical anthropological imaginary takes on nearly God-like features:

> Regardless . . . of the political goals to which it may lend itself, anthropology is *ontologically political* inasmuch as its operation presupposes, and is an attempt experimentally to 'do', difference as such: the politics of indefinitely sustaining the possible, the 'could be'. It is an anthropology, then, that is analytically anti-authoritarian, making it its business to generate vantages from which established forms of thinking are put under relentless pressure by alterity itself, and perhaps changed. (Holbraad and Pedersen, 2017: 296–97)

The critical politics of anthropology armed with indigenous analytics is that of enabling the critical but latent power of 'alterity itself'. Here we see the full hubris of ontopolitical anthropological thought in its pretence to write the subject out of critique and replace it with life itself, understood as the ceaseless differentiating power of 'alterity'. Western anthropologists have replaced the hubris of the modernist 'God's eye view from nowhere' (Haraway) with the no-less hubristic God's eye view from everywhere, from life itself.[7] This is a transformation in the form of knowing while maintaining its hierarchical content, through (once again) erasing the positionality of the anthropologist as knowing subject. It is achieved through the engagement with and transvaluation of indigenous knowledge.

One problem we have with taking at face value the articulation of indigenous knowledge as method is that it effaces the reality of being indigenous. Indigeneity is transformed into a way of being and knowing that has little to do with the rich plurality of the lived life of indigenous groups. This exoticisation of indigenous knowledge is widely prevalent in critical theory. To take one example of how the reality of indigenous being is neglected in the white, predominantly Western fantasy of 'becoming indigenous', Donna Haraway, perhaps the most widely known and cited critical feminist scholar, reveals a lot about the radical expropriation of indigenous knowledge as method in her book *Staying with the Trouble* (2016). Here, Haraway retells the 'Camille Stories' collectively written in a speculative narration workshop, staged with Isabelle Stengers. This speculative fiction is a story of 'Communities of Compost' of multi-specism, which instrumentally 'birthed symbiogenetic children for the work of rehabilitating ruined lands and waters through the coming generations' (Haraway, 2016: 154).

The 'Camille Stories' span five generations of Camille and her offspring born into a dystopian world of environmental devastation. These fictional 'future humans' provide a narrative story of 'becoming indigenous' as they seek to build a 'life in the ruins' (Tsing, 2015) through 'sympoietic creativity' (that is, becoming with others both human and nonhuman) 'making kin in innovative ways' (Haraway, 2016: 138). 'Becoming indigenous' as an analytic of sensitivity is at the heart of this story.

> Bodily modifications are normal among Camille's people and at birth a few genes and a few microorganisms from the animal symbiont are added to the symchild's bodily heritage, so that sensitivity and response to the world as experienced by the animal critter can be more vivid and precise for the human member of the team. . . . The animals themselves were not modified with human material; their roles in the symbiosis were to teach and to flourish in every way possible in dangerous and damaged times. (Haraway, 2016: 140–41, 147)

Here, the use of medical science to transfer genetic materials seeks to achieve the 'becoming other' of the Shaman, enabling the sensitivities to the world in its worlding that merely remaining human could not; enabling Camille to understand 'the biological, cultural, historical worlds of these clusters of [M]onarch [butterflies]' (Haraway, 2016: 153). Crucially this human-nonhuman symbiosis required the skill set of indigenous knowledge:

> Of course, as an important component of [Camille]'s education and working alliances as both child and adult, Camille 1 had studied with Native American, First Nation, and Metis teachers, who explained and performed diverse practices and knowledges for conjoined human and other-than-human becoming and exchange. (Haraway, 2016: 153)

Camille 1 is given some of the genetic material of the Monarch butterfly, helping her taste chemical signals in the wind and cope with the toxic alkaloids in the Monarch diet (Haraway, 2016: 148). The second generation, Camille 2, goes further having chin implants of butterfly antennae to sense better the butterfly world (ibid.: 152). In the process of 'becoming butterfly' Camille 2 goes to 'the overwintering habitat of the eastern migration to meet with indigenous people and campesinos who were rehabilitating damaged lands' (ibid.: 152). And from the second generation on 'decolonial work . . . had to be intrinsic to every form of sympoiesis with the monarchs' (ibid.: 154–55). And the indigenous community were confident that the symbiont 'would become an apt student of their own human-butterfly worldings, and so a useful ally . . . to join in the work of human and other-than-human rehabilitation and multispecies environmental justice in indigenous territory' (ibid.: 155).

Here the posthuman Camille needs the assistance of the nonhumans and the indigenous skills whereby nonhumans can be understood and related to only by letting go 'of colonialist notions of religion and secularism to begin to appreciate the sheer semiotic materiality' of the world (Haraway, 2016: 157).

In fact, the further down the line of future posthuman generations Camille goes, the more indigenous knowledge as method is necessary as an enabling factor. Camille 5, the last in the narrative time-span is trained in Susan Harding's 'experimental animism' (ibid.: 164) and in Viveiros de Castro's multi-naturalism and perspectivism (ibid.: 165). The Camille Stories are literally the white liberal fantasy tale of becoming posthumanly attuned to nature through 'becoming indigenous'.

We are not the first to raise the problem of 'exoticism'. As Bessire and Bond state (see also our discussion of 'dispossession' in chapter 2): 'the apparent fusion of nature and culture attributed to indigenous peoples is itself a long-standing conceit whose genealogy can be traced to colonial property regimes in which the commons was assigned to Indians while private property was reserved for Spaniards' (Bessire and Bond, 2014: 444). However, the problem of exoticism is often misunderstood as somehow giving indigenous groups a special insight into non-modern ontologies and epistemologies. This is not really the case. In fact, it could be argued that the reality is worse. One problem that the advocates of indigenous knowledge as method face is why the arguments and frameworks that they derive from their 'ethnographic experiences on the ground' always ends up being very similar to what Deleuze and Guattari and other continental philosophers have been arguing for decades. Therefore the anthropological promise that indigenous analytics can enable the infinite variety of life's alterity to emerge, to challenge Western analytical colonial hegemony, seems rather disingenuous. These radical anthropologists might just as well have stayed at home and attended workshops on speculative narration.

A typical example occurs in the work of Marisol de la Cadena, at the University of California, Davis, who states that she is taking her cue from Isabelle Stengers (2010: 336; 346) in developing a 'multinatural' cosmopolitics, centred on the alternative ontology of indigeneity. Here's a sense of how these 'cosmopolitical' sensitivities work out on the ground, as she describes two of her interlocutors:

> Graciano Mandura (Major of Ocongate, bilingual in Quechua and Spanish, holding a university degree) and Nazario Turpo (pampamisayoq in Ocongate, monolingual Quechua speaker, and not knowing how to read or write) participate in indigeneity from two different positions—one more capable through literacy, the other *better able to interact with other-than-human beings*—but both connected to the worlds that their lives make less than two. (de la Cadena, 2010: 348; emphasis added)

The ease at which the differentiation between different indigenous perspectives is understood in the most essentialising terms—literacy equals modernist ontology separating nature and culture, while illiteracy equals non-modern ontology 'better able to interact with other-than-human beings'—would be shocking if it was not written in good coin by a well-respected ontopolitical anthropologist. Once again, this repeats all the hoary colonial prejudices already rehearsed in Haraway and Stenger's speculative fiction workshop.

Holbraad and Pedersen, to their credit, take up the challenge, asking: 'Should we take the similarities between ontological turn-style analyses as an indication that the ethnographic situations that precipitate them are not, after all, as different from each other as we might imagine?' (2017: 279, n.11). The idea that all across the world the anthropological experience might be the same clearly doesn't say much for the discipline's investigative powers or ability to uncover new ways of thinking and doing! If this latter view, that anthropological investigation itself was the source of this similarity, were to be true, then they argue: 'This would be dismal, since it would effectively amount to the ontological turn admitting that its prime task, that of creating the conditions for ethnographic differences to make a difference, had effectively failed' (ibid.).

The 'convergence' of Western critical thinking, informed through the 'ontopolitical turn' in anthropology, thus celebrates indigenous knowledge at the same time as denying an indigenous voice independent of this 'methodological' framing. As Bessire and Bond argue, this is:

> what makes the implications of ontological anthropology so problematic. The paradox is this: Although it poses as a mechanism to promote the 'ontological self-determination of peoples' by 'giving the ontological back to the people', multinaturalist ontology cannot be taken as a general description of actually existing Indigenous being without becoming ensnared in empirical contradictions. The only way it can often be sustained is by a targeted erasure of ethnographic evidence and an artificial standardization of alterity itself. (Bessire and Bond, 2014: 443)

They continue:

> Is there anything more banally modern than that orthodox dialectic of Otherness wherein Indigenous ontological legitimacy is restricted to the terms of an alterity grounded in myth with which many do not agree and from which many are always already excluded? . . . To unsettle one modern binary, he or she must presume the validity of another: the incommensurability of the modern and the nonmodern. (Bessire and Bond, 2014: 444)

The problem of exoticism is precisely that critical anthropologists, so keen to distil indigenous knowledge as method or analytics, reduce their field studies to an homogenous whole: one which seems very much based on their readings of contemporary US and European writers engaged with the problems of continental philosophy. Rather than facilitating and enabling any plural or differential power of life to inform their critical perspectives, the project of extracting indigenous knowledge as a fungible method or analytic for Western critical theorists reduces indigenous societies and practices to mere props or backstops for the story of how the anthropologists themselves operate to 'do difference differently'. Rather than 'exoticising' indigenous practices, we argue that critical or ontopolitical anthropology instead 'objectifies' its subject matter. In treating indigenous knowledge as method or analytics they, in fact, reduce indigenous society to the level of any other object or appearance in the world that catches their attention and then becomes used to enable their own creative critical capacities. When Holbraad and Pedersen argue that they also want to treat things in the same way as they treat indigenous practices this 'objectification' becomes clearer.

The anthropological respect for the 'conceptual self-determination' of indigenous people is no different from their 'respect' for any other object. Holbraad and Pedersen state that rather than assuming to know or to represent 'things': 'Rather, the strategy must be one that is capable of effectively *de-theorising* the thing, by emptying it out of its many analytical connotations, rendering it a purely ethnographic "form" ready to be filled out contingently, according to its own ethnographic exigencies' (2017: 211). This 'is the prime step towards allowing things to dictate their own terms of analytical engagement' (ibid.). The task of critical anthropology, in applying indigenous knowledge as method, is to enable any 'thing' to have 'conceptual self-determination': to be able to be known through its '*conceptual* affordances' (2017: 218). Rather than generalising through abstraction and reducing life to more or less of the same, critical anthropology claims to render things *more concrete* (2017: 235), seeing how things or artefacts 'analyse themselves', through initiating trains of thought (2017: 234). Thus, indigenous knowledge as analytics does not make practices or things more 'exotic' but rather 'objectifies' the world to being merely a set of transmutable effects available for the speculative anthropological imagination.[8] In effect, indigenous analytics empties the world of things of all meaningful content, reducing the world to a mere foil for speculative thought. As Mark Jackson states: 'in matters concerning being-with others, human and nonhuman, *all our everyday materialities hold the capacity to indigenise*, that is, to render socio-natural forms of belonging that enfold and so create worlds otherwise' (2014: 76; emphasis added).

CONCLUSION

We find the conflation of a very white, very Western, very Eurocentric concern with the crisis of the modern episteme with the real political and life struggles of indigenous groups and communities to be dishonest and, indeed, parasitical. This conflation happens through a specific form of 'translation', through which radical Western conceptual critique becomes reconstructed through the injunction to 'become indigenous'. This process of 'becoming indigenous' is not the fantasy of literally pretending to be indigenous, nor is it necessarily a political act of solidarity with indigenous struggles for rights, land or resources. Indigeneity can become imagined as an ethic to be taken up by 'woke', 'aware' and concerned white people on the basis of transforming indigenous ways of being and of knowing from a 'culture' or alternative 'knowledge' that requires respect, but would always to some extent exclude white people (see, for example, Brigg, 2008), to a 'transferable skill set' or set of practices or speculative analytics that anyone can adopt.

The injunction to 'become indigenous' only works on the basis of universalising indigeneity as a set of analytical skills open to all. The sphere of thought through which indigeneity shifted from being seen as a distinct set of cultural practices and beliefs (closed off to complete modern understanding) to being a set of analytical or methodological tools open to all, was of course anthropology. Anthropology's 'ontopolitical turn' is thus key to understanding the conditions of possibility for 'becoming indigenous'. It was work in the field of anthropology that transformed indigeneity from an 'outside' of modernity to the 'inside' of a speculative non-modern condition. The Anthropocene, seen as the end of the modernist construction of a divide between nature and culture, is held to necessitate 'becoming indigenous' as an injunction necessary for Western survival. As we will consider later (chapter 5, 'Pluriversal Politics'), it is this process of 'ontologizing' indigeneity which has enabled the idea of Amerindian perspectivism to be translated from a speculative methodology into a 'decolonial' phenomenology of being, constituting a 'pluriverse' of 'many worlds'. These analytical tools are also deployed (see chapter 6, 'Resilience') in discourses of governing through resilience, which ontologically assert that complex adaptive systems require precisely these speculative and adaptive skills.

NOTES

1. As Luca Bessire and David Bond state:

the resulting awe of alterity holds up only so long as the ground of ontology is kept clean. Coca-Cola cans, shotguns, soccer balls, evangelical icons, petrochemical pollution, trinkets for tourists, and T-shirts from Grand Rapids—to name a few of the things we have encountered in far-flung Indigenous villages—are brushed aside, as the dreams of dogs and chants of elders come to stand in for the most pressing form of material becoming. This rarified multinaturalism is only strengthened as the figure of ontology shifts attention from domestic or working relationships with the natural world to priestly assertions of it. Thus, many in the ontological turn attempt to convince fellow anthropologists that shamanic visions of vibrant actuality are the only version that really counts. (Bessire and Bond, 2014: 447)

2. Returning to Haraway's ground-breaking article 'Situated Knowledges' from 1988, it is notable that 'Southwest native American accounts' of the 'Coyote or Trickster' are used to support 'feminist visualizations of the world' rather than to instantiate a non-modern ontology (1988: 593).

· 3. As Latour notes (2009: 2) Amerindian perspectivism is 'a bomb with the potential to explode the whole implicit philosophy so dominant in most ethnographers' interpretations of their material'.

4. 'Life is not the miracle—the dynamic opposed to the inert of rocky substance. Nonlife is what holds, or should hold for us, the more radical potential. For Nonlife created what it is radically not. . . . Life is merely a moment in the greater dynamic unfolding of Nonlife' (Povinelli, 2016: 176).

5. As Eduardo Kohn describes his response to being challenged with the question of whether he was still just talking about a cultural system: 'My response was, "Oh, you think that how people see a jaguar seeing the world is a cultural product? Well, go out in the forest. When you're out in the forest, you have to get how the jaguar sees the world right, or else" (Kohn, 2017: 163–64).

6. This is why indigenous knowledge as an analytic is a distinctive part of what is often called the 'ontological turn' to material ways of being in the world. As Holbraad and Pedersen write, in the early 1990s, the focus in anthropology was upon phenomenology, alternative ways of being in and thereby perceiving the world, held to be prior to language and conceptualisation (this was thereby another way of interpreting or understanding indigenous cultural distinctions). The difference in the shift to indigenous knowledge is that this is seen as a specific method for theorising and conceptualising from reality itself (Holbraad and Pedersen, 2017: 284).

7. As Claire Colebrook (2014: 163–64) states:

Humanism posits an elevated or exceptional 'man' to grant sense to existence, then when 'man' is negated or removed what is left is the human all too human tendency to see the world as one giant anthropomorphic self-organizing living body. . . . When man is destroyed to yield a posthuman world it is the same world minus humans, a world of meaning, sociality and readability yet without any sense of the disjunction, gap or limits of the human.

8. As Bessire and Bond state:

These imaginaries redefine critique by displacing it in time and space. Critical theory, of course, has long been concerned with working out the coordinates of critique from the subaltern positions of real people: their fraught ways of knowing as well as their unruly ways of being. Ontological anthropology rejects this operation. Instead, it imagines resistance as a future fait accompli that does not require the foil of present domination. In this model, critique is not located within the historically specific subject position of the Indian but in the impending utility of his or her timeless cosmology. (2014: 449)

Chapter 4

Perseverance

Perseverance, the ability to stick to a commitment, continue steadfastly and persist in its fulfillment, is an attribute regularly assigned today to indigenous peoples, as much by indigenous peoples themselves as by their purported allies (Clark, 2012; Pechenkina, 2017; Pedri-Spade, 2014). Scholars typically remark on the 'astonishing resilience and persistence' of indigenous peoples in their struggles to maintain their existences and identities in the face of strategies of nation-states and associated powers aimed at wiping them out (Granville Miller, 2003: 6). In a way it is a paradox that indigenous peoples, identified as existing in a state of peril, struggling to survive collectively and individually, and at high risk of suicide, should be those subjects in which a power of perseverance is more developed than in others. The indigenous peoples of Canada especially, and their youth in particular, have 'the highest known suicide rate of any culturally identifiable group in the world' (Chandler et al., 2003: 3). Yet it is precisely these peoples, most at risk of death, individually and collectively, in which perseverance is identified as a notable and particular trait. To be indigenous is to be good at being perseverant, exemplary even, at surviving, keeping going, in a struggle to the death. Disappointment and defeat just seem to spur these particular peoples 'to still greater effort' (Granville Miller, 2003: 4)

PERSEVERANCE

One such example are the Mi'kmaq peoples, indigenous to Eastern Canada, the territories of which are known as Mi'kma'ki, covering Atlantic Canada and the Northeastern United States, who have suffered a long history of colonisation involving many attempts to eradicate their ways of life (Prosper et al., 2011: 3) Yet, as one group of anthropologists have argued, 'Mi'kmaq resilience and inherent rights could not be erased and today are being reshaped in the reclamation of their own history' (Prosper et al., 2011: 3). Indeed the Mi'kmaq themselves proclaim their own perseverance. 'Our perseverance and continuum as a People; our Community of Mi'kmaq/Aboriginal Peoples, "the forgotten people", can no longer be denied or ignored' declares the Native Council of Nova Scotia, the self-governing authority for the large community of Mi'kmaq/Aboriginal peoples residing off-reserve in Nova Scotia throughout traditional Mi'kmaq territory (Native Council of Nova Scotia, 2018). 'Our Community of Mi'kmaq/Aboriginal Peoples continuing on our traditional ancestral homelands never surrendered, (and) by our courage, perseverance, capacity, merit and dignity, continue to denounce the government policy and we remain Mi'kmaq on Mi'kma'ki' (Native Council of Nova Scotia, 2018).

The celebration of perseverance as a trait and ability is of course not limited to indigenous peoples. In recent years we have seen a veritable explosion in popular scientific knowledge concerned with understanding and promoting it. The American psychologist Angela Lee Duckworth calls the combination of perseverance with passion 'grit' and argues it to be at least as important as talent in determining the relative success and happiness of all human beings, regardless of their being indigenous or not (Duckworth, 2016). There exists some research on the racial and cultural determinants of 'grit' (Zentner et al., 2016) but it is, in fact, not a discourse to be found often being applied to indigenous peoples. Duckworth's studies of grit avoid discussing 'mediocre or moderately successful people' at all and focus on corporate 'high achievers' like Jeff Bezos, the founder of Amazon, and Jamie Dimon of JPMorgan Chase (Denby, 2016). She notes that genes are 'in part' responsible for our grittiness (Duckworth, 2016: 79–83) and that particular cultures, such as that of the Finnish people, may prize grit more than others (Duckworth, 2016: 250–53), but her main message is that grit is an attribute that can be grown (Duckworth, 2016: 269).

Yet perseverance is arguably not a particularly human trait at all. It's a resource we are, as humans, likely to lack rather than possess in abundance, which is arguably why psychologists like Duckworth are concerned with how humans might 'grow' it (Duckworth, 2016). If we want exemplars of perseverance we would do well to look outside of the distinctly human realm of endeavours and focus, for example, on plants, whose perseverance is indeed often admired. The philosopher Michael Marder has argued precisely this. Plants, he argues, can and do inspire humans to act like them, and learn how to persevere

(Marder, 2012: 24). They are exemplars of beings which, unlike humans who in their suffering of defeats and losses are likely to be deterred from continuing on the paths which led to their suffering, continue and only seem to grow stronger from setbacks. 'The more the plant loses, the more it grows. Proliferating from pure loss, plants offer themselves with unconditional generosity. Silently they extend themselves in space, exposing their vegetal bodies in utter vulnerability to being chopped off or plucked, harvested or trimmed, broken by a hurricane or burnt by the sun' (Marder, 2013: 73–74).

Unlike Duckworth, who writes to address the would-be chief executive officers of the corporate world, Marder is writing for the downtrodden, oppressed 99 per cent who have been seeking to resist the corporative powers whose economic success supposedly depends on gritty leaders like Bezos and Dimon. Since 2011 a movement has developed worldwide, and significantly in the United States, aimed at resisting neoliberalism through the development of new tactics of the occupation of space (Marder, 2012: 24–26). The Occupy movement is of course the prime example of this. As Marder describes it:

> The politics of the Occupy movement is the politics of space, not of time, and it extends its reach by replicating itself in different locales around the world, not by formalizing its program in an effort to attain a stable temporal identity. While it continues to resort to the traditional tactics of marches, support for labor unions on picket lines, and demonstrations, the core of the Occupy movement is made of the determination to dwell in the uninhabitable, to inhabit a previously depersonalized, depopulated, abandoned, but highly symbolic and central place in the public sphere. Its staying power is bound to the protesters' staying in their chosen gathering place, *their defiant perseverance in a locale*. (Marder, 2012: 25)

But lest we think that this championing of perseverance is a relatively recent trend in thinking on both left and right let us not forget that, in the West at least, long before the contemporary veneration of plants, we were taught to associate it with Christian saints; beings inspired by powers gifted to them by gods from other worlds (Berkouwer, 1958). It is particularly crucial to the doctrine of Saint Paul and bound up there with hope, which itself 'pertains to endurance, to perseverance, to patience' (Badiou, 2003: 93). Perseverance, then, is an attribute of a wide range of different kinds of subjects. It is a property which binds together indigenous peoples—in their struggles to maintain their existences in the face of colonial projects dedicated to destroying them—with the chief executive officers of corporations like Amazon and JPMorgan Chase, the leftists occupying Zuccotti Park in New York, Christian saints, and the vegetal life of plants.

As already stated, in her book *Grit*, Duckworth makes no mention of indigenous perseverance. And indeed in accounts of their own perseverance indigenous peoples do not tend to represent themselves either as 'gritty' or as particularly happy or successful. To return to the Native Council of Nova Scotia is to return to a description of the suffering which perseverance can bring. 'Our Community of direct descendent Mi'kmaq continuing to live throughout our traditional ancestral homelands, have suffered greatly for our perseverance to resist: government denial of our true identity, forced dispossession and dislocation from our homelands, and the denial of the Mi'kmaq people as the Mi'kmaq Nation of People on the east coast of Canada', they declare (Native Council of Nova Scotia, 2018). Whether the suffering and travails which the indigenous continue to register on account of their treatment at the hands of colonisers is as affirmative for them as it is alleged to be for the saints, on whom it confirmed beatitude, or the plants, which only grow stronger from it, or for financiers, who need to bounce back from losses and negotiate tough bargains, is of course highly questionable.

THE COLONIAL ROOTS OF
INDIGENOUS PERSEVERANCE

Indeed perseverance is an attribute of indigenous subjectivity that the creators of indigenous suffering, their colonisers, have also admired, ever since their first encounters. The arrival of the Astorians in the early nineteenth century in the Pacific Northwest of the United States is documented in Alexander Ross's *Adventures of the First Settlers on the Oregon or Columbia River* and recounted in Richard White's excellent history of the Columbia River at the mouth of which they set up base in 1811 (White, 1995). One of these Astorians, Robert Stuart described with awe how the Indians, when the river capsized their canoes, would simply empty them, and 'with the greatest composure', get back in and proceed to attempt to navigate it again and again (White, 1995: 8). Ross himself described his own faith in the 'zeal, fortitude, and perseverance' of indigenous peoples that led him to hire indigenous labour in place of white Western labour in conducting expeditions westward (Ross, 1855: 29). He then went on, however, to describe the misplaced nature of this faith, as the indigenous guide and 'companions' he took with him on his expedition deserted him, apparently frightened by the weather conditions, and how after trying and failing 'to infuse some ambition and perseverance' into them, he concluded as to their destitution of 'moral courage, a characteristic defect of their race', and having been taught a lesson, determined never to put his faith in indigenous people again (Ross, 1855: 38).

The lack of perseverance Ross thought he met in the indigenous subjects he attempted to exploit might today as well be described, of course, as resistance. The fright of the indigenous guide who Ross took with him, when witnessing the effects of a storm on their passage, and his decision to desert Ross and return back the way they came, might as well be described as indigenous wisdom, indicating the greater respect of the indigenous for the superior forces of nature over humanity. The true perseverance of indigenous peoples lies, of course, we are told, in their success in having survived and maintained not just their existences but ways of life, despite the exploitative denigration of colonisers such as Ross. It is this remarkable achievement which, even if it has involved suffering, nevertheless still creates the possibility of an 'end to the assault of demeaning subjugation' (Native Council of Nova Scotia, 2018) against indigenous peoples everywhere.

Or does it? Today the discourse of perseverance has returned. It is, at times, invoked by indigenous peoples themselves, including the Mi'kmaq, when they describe their survival over historical time, and despite the attempts of colonisers to wipe them out. Other times it is invoked by the powers that govern them, such as the Arctic Council, when it describes the perseverance of indigenous cultures and promises strategies designed to help foster their persistence further (Arctic Human Development Report, 2004: 45–68). It is also utilised by authors and activists, sometimes referring to themselves as the 'friends' of the indigenous, whose subject positions are non-indigenous, but who nevertheless want to decolonise political struggles (Granville Miller, 2003: 6). In these latter discourses, the ability of indigenous peoples to persist is seen less as a key to their survival in the past and more as a capacity they are going to require forever into the future (see Rubis and Theriault, 2019). Wary of making promises about future emancipation, these current discourses often transpose perseverance into a capacity that equips the indigenous as much for the future as it has enabled them to survive until the present.

PERSEVERANCE IN THE ANTHROPOCENE

We ourselves are wary of these latter discourses. It seems to us that the discursive representation of indigenous peoples as perseverant is being mobilised to connect with and give support to the neoliberal project, concerned as it is with the deconstruction of the political subject and its replacement with the resilient, perseverant and dispossessed subject of the Anthropocene. We recognise, of course, that indigenous peoples can be seen on the left as 'the canary in the coal mine', a pure kind of subject, capable of throwing 'a wedge into the universalising logic of the Anthropocene' (Demos, 2017:

44), because they bear no responsibility for the degradations of the planet done by the West. But the reality is much more complex. The function of the reification of indigenous perseverance is that of making us all, whether indigenous or not, learn perseverance as a coping mechanism for dealing with catastrophic futures. Here discourses on indigenous perseverance dovetail nicely with the psychological literatures that celebrate perseverance as 'grit' such as that of Angela Lee Duckworth (Duckworth, 2016). Grit functions as that uncanny resource which any subject struggling to succeed 'against the odds', sutured in relations of inequality and disadvantage, is required to possess (Clay, 2019: 30).

The invitation to 'become indigenous', then, not only deconstructs the liberal subject of old. It also disciplines and produces, as we have seen and as we can yet further see, a particular kind of alternative to it. The production of this alternative subject is as much a function of a homogenising approach to indigeneity as it is of literatures on political subjectivity as such. This alternative is a subject that has learned the lesson of perseverance from indigenous peoples and their struggles, as well as from a variety of other struggles and sites of experience not traditionally valued on the left, including those of plants (Marder, 2012) as well as the Christian saints (Badiou, 2003). It is a queer kind of subject, whose ability to persevere continuously demonstrates its capacities to be responsive and relate to the world around it, reflectively critical of itself, its relationship to others as much as their relationships to itself, suspicious of normalising practices, and creative of new and resistant ones. Since at least the advent of the Occupy movement, which emerged out of the popular protests that took place throughout 2011, the idealisation of this new kind of subject has taken hold.

Occupy experienced a somewhat vexed relationship to indigenous struggles and movements, and some critics argued that it did not take the indigenous question as seriously as it ought (Barker, 2012; Kilibarda, 2012)—after all, Wall Street, the central space of occupation for the movement, was itself built on the dispossession of land from an indigenous people, the Lenape (Kauanui, 2016). However, the Standing Rock protests of 2016 are argued to have corrected that, combining '#occupy with #decolonize' and 'creating radical possibilities for an ongoing intersectional movement' (Larkey, 2017). This convergence is not a product merely of adapting to sensitivities, previously ignored. To occupy, in the evolving subjectivity of radical politics, is precisely not to possess but to advocate a way of mutualist being in the world.

Fundamental to the politics of much contemporary protest is the attempt to articulate this new form of perseverant subject, which takes inspiration from indigenous knowledge and practices. However, the inspiration taken from indigenous approaches is not that of political or tactical forms of organisation or expression, nor that of a concern for care of nature or the environment per se. Rather, it is the appropriation of a particular form of subjectivity, subject positionality or way of being. We suggest that this form of subjectivity derives from an image of indigeneity constructed through contemporary discourses of perseverance. We wish to highlight that this construction of a mode of being that enables perseverance is not specific to discourses of indigeneity but rather a lens which we see to be highly reductive and essentialising.

We saw in the chapter on dispossession how closely related the discussion of indigeneous perseverance has become today to the understanding of other modes of perseverance, for example, that of plants (Kimmerer, 2013). This interconnection around an imaginary of a shared way of being or approach to the world highlights the power of contemporary framings of what it means to know how to persevere against powerful and oppressive forces. This knowledge is held to be as vital for today's political movements as it was for indigenous life before them and is perhaps exemplified in the increasingly widespread understanding that these strategies of resistance and survival can be abstracted and generalised on the basis of modelling the life and behaviour of plants; resisting constraints, probing possibilities but always, seemingly, through assembling collectives and collaborations with other life forms rather than imposing their own.

This perspective comes across strongly in the work of Natasha Myers, and in her view of 'Planthropocene' thought and practice, enabling us to 'change the terms of encounter' with nonhuman others (2017: 299–300). Picking up on a range of associated work, such as Anna Tsing's ideas of 'collaborative survival' (2015), Marisol de la Cadena's view of cultivating relations with the 'anthropos-not-seen' (2015), and Maria Puig de la Bellacasa's specula-tive ethics of care (2017), she argues that we need to learn from and listen to nonhuman modes of living, 'find ways to *vegetalise* our all-too-human sensorium, and learn how to involve ourselves with plants' (Myers, 2017a: 300, italics in original). If we are to decolonise ecology and resist 'colonial imaginations of nature and culture', new speculative and nonhuman forms of sentience and attention are necessary (Myers, 2017b: 7).

As Michael Marder has put it, the idea is to 'resist like a plant!' (Marder, 2012). After all, what is more perseverant than a plant when it comes to the ability to occupy a space and to stay in one place (Marder, 2012: 25)? Like indigenous peoples everywhere (Kimmerer, 2013), if we are to believe what we are told, these movements have learned how to be perseverant, even how to conduct their conflicts and struggles wholesale, from the vegetal life of plants (Marder, 2012: 26). For Marder at least, the perseverance of the plant owes to its 'non-oppositional being', which, unlike that of the animal (which opposes itself to its place by dislocating itself), is 'shackled to its environment' (Marder, 2012: 26). This means that:

> When environmental activists chain themselves to trees that are about to be felled, they replicate, to some extent, the mode of being of these vegetal beings: confined to a place, bodily manifesting their bond. . . . And when protesters pitch tents in parks or on city squares, they reinvent the strange modern rootedness in the uprooted world of the metropolis, existentially signifying their discontent by merely being there. (Marder, 2012: 26)

Emergent from this convergence of environmental philosophy with indigenous knowledge and political practice is a profound displacement of the instrumental temporal politics of future ends with an experiential politics of being in space (Marder, 2012: 25). The body, as we will see, is central to the development of this new politics of space and its strategy of perseverance. The image of the body at stake here is also particular, however. It is not a body made to ever master the space it occupies but which indeed foregoes mastery deliberately. It is a body that 'extends its reach by replicating itself in different locales around the world, not by formalising its program in an effort to attain a stable temporal identity' (Marder, 2012: 25). Its aim is not to master the spaces into which it moves but 'to dwell in the uninhabitable' (Marder, 2012: 25) in exactly those ways by which weed species dwell in seemingly uninhabitable spaces. Though, in what is apparently not a paradox, Marder himself does write of the ways in which plants have 'mastered this way of being' (2013: 51). Plants, we have to assume, are the new masters of 'being in being', and we, or at least the non-indigenous who are still learning how to be, are their pupils.

The radicalism of turning to indigenous knowledge or indigenous modes of being is seen not merely to apply to political protest but to resistance to Western and colonial forms of knowing and acting in general, as Natasha Myers argues:

> I am looking for ways of knowing that can expose the colonial and extractive logics of the sciences, while holding scientists, their publics, governments, and industry accountable to asking better questions and cultivating more robust modes of inquiry. I am holding out hope for a mode of inquiry that can be responsive to the needs of communities, such as those living downstream from the toxic flows of late industrialism, and in the wake of climate change. I want to support the creation of knowledge forms that can help us to contest constrained regimes of evidence, unsettle ideas about what modes of attention, objects, methods and data forms are proper to the sciences, and disrupt assumptions about whose knowledge counts. (Myers, 2017b: 3)

The argument of many contemporary critics, particularly those who advocate queer, feminist and decolonial political approaches, is that this way of embodying perseverance is necessary as a turn against the liberal tradition of thinking about political subjectivity, based as it supposedly has been on the assumption of a body which masters, possesses and improves the space it occupies. This theoretical turn combines with the valorisation of the environmental adaptivity of the indigenous body whose perseverance in space is increasingly seen to be an inherently ecological capacity of bringing together human and nonhuman worlds grounded in mutual and beneficial processes of becoming against the closures of colonial and modernist thought and practices.

What we see happening here, then, is an important reversal of the ways by which the political subject relates to space. Politics is no longer the art of invading and holding space, occupying it, and persevering in the occupation of that space, against the odds of one's ejection, by forces and powers that claim possession of it, and which seek to be its master, as well as to develop it. Politics is no longer a claim over space—about rights to territorial self-determination or self-government—but now is ontologised: a claim of how to be in space in ways in which perseverance is a collective process of working with the other in mutual and non-exploitative or extractive ways. In other words, what we have here is an ontologisation of the very spatial conditions on which indigenous subjugation has been based historically. A politics which functions by naturalising the struggle to hold on to a way of being in a space against powers which claim formal possession of it and of how it is to be managed. A politics, in other words, which ontologises the very conditions that indigenous peoples have been struggling with since the very first arrivals of colonial powers at the birth of modernity and ever since.

THE DOUBLE-BIND OF
INDIGENOUS PERSEVERANCE

In philosophical and theoretical terms the capacity for perseverance is crucial to the view, said to have emerged in the seventeenth century with Spinoza, that basically all living things seek to persevere and that therefore anything of which perseverance can be observed may be said to be living and have life. As he put it in his *Ethics* 'everything in so far as it is in itself endeavors to persist in its own being' and 'the endeavor wherewith a thing endeavors to persist in its being is nothing else than the actual essence of that thing' (Spinoza, 1972: 91). Whether this underlining of the importance of perseverance by Spinoza actually amounts to the assertion of a 'life drive' is seriously disputed (Williams, 2016). Nevertheless, influential interpreters of Spinoza today argue the case that not only do all things which live persevere but that all things which persevere ought to be accorded the same right to life because they are all of equal value (Povinelli, 2012: 465). If perseverance can be said to be a particular virtue of indigenous peoples then perhaps that is because they have greater access to the most fundamental law of living systems than other peoples.

The work of the anthropologist Elizabeth Povinelli has been central to this new discourse on indigenous perseverance, as well as the wider claim that perseverance is fundamental to political subjectivity per se. Povinelli describes herself as concerned with the questions of '[How] new forms of social life maintain the force of existing in specific social spacings of life? How do they endure the effort it takes to strive to persevere?' (Povinelli, 2012: 462). At the same time, Povinelli has been pushing the boundaries of the limits of the kinds of space with which we are taught to associate perseverance as a capacity of things, not just by multiplying the forms of life in which we identify the capacity to strive and persevere, but by shifting from life to non-life, bodies to assemblages, and the organic to the non-organic (Povinelli, 2015: 440–41).

Others have picked up on Povinelli's argument that qualities of perseverance as well as endurance are 'defining characteristics of the late liberal present in settler democracies such as Australia', where Povinelli has conducted most of her fieldwork (Povinelli, 2011; Rickards et al., 2017). In these contexts, the assignation of these qualities of perseverance and endurance to indigenous peoples is exposed as a discourse of state and subjugating political power. As noted perceptively by Lauren Rickards and her coauthors, the perseverance of indigenous peoples 'is co-opted into legitimising narrations of the settler nation' while 'the same perseverance is simultaneously undermined by continuing racialised governmentality' (Rickards et al., 2017: 472–73). As Rickards et al. argue, in extension of Povinelli, such discourses of perseverance rest also on the messianic promise that 'persistence under present suffering—including suffering imposed by the state—will be redeemed in some anticipated future' (Rickards et al., 2017: 473). In other words, perseverance is often linked in these discourses also to the governmentality of a Christianised form of 'hope' (Rickards et al., 2017: 472).

Radical political theorists and activists are among the last people who would like to be associated with the colonial projects which forced the subjugation and exploitation of indigenous peoples, and yet when we read their work we encounter similar kinds of awestruck observation as to the remarkable perseverance of the indigenous, which can be dated back to the origins of colonial encounters of settlers with indigenous peoples. Such colonial ways of representing the indigenous subject, particularly the perseverance that supposedly defines it, find traction, for example, in Povinelli's much lauded *Economies of Abandonment* (2011: 33), which, via an engagement with indigeneity, aims to theorise political subjectivity as such.

Here, again, we encounter the same paradox as that which we saw emerge from Butler and Athanasiou's engagement with indigeneity in the earlier chapter on dispossession. The conditions of indigenous subjugation to liberal colonial power function also to provide the attributes for the subject of resistance to that subjugation. In Butler's case that paradox played out through her theorising of the condition and concept of dispossession. Dispossession is not simply what has been done to the indigenous—it is also the precondition for a new form of political subject: one that transcends the desire to turn the world into property. In Povinelli's case, this paradox plays out through her theorisation of the condition and concept of perseverance. Perseverant is not simply what the indigenous have had to be in order to survive the experience of colonisation; it is the capacity which acts as the font of political subjectivity as such, be that the political subjectivity of indigenous or non-indigenous communities. In this context, we can see how perseverance connects with a range of other concepts and conditions: especially those of immanence and potentiality.

Indeed indigenous 'understandings of the immanent geontological source of life and its possibilities' are identified by Povinelli as being an answer to her own philosophical project of immanent critique, aimed as it is at finding 'a source of a social otherwise outside a gesture of transcendental consciousness' (Povinelli, 2011: 16). Not only, therefore, is the indigenous subject fully equipped, despite its condition of subjugation, to resist the very strategies of subjugation by which it came to be subjugated, so, also, does it provide the answers to the broader social and political project which Povinelli seeks to advance, concerned as she is with theorising the life of the subject in its potentiality, at the thresholds between being and non-being, other than and against the capacity for transcendence which she, like Butler, identifies with the liberal subject, which is to say, the subject responsible for the subjugation of the indigenous.

If the philosophical question, Povinelli asks, then, is that of how forms of life are able to maintain their force of existence, persevere and endure—surviving, in specific organisations of social space (Povinelli, 2011: 9)—then her political question is that of how the indigenous can maintain their life in the context of the structures of subjugation set in place to stifle and constrain that life. Either way, this is a subject the life of which lacks the force 'to act in the sense of making anything like a definitive event occur in the world' but which, nevertheless, persists in its being, staring back at us without necessarily being able to speak back to us (Povinelli, 2011: 30). This capacity for persistence, and not transcendence, is the font of political subjectivity, Povinelli argues, as well as being a particular kind of virtue we can find specifically among indigenous communities and subjects.

The embrace of the perseverant subject that lacks the force to act, to produce events, to master its world, is a signature of course, not just of the works of Elizabeth Povinelli or Judith Butler, nor of indigenous studies, but of wider and deeper trends in the culture of critique which we have already made reference to. For a while now the social sciences have been beset by an obsession with the 'other-than-human' and idea of moving 'beyond the human', and for a long time that has meant a shift toward discovering the connections between human and other nonhuman life forms. Today, and as indicated by a range of works which back up Michael Marder's treatment of the topic, it is increasingly plants which are inspiring 'conceptual advances' in these sciences (Head et al., 2014: 863).

The driving force here is, of course, neither the real struggles of indigenous peoples nor those of plants themselves, but the theorists and conceptual entrepreneurs appropriating whatever forms of life they can to subjugate them to their own ends. Alcida Rita Ramos, for example, notes the remarkable similarities in ethnographical interpretations of indigenous modes of life and the ways in which indigenous thought is appropriated as 'Other' to an equally homogenised thought of the West (2012; see also Agrawal, 1995, 2005). It would appear that, increasingly, all forms of existence are able to play the same speculative role, highlighting the prevalence of this appropriative form of critique. Joe Crowdy, for example, has argued weeds and undergrowth to be especially queer, by 'showing no respect for human norms and private property' (Crowdy, 2017: 425). They are equivalent to 'insurgents', he argues, in the otherwise normalised space of the garden (Crowdy, 2017: 425). Humans who weed the weeds are practicing 'mastery over the life and death of plants' (Crowdy, 2017: 425). Catriona Sandilands argues plants possess a shocking, complex and queer agency, on account of their refusal to submit to the biopolitical imperatives through which life is otherwise governed (Sandilands, 2017: 425–26). The growth of weeds is not normal but 'obscenely vigorous', 'wild and rank', shocking to the civilised (Crowdy, 2017: 425). Their nature is to resist, and they can never be eradicated fully (Crowdy, 2017: 425). Their natural space of occupation is the wilderness, from which they invade the cultivated spaces of humankind, by following the winds and the movements of the soil (Crowdy, 2017: 425).

In other words there is much to compare between the life and agency of plant life, particularly that of weeds, and that assigned to the indigenous. Anna Tsing, for example, uses 'weeds' as a conceptual lens for thinking through inter-species storytelling, where life escapes the constraints of human engineering and colonial imaginaries (2017). Weeds queer and disturb the projects of social and environmental engineering and thus create new potentials and opportunities. She argues: 'So many of us are Anthropocene weeds. Weeds are creatures of disturbance; we make use of opportunities, climb over others, and form collaborations with those who allow us to proliferate. The key task is to figure out which kinds of weediness allow landscapes of more-than-human livability' (Tsing, 2017: 17). Indigenous studies, critical and queer approaches increasingly share an interest in the propagation of certain forms of indigenous being, seen to practice perseverance and to be part of speculative projects of 'everyday decolonisation' and the practice of 'queering', facilitating the critical deconstruction of normative knowledges, identities, behaviours, and spaces' and increasingly as a major tactic of decolonisation itself (Hunt and Holmes, 2015).

LOVING WHAT HURTS

In the struggle to decolonise Western, subject-centred approaches, it is common to see the queering of critique itself. In queer theory this project has led to a distinguishing between criticism and critique. Criticism, in Robyn Wiegman's terms, is defined in distinction to critique, and 'queer feminist criticism' in particular (Wiegman, 2014). The person who inhabits critique is one who claims to know what others do not, 'the hidden contingencies of what things really mean' (Wiegman, 2014: 7). For queer criticism, in contrast, the critic neither claims nor seeks to know or master the object of her study, but instead seeks 'new environments of sensation' in which to relate to that object, displacing 'critical attachments once forged by correction, rejection, and anger with those crafted by affection, gratitude, solidarity, and love. Under these affective terms, the critical act is reconfigured to value, sustain, and privilege the object's worldly inhabitations and needs' (Wiegman, 2014: 7).

Partly this is an outcome of the fact that 'faith in the equation between knowledge and political transformation has undergone enormous attrition' (Wiegman, 2014: 7). Critics are no longer so assured of what they can claim to know, or that any such knowledge, no matter how it is claimed, can lead to prescriptions concerning what is to be done. But it is not simply the outcome of a search for an alternative to traditional critique on strategic grounds, Wiegman argues, but a way of compensating for the damage that critique has historically done to its object. In the context of indigenous studies that damage is well testified to. The corrective and developmental discourses of critique, for so long directed at indigenous peoples in the name of progress, are displaced by affective discourses aimed not at correcting or developing but valuing, sustaining and privileging habitats and ways of being indigenous. For Wiegman, this is a reparative rather than simply a strategic move. It expresses the desire to repair the relation between the critic and their object by assuring the object as to the value and worth of what the object thinks it knows, how it lives and what it feels, and forging an affective solidarity with that knowledge, life and system of values.

The move to mobilise queer theory as an approach to knowledge and critique for indigenous peoples is already wide in its deployment. It is testified to, for example, in the work of Andrea Smith, and her argument for the application to indigenous studies of what she and other queer theorists call 'subjectless critique' (Smith, 2010: 44). A subjectless critique is one that refuses the positing of any claim to be able to determine the subject or object of the field of indigenous studies by insisting that queer is without fixed political referent. Instead a subjectless critique attempts to widen the range of understanding of the field of indigeneity as far as possible. It denies any claim to determine the who and what of indigeneity as much as any claim to determine the who and what of settler colonialism. One could easily be confused by the differences and contradictions in nomenclature when comparing subjectless critique with queer criticism. Both contribute to more or less the same prescriptions. For a subjectless critique to succeed it must disavow any line of critique that might bring into being a subject as such. And likewise for a reparative approach to the indigenous to win out, it is necessary for the critic of such criticism to combat the deployment of critique, which requires vigilance in advance of the appearance of critique.

Critique is distinguished by the following hallmarks: it is anticipatory, concerned with knowing and seeing what others cannot know and see; it believes in the efficacy of what it can know and what it can see, political agency arises from its abilities to expose how power works; making the workings of power visible and known detoxifies power and increases the security of the knower. Anyone wishing to practice the reparative approach must be able to identify critique, by way of these hallmarks, when and where it appears in their vicinity. They must combat critique by practicing in its place a reparatory approach. In contrast to critique, reparatory knowledge does not aim at seeing the future. Instead it is concerned with changing the present, adjusting our relation with the suffering the world sends us, not so that we can become more secure from the possibilities of it arising, but so that we can learn to live with it. As Wiegman puts it, 'it is about loving what hurts' (Wiegman, 2014: 11). Instead of preparing for a vigilant stand against the possibility of the repeat of suffering, it urges us to embrace suffering as constitutive of the richness of the world, and persevere. It is in the words of another queer theorist, Eve Sedgwick, 'to surrender the knowing, anxious paranoid determination that no horror' shall ever befall us and accept as realistic and necessary the experience of suffering (Sedgwick, 1996: 279). It is a form of knowledge grounded in disillusion, opposed to all fantasies of omnipotence, accepting and celebrative of the dangerousness of the world (Wiegman, 2014: 11).

Here we encounter a comparatively similar paradox to that which we already met in the theory of the dispossessed subject. As we recognised when reading Butler and Athanasiou, prizing dispossession requires dispossessing the dispossessed of any future will to possess—it performs the very act it deplores. Likewise the building of a reparatory knowledge requires the very tools—vigilance and exposure—it denounces in the other of reparation, critique. It renders critique an object of suspicion, such that, were it to appear as a practice of the indigenous, it would need to be denounced. In this sense reparatory knowledge demands much of the indigenous, in much the same way that dispossession demands much of them. Pitched against the sovereignty of critique it makes, nevertheless, sovereign kinds of demand. In effect it is not so much about the object of critique, the indigenous or whomever, but the critic, and his or her legitimacy in the face of a world in which its traditional modus operandi has been discredited. How might the critic save herself from the accusation of contributing to 'statist logics' and 'imperial knowledge forms' (Lea, 2012)?

DWELLING

The critic must learn, as Povinelli prescribes, to 'dwell within' the world of the indigenous (Povinelli, 2011: 32–33). As Tess Lea has also argued, it is by

> living alongside and yielding to networks and relationships, sharing cups and illnesses, learning languages and codes, and attending politically to distributed differentialities, not as colonial intermediaries but as co-creators. This is to reassert unabashedly the cultural critique possible in deep ethnography, alongside a willingness to embrace the demands, openings, and restrictions that collaborations with indigenous people require. (Lea, 2012: 196)

This notional practice of 'dwelling', which both Povinelli and Lea demand of us, and which we already encountered in Marder's celebration of the attributes of plants, is also described and celebrated by Jarrett Zigon; it is 'being-in-the-world in such a way that as part of that world one is intimately intertwined with and concerned for it and its constituent parts' (Zigon, 2014: 757). Dwelling is, as such, 'an ethical imperative', if we follow Zigon (Zigon, 2014: 757). It is a plant-like attribute of the human that is often identified with indigenous peoples in particular. Like plants, the indigenous subject does not need any lessons in how to dwell. It is the indigenous who instructs the Westerner as to how best to fulfil this imperative.

'Indigenous intelligence' is the term coined by Laura Rival to describe the capacity which enables the subject to learn how to dwell; to be in the world in such a way that, in being so, one is intertwined with and concerned with its care, such that the very act of care for the world functions as self-care (Rival, 2009: 310). It is a form of intelligence which Rival, in her anthropological research, details the existence and traits of among indigenous peoples, such as the Makushi, who live in the borderlands of Northern Brazil and Southern Guyana, as well as the young environmental activists who Rival has met in Brazil who are learning how to dwell and thus 'becoming indigenous' in her terms (Rival, 2009: 310). 'Living well' for the activists Rival describes 'means thinking and acting in a world where built environments are not severed from wilderness, as all spaces need to be meshed within a web of relationships that unfolds into seamless socio-ecological spaces of dwelling' (Rival, 2009: 308). These are people for whom 'there is absolutely no difference between "caring for the earth", "caring for people", and "caring for the self". It's all part of the same ethics, all part of the same challenge' (Rival, 2009: 308). Indigenous intelligence, enabling the capacity of the indigenous subject to dwell, is the attribute that underwrites indigenous subjectivity from its existence in the savannahs of the Guiana shield to the coasts of California.

CONCLUSION

This chapter has outlined the problematic nature of the discourse of indigenous perseverance. As an attribute, perseverance is asserted and privileged not only by indigenous peoples themselves, but also by Western scholars of indigeneity. However, it is a colonial concept and perseverance has been attributed to indigenous peoples by Western observers since the very first colonial encounters with indigenous peoples by settlers dating back to the origins of the colonial project. Today the resurgence of the discourse on indigenous perseverance can only be understood in the context of a much wider valorisation of perseverance, among right-wing psychologists concerned with convincing their readership that anybody can become a chief executive officer of a major corporation, as well as by leftists writing for the downtrodden 99 per cent who have already given up hope of being able to 'make it' under existing socio-economic conditions and want to believe in another world beyond capitalism. It is also celebrated within broader contemporary strands of radical political and social theory. It plays into epistemological shifts within critique that aim at dehumanising critique, promoting the ways of nonhuman life, particularly that of plants, as the model on which to reshape human subjectivity. In this context, we argue that this discourse of perseverance, whether in its application to indigenous peoples, or to other peoples, needs to be rejected.

Chapter 5

Pluriversal Politics

Pluriversal politics is, we argue, the logical corollary of indigenous analytics (discussed in chapter 3). In its decentring of Western or modernist assumptions of a 'one world' world (Blaney and Tickner, 2017; Danowski and Viveiros de Castro, 2017; de la Cadena and Blaser, 2018; Escobar and Law, 2015), that is, a world amenable to universal or 'objective' understanding, we argue that the politics of 'becoming indigenous' constructs a new speculative uniformity. The paradox of pluriversal politics is that the cost of the enhancement of the world—in its liveliness and differentiation—is bought at the reduction of human agency. Pluriversal politics necessarily suborns human subjectivity to the world of pluriversality, the world in its processual becoming.

We need to be very clear at the outset: pluriversal politics is distinct from modern pluralist politics. In fact, it is its very opposite. Whereas under pluralism there are many cultural perspectives or ways of knowing one world, for pluriversalism, there is one way of knowing, or worlding, but many worlds. For pluralism the differences are epistemological (that is, about ways of knowing); for pluriversalism, the differences are held to be ontological, about world-making. In short, a pluriverse of 'one culture, many natures/worlds' is contraposed to a modernist view of 'one nature/world, many perspectives/cultures'. For Walter Mignolo, who developed the use of the concept from the late 1990s (Mignolo, 2013), the concept is closely linked to second-order cybernetics, especially Humberto Maturana's conception of a 'multi-verse' (Mignolo, 2011: 70–71). For Arturo Escobar and Boaventura de Sousa Santos, 'the diversity of the world is infinite . . . the world is made up of multiple worlds, multiple ontologies or reals that are far from being exhausted by the Eurocentric experience or reducible to its terms' (Escobar, 2016: 15).

In pluriversal politics we are all—ontologically—assumed to have 'become indigenous', to engage within the world in its becoming, speculatively. In place of one form of universalism a new one therefore emerges. In place of a universal world there is instead a universal subject, one that can no longer act upon the world but only speculatively adapt within it, suborned to processes beyond its control. In the place of a linear temporality of past, present and future, there is only a presentism, in which being is always destabilised through processual uncertainty and the capacity to know recedes, displaced by the continuous work of speculative and futural adaptivity. The logic of pluriversalism, we argue, reduces human existence to the speculative becoming of life itself. While influential critical theorists, especially in the United States, have sought to celebrate this ontoethical politics of 'becoming' (Connolly, 2011), we seek to stand against this ontopolitical demand, which is today being couched in the invitation to 'become indigenous'.

This chapter thus seeks to develop further the political problems entailed by the ontologisation of indigeneity as a mode of being. The mapping of indigenous knowledge onto certain modes of being can easily lead to phenomenological understandings of ways of being as productive of different, distinct and unique ways of knowing. Taken to its logical extreme, speculative knowledge would be infinite in its differences and distinctions as every knowing entity and context differed from one second to the next, as is wonderfully demonstrated in the work of speculative theorist Alfred North Whitehead (1978). Thus, rather than extracting indigenous knowledge as an alternative analytic of speculative realism, 'perspectivism' would impose a literal ontologisation of difference. Every living agent would always know differently from every other, including its own past ways of knowing (this idea is in itself quite easy to grasp: we know from our own experience that our reading, enjoyment or experience of the same book or film or any other object for a second time differs from the first).

While the desire to 'pluralise' or to 'decolonise' the academy is not problematic in itself, we argue here that the ontologisation of indigeneity can have unintended side effects—not merely in terms of the homogenisation, essentialisation and exoticisation of indigeneity (already discussed)—but in terms of how this understanding of indigenous knowledge as constituting part of a 'pluriverse' of 'many worlds' sets up these differences as ontological rather than merely epistemological. While the modernist world was hierarchically ordered and reified on the basis of universalist frameworks of objective knowledge (which marginalised different ways of knowing or of being in the world), there is a danger that the world can also be reified in other, ostensibly more pluralising but equally problematic, ways. In short, we argue that the 'political ontology' of the pluriverse, in reversing the modernist culture/nature binary, does little to take us beyond it. In fact, we argue that this is profoundly depoliticising for two reasons: first, if perspectives on the production of knowledge were ontologised there could be no possibility of discussion or the exchange of views; secondly, there could be no perspective beyond the infinite multiplicity of this 'pluriverse', making all knowledge situated and embodied and thereby purely speculative.

This chapter is set out in three sections. First, we suggest that indigenous knowledge is problematically deployed as ontologically distinct in some pluriversal approaches, which seek to argue that only the Western or modern episteme is essentialising in its attempt to ground itself as universal. We analyse this framing through highlighting the influence of cybernetic constructions of embodied difference, underpinning some anthropological approaches, from which pluriversality draws. In the second section, on the problem of alterity, drawing on analogous framings of object-oriented theorising, we argue that, for the thesis to be logically consistent, all ways of knowing would have to be seen as purely speculative. If 'becoming indigenous' involves the ontological imaginary of a 'pluriverse' of worlds side by side (and logically also atomised, second by second, temporally), without an external God's eye view that could enable other ways of knowing to be a matter of conscious choice, the problem becomes that of the impossibility of knowledge itself rather than that of a particular claim to reality. Or rather the two become necessarily conflated: knowledge claims to represent an external reality are necessarily speculative: selective, reductionist and prone to unintended consequences. In the third section, drawing on the work of Eduardo Kohn, Anna Tsing and others, we highlight that if knowing cannot be separated from our embedded embodied being in the world, knowing can only be speculative (that is, adaptive rather than transformative). Knowledge rather than being liberating would then only serve to affirm and to reify the infinite flux of being itself. The aspiration to dissolve the subject into its context—to reduce knowing to the self-awareness of our being—is therefore, we argue, a seriously limiting one.

THE PLURIVERSAL PROJECT

As we discussed in the chapter on ontopolitical anthropology, critical approaches have increasingly stressed the distinctive ontopolitics of indigenous thought, rather than the hybrid, inter-related, aspects of cultures, which largely share the same approaches, although with different levels of technological and scientific opportunities. As Philippe Descola notes, this stress on difference was a political wager, driven by the desire to pluralise, to decolonise or to provincialise the Western episteme, removing modern thought as the 'standard' by which all else was to be judged:

> I agree that it may have been useful, in a particular period, to declare that peoples long considered 'savages' were nevertheless not in thrall to Nature since, just like us, they were capable of conceptualizing its otherness. The argument was effective when used against those who doubted the unity of the human condition and the equal dignity of all its various cultural manifestations. But there is now more to gain from trying to situate our own exoticism as one particular case within a general grammar of cosmologies rather than continuing to attribute to our own vision of the world the value of a standard. (Descola, 2013a: 87–88)

Key to this shift, away from highlighting the shared and universal forms of knowledge production, is precisely the point highlighted by Descola in relation to the indigenous separation from nature. What was once seen as a racialising move, enabling the colonial domination over and exclusion of indigenous peoples on the basis of their inability to separate themselves from nature, has become entirely transvalued. Today, it is more likely that accusations that indigenous peoples are 'just like us', in distinguishing human agency from that of nonhumans, will be met with the counter-charge of reinforcing the long history of colonial domination and suppression. If we are to be resilient and to cope with the coming catastrophes of the Anthropocene, the inclusion of distinctive indigenous ways of being and of knowing are held to be essential. And, most importantly of all, it is held to be the indigenous view of nonhuman agency that needs to be revived and reappraised:

> Decolonizing ecology demands disrupting our well-rehearsed retorts to the suggestion of more-than-human sentience. We are all familiar with the quick dismissal that reduces claims about nonhuman sentience to primitive expressions of animism or anthropomorphism. Consider for a moment however, that the very taboos against animism and anthromorphism are grounded in colonial imaginations of nature and culture, and that this disavowal of nonhuman sentience is intimately bound up in colonial projects . . . ongoing protests against the very conception of nonhuman sentiences risk re-colonizing the past, reviving a colonial present, and ensuring that colonial rule over settled lands and bodies endures well into the future. (Myers, 2017: 7)

Our concern is that the project of Natasha Myers (cited previously), Descola, Latour, Blaser, de la Cadena, Danowski, Viveiros de Castro and a growing army of critical scholars, of provincialising the Western canon in terms of epistemological methods and approaches, has become the basis upon which much more essentialising claims are being made. We see this as due to the influence of anthropological work, which has ontologised cultural difference as the product of different ways of being in and experiencing the world. This approach to phenomenology, which we find to be essentialising and reductionist, imagines that different 'life-worlds' cannot be distinguished from different ways of knowing. In a circular or tautological logic of argumentation, the division of life into different ways of 'worlding' is held to produce or 'world' different worlds. It is for this reason that Blaser and de la Cadena argue that pluriversal politics presuppose the capitalised concept of 'Political Ontology', 'inasmuch as knowledges are world-making practices' (Blaser and de la Cadena, 2018: 6). Thus knowledge is always in process and is always a matter of politics, in that knowing can never be separated from the ongoing process of world-making. As intimated in the previous reference to the work of Whitehead, the processual logic inherent to the worlding of multiple worlds would be the 'occasionalist' position where every finite moment (occasion) was composed of infinite worlds (Harman in Latour et al., 2011: 29–30) constantly becoming and perishing.

Perhaps the key anthropological influence on the politics of pluriversalism was Claude Lévi-Strauss, who sought to apply semiotic analysis to anthropology, arguing that the task of social anthropology was to reveal the 'unconscious mental structures' of 'symbolic thought' that enabled practices in 'archaic' societies to have social meaning (cited in Dupuy, 1999: 556). Lévi-Strauss sought to go beyond the modernist subject-centred framing of knowledge to reduce thought to a mathematical theory of communication, gleaned from his readings of cybernetic theory, Weiner's *Cybernetics* (1948) and Shannon and Weaver's *Theory of Communication* (1949) (Dupuy, 1999: 556). For Lévi-Strauss, the key insight of cybernetic thought was that the mind (or the living system concerned) does not know an objective independent reality that exists externally to it but develops ways of knowing and sensing that serve its own functional needs of survival and reproduction.[1]

Knowledge is thereby not capable of serving any transformative project but rather can only contribute to strategies of continuous adaptation. Every form of being or way of life develops its own phenomenology of 'knowledge', its own way of interacting with its environment and thus experiences and knows or 'worlds' its own world. Cybernetic approaches pluralise knowledge as an active process of communication between systems and their environments. Knowledge is not epistemologically relative (that is, a product of different perspectives of the same world), but ontologically distinct, the experiential practical production of worlds that differ depending upon the embodied and relational context of the 'knower'. As leading cybernetic anthropologist

Gregory Bateson argued: 'the cybernetic nature of self and the world tends to be imperceptible to consciousness' (Bateson, 2000: 450; see also Beradi, 2015: 15). Thus the key problematic of cybernetic approaches for the social sciences, and for anthropology in particular, was how to develop ways of knowing within an interactive and emergent world, rather than objective universal knowledge about an external, fixed and static world (Pickering, 2010: 402).

Cybernetics heavily influenced anthropology in the work of Harold Garfinkel, Clifford Geertz, Gregory Bateson, among others (see Vrasti, 2008) and has been central to the construction of pluriversal or decolonial approaches, increasingly taken up across the humanities and social sciences.[2] Turning 'knowing' from a process of abstraction, or of distancing the subject from the world, allowing the subject to survey the world from above, to a process in which subject and world are indistinguishable, profoundly destabilised modernist assumptions. Thus, pluriversal, interactive, communicative, semiotic or worlding practices of becoming stake out the importance not of a modernist right of 'access to knowledge' but of a more radical claim of the political struggle for recognition of other 'ways of knowing' and also inform the pluriversal underpinnings of many posthuman, new materialist, actor-network and object-oriented approaches to knowledge.[3]

As yet, there have been few attempts to bring to the surface the potential political problems caused by the cybernetic and phenomenological underpinnings of pluriversal politics outside of anthropology, where there has been a lively debate considering the ontological or phenomenological practices of knowledge production over the last decade (for example, Carrithers et al., 2010).[4] Under modernity, understandings of plurality and entanglement were relegated to the margins on the basis of universalist forms of religious, natural and social scientific reasoning, justified on the basis of Western or European power and superiority (Toulmin, 1990). A leading proponent of cybernetic and pluriversal understandings, Jamaican philosopher Sylvia Wynter (2003), traces the development of the modernist episteme through two stages. First, the European Renaissance displacement of Christian theology, enabling a theocentric order to be replaced by a *ratiocentric* hierarchy of universal reason. Secondly, the displacement of this order, in turn, with the bourgeois revolutions and the rise of *Homo economicus*. Thus the modern episteme, far from being universal or objective, is seen to be the product of a Western, Eurocentric or White, modernist, universal 'perspectivism', understood as a 'perspective internal to Western civilization itself' (Mignolo, 2011: xviii; see also Acharya, 2014; Beier, 2005; Chakrabarty, 2000; Inayatullah and Blaney, 2004; Ling, 2002; Quijano, 2000): one that vastly 'overrepresents' the perspective of the elite against the rest (Wynter, 2003: 262, drawing on Bateson).

Thus it is important to note that, from the perspective of pluriversal approaches, the problem is not that modernist knowledge has been colonised by Western power but rather that the modern episteme is itself colonising or racialising in devaluing and dismissing alternative ways of being and knowing (Mignolo, 2011: 205). As Robbie Shilliam (2015) highlights, the gaze of 'colonial science' structures and produces knowledge through imperial hierarchy dispossessing its Others. Starting from the position of the knowing subject with the known as objects, Western hubris 'resulted in conjoining epistemic and ontological differences' (Mignolo, 2011: 193) where the power position at the apex of the colonial matrix meant that Western ways of knowing were imposed as objective vis-à-vis other ways of being and knowing which were excluded (see also Mignolo, 2015: xv).

The pluriversal problematic is thus not that of improving modernist ways of knowing but deconstructing their provincial bias and articulating alternative possibilities of being and knowing; ways of 'living otherwise-relationally . . . and accepting that we are not metaphysically committed to a common world' (Rojas, 2016: 370). For de Sousa Santos: 'The call is not just for a new epistemology and a new politics but for a new relationship between epistemology and politics' (2016: 72). As Mignolo states, the project broadly interpreted—in *sensu largo*—seeks to 'articulate a new politics of knowledge rather than new contents' and, more narrowly—in *sensu strictu*—is used among indigenous intellectuals across the globe in connection with scholarly activism based on developing alternative knowledge practices (2011: 58). Thus, for example, for pluriversal political approaches, instead of 'Asian studies', where Asian ways of thinking and doing are merely an object for Western knowledge (as in 'area studies') a new 'decolonial' dimension is brought in through thinking 'Asia as Method', seeing Asia not as an object of knowledge but as a method of knowing and thus taking its subject matter more seriously, deploying it speculatively to disrupt the hegemonic positionality of the Western 'knower' (see also Chen, 2010).

At the heart of the pluriversal project is thereby the shift from the construction of universal perspectives toward the appreciation of the speculative pluriversal production of worlds. As Boaventura de Sousa Santos argues:

Structural (not functional) diversity is as seductive as it is threatening. It is seductive for those who see in it the reason for the end of dogmas and the opportunity to imagine and create other life possibilities. If the diversity of the world is inexhaustible, then utopia is possible. All possibilities are finite, but their number is infinite. The constituted experience is nothing more than a provisional and localized concretization of the constituent experience. . . . The affirmation of the diversity of the world marks a turning point in Western exceptionalism. (de Sousa Santos, 2016: 15)

It is with this shift that the speculative (that is, embodied, relational, more-than-human or cybernetic approaches) comes to the fore: rather than reproducing the Western self-understanding of knowledge as abstract theorising, ways of producing knowledge are understood to be materially embodied: the 'geo- and body-politics of knowing and sensing' is thus argued to be 'foundational in decolonial thinking' (Mignolo, 2011: 203). This is without doubt a radical disavowal of the modern Western episteme; one which puts phenomenological limits to knowledge claims as merely projections of one's own embodied being onto the world. Key to the pluralising framing of the pluralist project is that the problem is constructed as one of phenomenology, the way in which the world appears and is experienced through interactive practice or world-making of the subject. Thus, beyond the limits of modernity, other worlds sit alongside in an 'ecology of knowledges' (de Sousa Santos, 2016: 111; Rojas, 2016: 380).

ALTERITY AND THE
PROBLEM OF KNOWLEDGE

For pluriversal approaches, the systematic exclusion of other (non-modern) ways of knowing the world is a product of the embodied limits of the Western way of knowing—rather than the what of knowing, the content of knowledge. The problem is not epistemological (that is, a matter of how to know the world); the problem is ontological in that all knowing can only be speculative. A key political theorist to mark this fundamental break, taking on board the ontological turn in anthropology, clearly articulating the problem of knowledge as one of phenomenology, is Gayatri Chakravorty Spivak. In her seminal piece, 'Can the Subaltern Speak', she forwarded a scathing critique of Foucault and Deleuze: stating that the non-Western and non-modern 'Other as Subject is inaccessible' to radical continental philosophers (1993: 78). The reason for this was that 'the colonized subaltern *subject* is irretrievably heterogeneous' (ibid.: 79), too multiple in its interrelations to be capable of being represented. Here, '"the peasant"—is marked only as a pointer to an irretrievable consciousness' (ibid.: 82) available for signification by intellectuals. Thus the project of accessing the Other, for Spivak, is merely one where the 'ethnocentric Subject establishes itself by selectively defining an Other', concluding: 'This is not a program for the Subject as such; rather it is a program for the benevolent *Western* intellectual' (ibid.: 87). Here, Spivak presciently points to the epistemic limits of phenomenology and the inevitable failure to grasp alterity:

> the assumption and construction of a consciousness or subject [as a subaltern woman] . . . will, in the long run, cohere with the work of imperialist subject-

constitution, mingling epistemic violence with the advancement of learning and civilization. And the subaltern woman will be as mute as ever. (1993: 90)

The subaltern cannot be known or given voice any more than Western anthropologists can know, rather than construct, the 'Other' (Carrithers et al., 2010) or any more than modernist science can know complex reality rather than produce its own reality in a laboratory (Barad, 2007; Latour and Woolgar, 1986). The subaltern, human or nonhuman, cannot be known or represented. The problem is the attempt to know or to represent the Other itself. Spivak highlights the need to go beyond the limits of 'correlationism', the view, from the time of Kant onwards, that knowledge is a product of the knowing being and cannot be separated from 'the knower' (see Meillassoux, 2008). Rather than just point to a limit of knowing, Spivak's piece can be read as arguing that other ways of knowing necessarily exist, precisely through the self-knowing subject's 'ways of being otherwise'. However, while this knowledge may not be accessible to other actors it nevertheless exists and is reflected in the interactions and practices of the subaltern. The problem then becomes not so much the failure of a modernist aspiration to truly know the Other, but the failure to recognise that 'other worlds' will always be withdrawn, exterior to any forms of 'epistemic domination' (see also Shiliam, 2015: 5–7). It is this shift, and what is at stake in it, that is at the core of pluriversal politics and the international appropriation of a speculative indigenous analytical imaginary.

We want to suggest that, despite the increasing popularity of pluriversal approaches in the social sciences, the critique of Western knowledge can be problematic to the extent that the focus of the critique inevitably tends to become that of representation per se rather than of the power hierarchies and racism underlying them.[5] The problem for speculative approaches is that while pluralising knowledge is possible, critique is necessarily limited to claims that any one way of knowing can be superior to any other. It is the claim to knowledge that then becomes problematic and colonising rather than the conditions of possibility enabling and reproducing these claims. Thus pluriversal approaches become a vector for the shift from Marxist and poststructuralist frameworks towards the speculative or posthumanist ones of object-oriented philosophy. If Katherine Hayles is right to argue that the analysis of the development of cybernetic thinking helps us understand 'how we became posthuman' (1999), then perhaps the study of pluriversal approaches helps clarify the unfolding of this process within the disciplines of politics and international relations.

Cybernetic or posthuman approaches highlight that all knowledge claims are necessarily speculative ones (grasping only certain aspects of an interactive reality). Knowing is problematic, in the sense that all knowing is reductionist and essentialising, thereby constituting hierarchies and exclusions. The knowing subject cannot be other than a self-oriented subject. This is accepted (even celebrated in its inevitability) in some of the most influential pluriversal literature where, for example, Mignolo (2011: 331) and Dabashi (2015: 3) argue that they are happy for the Europeans to be Eurocentric (what else could they be), what they are unhappy with is that these ways of knowing are claimed to be universal. Thus they argue for the pluralisation of knowledge: 'knowledges' not knowledge. The indigenous, cybernetic or ontological turn necessarily constitutes the world as a 'pluriverse' of multiple worlds (see Rojas, 2016). In this respect, Sylvia Wynter's work is axiomatic. She argues:

> Here, the Argument, basing itself on Fanon's and Bateson's redefinition of the human, proposes that the adaptive truth-for terms in which each purely organic species must know the world is no less true in our human case. That therefore, our varying ontogeny/sociogeny modes of being human, as inscribed in the terms of each culture's descriptive statement, will necessarily give rise to their varying respective modalities of adaptive truths-for, or epistemes, up to and including our contemporary own. (Wynter, 2003: 269)

For Wynter, knowing is being: the mapping of our ways of knowing onto the world with the function of worlding the world 'for-us'. Thus different ways of being in the world manufacture different 'adaptive truths-for and, as such, ethno-astronomies, ethno-geographies', etc. (2003: 271). The alleged error of modernity as opposed to Medieval Christianity was that the otherness of Others was no longer seen to be legitimate or recognised, difference was not to be taken seriously and alongside this, the 'adaptive truth-for' nature of Western knowing was concealed while becoming hegemonic on the basis of European colonial power. As Sara Ahmed (2007) argues, 'whiteness' is a 'phenomenology'—a way of being in the world—an orientation that enables some things rather than others. Problems are always 'problems for us', never constructed in the ways in which they may appear for other forms of being or ways of existing. The perceived need to overcome or to bypass these limits increasingly links pluriversal approaches with posthuman, actor network and speculative realist approaches but has a particular ontologisation of perspectivity which most closely aligns with approaches of object-oriented ontology. For example, object-oriented theorist Levi Bryant (2012) states:

> A phenomenology-of investigates how *we*, us humans, encounter other entities. It investigates what entities are *for-us*, from our human perspective. It is humanist in the sense that it restricts itself to our perspective on the beings of the world. ... The problem is not markedly different from that of understanding the experience of another person. Take the example of a wealthy person who denounces poor people as being lazy moochers who simply haven't tried to improve their

condition. Such a person is practicing 'phenomenology-of', evaluating the poor person from the standpoint of their own experience and trying to explain the behavior of the poor person based on the sorts of things that would motivate them. They reflect little understanding of poverty. (Bryant, 2012)

The key point at stake for anthropologists, in the turn to ontology, to embodied knowledge practices was the need to speculatively go beyond the study of 'culture'. The concern was that focusing on cultural understanding could never take alterity seriously enough (Candea in Carrithers et al., 2010: 175): the study of different cultures affirmed the modernist worldview (of 'phenomenology-of') rather than questioning the hegemonic Western assumptions about the universal nature of knowledge. This was because the study of cultural difference started with the assumption that the world was single and uniform and that culture depended on plural ways of representing or thinking about this world (Holbraad in Carrithers et al., 2010: 181). The nature/culture divide is thus affirmed rather than challenged through the study of culture or the focus on epistemological differences only. Blaser argues that the side effect of culturalist approaches is that differences become minimalised and the modern ontology naturalised in a process of 'Sameing' rather than Othering (2013: 549), thus the pluriversal turn to ontology 'radicalises' modernist critical and postcolonial theory by taking difference more seriously (Blaser, 2014: 52).

For Blaser (drawing on the work of actor network and posthuman approaches of Latour, Law, Haraway, Mol and others) the speculative work of thought is key: the pluriversal turn to ontology in anthropology should not assume that realities are 'out there' rather than continually and multiply enacted or performed (2013: 551). Here the work of Annemarie Mol is seen as particularly useful; 'understanding ontology as performance or enactment brings to the fore the notion of ontological multiplicity', where different stories and practices are neither describing something existing ultimately 'out there' nor are they mistaken or metaphorical, but actually enact or 'world' (Blaser, 2013: 552; see also Mol, 2002). Rather than literally taking as given the multiple ontologies of anthropology and thus reducing ontology to culture, ontologies must be practiced or enacted rather than merely mapped, studied or collected (Blaser, 2014: 54; Palecek and Risjord, 2013: 21).

The work of Silvia Rivera Cusicanqui (2012: 107) and Robbie Shilliam (2015: 13) draws this out in their respective calls for 'our own science' or 'decolonial science' of the practical relational construction of alternative worlds. It is these enactments, performances and practices that bring new worlds into being. Whereas postcolonial approaches sought to challenge the knowledge claims of Western hegemony, pluriversal or decolonial thought seeks to bring other ways of worlding, seen as non-modern, into a relationship of equality and mutual respect. Thus, as Mignolo emphasises, the politics of geo- and body-knowledge particularly challenges modernist ways of being in relation to nature and the nature/culture divide, highlighted in the attention given to indigenous concepts such as *sumak kamsay/suma kamaña* and "right of Pachamama issues" in South America (2011: 64).

For us, there are two problems with the anthropologically informed politics of the pluralisation of 'knowledges'. The first, and most obvious, is that there would appear to be a methodological contradiction involved in selecting from a smorgasbord of 'ways of knowing'[6] and an obvious risk that (as we argue throughout this book) non-Western or non-modern approaches will be instrumentalised and assimilated into hegemonic ones.[7] However, the less articulated problem is that it does not begin to address the problem of phenomenology in seeking to avoid universalist forms of reification. We want to suggest that the focus on phenomenology rather than epistemology, or the content of knowledge, merely normalises or reifies the problem of the essentialising nature of knowledge. This is clearer in object-oriented ontologies, as alluded to previously, where it is not just Eurocentric philosophers who can only see the world through their own projections, silencing, marginalising and excluding other ways of knowing. All subject-objects relate to each other, and world themselves, through the self-projection of their own capacities or conatus, will to power/life.

All objects-subjects are irreducibly within their own worlds of experience and sensation: bees cannot see the colour red, dogs have terrible colour vision, humans have practically no sense of smell, etc. The reification of reality is rampant; it is not just humans who are the culprits. We all, humans and nonhumans alike, apparently essentialise in our worlding of separate worlds. As Graham Harman states: 'object-oriented philosophy holds that the relation of humans to pollen, oxygen, eagles, or windmills is no different in kind from the interaction of these objects with each other' (2005: 1). At this point it becomes clear that it is not so easy to separate knowledge, reification and universalism. Rather, it is the essentialisation of reality itself that is universal: all knowledge is necessarily a speculative moment in the worlding of the world. For example, in Levi Bryant's 'onticology':

> It is not simply that objects are, in themselves, fully actual and only withdrawn for other objects relating to them, but rather that objects are withdrawn in themselves. . . . [T]he distinctions or organization by which objects produce information for themselves are themselves withdrawn or invisible to the object that deploys them. . . . [E]very distinction necessarily contains two blind spots . . . objects can only see what they can see and cannot see what they cannot see. Moreover they do not see that they do not see this . . . objects are blind to their own operative distinctions. (Bryant, 2011: 282)

It would seem that geo-situated and bodily situated knowledge inevitably makes a claim to the universal as much as non-situated knowledge. In fact, from this perspective, there can be no difference between the two, as it is not possible to produce situated knowledge which is any less blind to its situatedness (de Sousa Santos, 2016: 137). The limits to the knowledge claims made by the situated subject will never be clear as the mechanisms of 'geo- or body-knowledge production' cannot be reflected upon without paradoxically stepping outside of the limits of knowing. As Sara Ahmed suggests:

> A phenomenology of whiteness helps us to notice institutional habits; it brings what is behind, what does not get seen as the background to social action, to the surface in a certain way. It does not teach us how to change those habits and that is partly the point. In not being promising, in refusing to promise anything, such an approach to whiteness can allow us to keep open the force of the critique. (Ahmed, 2007: 165)

While the phenomenological focus of pluriversality can promise to get rid of the hubristic assumptions of objective knowledge/the knowing subject—as all objects-subjects reify knowledge—it cannot legitimately promise to get rid of the essentialisation of reality. We would argue that the outcome is that reality is reified in a much more thorough way as the essentialisation of reality is now merely a universal attribute of being itself. We are thus necessarily left with only the possibility of speculation, thereby reversing the relation of the subject to the world. Speculative analytics pluralises the world on the basis that all forms of life world 'worlds' interactively. This realisation has been lost to the moderns on account of their belief in their separation from the world and the highly mediated forms of modern life, hermetically sealed from the world outside. Speculative analytics, at the heart of pluriversal politics, thereby assumes that we should recognise that knowledge is the product of the world working on us, and therefore consciously suborn ourselves to the process of opening to the world—as Blaser and de la Cadena state, 'where knowers dissolve themselves' (2018: 12)—rather than acting as subjects upon the world.

THE WORLD AS RAINFOREST

The influence of the pluriversal politics of embodied 'worlding' is increasingly key to the integration of indigenous knowledge as a specific form of ontopolitics in the Anthropocene. Calls for the pluralisation and decolonisation of the Western academy may sound like a radical challenge to the status quo, but rather than pluralising and opening up academia, we argue that it necessarily privileges an alternative understanding of knowledge: one without the possibility of subject/object distinctions requisite for transformative action. This is precisely the point argued by Mario Blaser and Marisol de la Cadena in their understanding of pluriversal becoming without the possibility of 'subject knowledge creating its object knowledge' (2018: 11). The embedded or embodied subject may know different realities or 'worlds' but it knows them all in the same way: as signs and signals that are to be speculatively adapted to. The price to be paid for the pluralisation of knowledge production is that there can only be one type of knowledge: adaptive or speculative knowledge.

Pluriversal politics argues that all knowledge is a product of embodied practices of world-making. All knowledge is therefore 'real', the task is then to be able to speculatively access these other, multiple 'realities': the cosmopolitical promise of 'many worlds'. It is precisely at this point that we can see the consequences of an ontologisation of the indigenous subject. Rather than Amerindian perspectivism framing one possible way of thinking about the relation between culture and nature—thinking speculatively beyond the 'correlationalism' essential to modernist thought which separates culture and nature—pluriversal perspectives implicitly argue that perspectivism is an ontological fact of the world. Thus the price to be paid for the ontologisation of indigeneity is a higher one than merely the poor anthropology of homogenising indigenous thought as necessarily speculative. There is a danger that in relativising ways of thinking and being as ontological there can only ever be one way of thinking. This is precisely the key facet of Amerindian perspectivism and multi-naturalism, enabling the construction of one culture (one way of thinking) and many natures (many worlds).

The one way of thinking, the way of thinking considered to be essential in the Anthropocene, is that of indigenous analytics, seen to be capable of speculatively working on the basis of pluriversal openness to alterity. As Blaser and de la Cadena ask:

> Could the moment of the Anthropocene bring to the fore the possibility of a pluriverse? Could it offer the opportunity for a condition to emerge that, instead of destruction, thrives on the encounter of heterogeneous worldings, taking place alongside each other with their divergent here(s) and now(s), and therefore makes of their taking place a negotiation of their going on together in divergence? Can the Anthropocene be the scenario of both the end of the world (as hegemonically conceived and practiced) and the inauguration of what Helen Verran calls 'a cosmopolitics as the politics of collectively doing cosmologies together and separately'? (Blaser and de la Cadena, 2018: 16–17)

This world (after the end of the 'one world' world) where it is necessary to 'thrive on the encounter of heterogeneous worldings' is thereby infinitely rich and intense in its inaccessibility: it is the world as rainforest. Indigeneity as futural analytics assumes that multiple (infinite) worlds which make the present world 'alive' can be lived within through a process of continual openness and speculative adaptation, where everything is not a potential 'object' of knowledge but a sign to be speculatively interpreted in order to guide adaptation: to become as part of the flux or process without any given causal determination. To 'world' within heterogeneous worldings is the ethical mode of being of pluriversal politics. This ethical mode of being thereby presents indigenous analytics as necessary for contemporary survival in the Anthropocene—not as an epistemological aspect of 'knowing' but ontologically, as becoming: as 'Political Ontology'.

The politics of pluriversality necessary involve an anthropology 'beyond the human' (Kohn, 2013), using the speculative study of appearances as a method of accessing alternative realities. As we have seen, indigenous knowledge as method is based on the inverse of modernist assumptions, rather than one world and many different (cultural) perspectives, it is assumed that different ways of being in the world constitute the world as different ontological realities. This doesn't just inverse a modernist episteme—'one culture, many natures/worlds' as opposed to 'one nature/world, many perspectives/cultures'—it also enables new actors and agents to enter the world. The world is held to expand using indigenous knowledge as method, whereas it is held to reduce using a modernist ontology. Eduardo Kohn perhaps goes furthest in this project, drawing upon the semiotics of American pragmatist Charles Peirce to argue that rather than equating indigenous and modernist methodologies (as Latour and Viveiros de Castro can be read to do), understanding the distinctions enables us to see the distinct advantages of indigenous knowledge as a methodology.

Whereas modernist thought depends on the power of abstraction, in its artificial bubble where meaning increasingly depends on internal semiotic relations rather than a relation to the external world of signification, indigenous analytics are constructed as externally orientated: 'The world is animate, whether or not we are animists. . . . And it is not just located in the here and now, or in the past, but in a being in futuro—a potential living future' (Kohn, 2013: 217). For Kohn, this speculative orientation is semiotic, and, drawing upon Peirce, he argues that there are three types of semiotic relation, the symbolic (specifically modernist), the indexical and the iconic, nested within each other. These are all forms of representation, but the indexical is key to indigenous knowledge as analytical method. In the 'iconic' form of signing or semiotics, there is no distinction between the sign and the signified. It is like a label; no interpretative act is necessary and nothing new is produced through it. The 'indexical', on the other hand, speculatively correlates the sign with something that is not immediately seen to be present. The sign is interpreted through its relation to another sign that it is an 'index' of. Indexical semiotics are not limited to the human: a monkey may jump at a loud noise, indexing a threatening large animal, a dog may react to the command 'sit' indexing it to its owner's praise, obviously without understanding it symbolically (though the internal relations of a language) (Kohn, 2013: 52–53). Kohn argues that the world, or 'life', works on the speculative basis of semiotic chains of signs, which all living beings engage in.

Elisabeth Povinelli's work with indigenous communities, for example, emphasises this speculative nature of thinking in terms of an 'analytics of entities' (rather than the passing down of 'cultural' or 'local' relational knowledge) as a way into an infinite world of interactive relations. This is distinct from conceiving of the world as a fixed set of signs or indicators, merely needing to be learnt and read off:

> Everything could be a sign pointing to something else, which interpreted the other thing. . . . It was within the field of interpretation that any one sign could reveal that all the previously understood signs, and thus the foundation of interpretation itself, had to be rethought. (Povinelli, 2016a: 123)

Povinelli makes the point that it would be 'seductive' to translate these analytics as a direct form of knowledge, without the need for speculative mediation, in terms of merely needing to 'listen to what the country is saying', enabling a new relational narrative of inclusion and attention, enrolling indigenous interlocuters and nonhuman actors and agencies into discussions of resilience and adaptation to climate change (2016a: 123–24). Yet she cautions against this view of relationality as making the world more meaningful, rather than stranger, for us: "The generosity of *extending* our form of semiosis to them forecloses the possibility of them provincializing us" (Povinelli, 2016a: 142). Objects do not just directly speak to us or act on our behalf, pointing the way to knowledge and understanding. Speculative thought is necessary because relationality is too intense: 'Objects do not stay one thing but become other things because of these forces of shaping and shifting and assemblage' (Povinelli, 2016b: 119).

For Kohn, human forms of representation, thought and culture work on the basis of a nested continuity with nonhuman ones. They are not radically separate: there is no divide between culture and nature. All life speculatively reads and reacts to the world as a system of signs. This is only possible because there are regularities in the world that enable forms of representation and correlation. Evolution as a process is one of semiotics, of sign and response, of adaptation to the environmental context, which changes both the nature of the subjects and the context. Here, Kohn's work very much follows in the lines of other speculative approaches (Brassier, 2007; Bryant 2011; Morton, 2013). Human thought emerges from the world rather than existing separately. The world emerges through responses as the lived reactions to signs that enable habits and ways of being to form which thereby constitute and amplify the patterns and regularities of the world.

Speculative thought is not separate from the world; it is in the world, and, in fact, makes the world (see also Grosz, 2017). Thought—processes of speculative communicative feedback and patterned interaction—is the way the world 'worlds' itself. Kohn argues that for indigenous knowledge as speculative analytical method; this is key to understanding how the world works. Rather than having some sort of backward 'culture', indigenous thought is a living method for seeing the world, as cybernetics implores us to, in its emergence, through the world's own pluriversal representation of itself: through signs and indexical correlation. The world literally signs, speaks or alerts us to what is happening and is therefore animate in very important ways. Indigenous knowledge as an analytic enables us to speculatively access this world in its 'worlding' in ways that are barred from modernist methodologies of old, but which develop in line with the new sciences which emerged after 1945 to bulwark the liberal order.

Modernist methodologies of old do not see the world as animated, but as flat, dead or lifeless, merely a product of cause-and-effect interactions. The advantage of seeing the world as an animated one is that it enables paying attention to it. For many indigenous communities, paying attention to the world and its semiotic processes of emergence is held to be crucial to maintaining their existence. It is precisely this 'attentionality' and sensitivity to feedback that is held to be essential for survival in the Anthropocene. For modernist thought the question does not arise of how to listen or to pay attention to the world. There is no concern with how nonhumans 'think' or sign the world. For indigenous knowledge as analytics this is central to expanding ways of seeing and knowing the world. Therefore, rather than being premodern, indigenous analytics are increasingly seen as a speculative method, to be learned from, precisely because of the ability to enrol nonhuman actors and agencies in the production of pluriversal knowledge. Indigenous knowledge as method does this through reverse anthropology, imagining what it would mean to take alterity seriously. What does it mean to think like a dog, a peccary, a mongoose, an anteater, a puma? Were this to be possible, the signs and interpretations that these nonhumans provide could be given attention and provide the basis for speculative knowledge.

As Kohn emphasises, understanding the world through a semiotic ontology enables speculative approaches because in a world that is full of immanence: 'All semiosis, then, creates future' (2013: 206). Seeing and relating through the interpretation of signs 'as "guesses", re-present a future possible, and through this mediation they bring the future to bear on the present' (ibid.: 207):

> Peirce refers to the past—the product of causes and effects—as fixed or 'dead'. Being in future, by contrast, is 'living' and 'plastic'. All semiosis, as it grows and lives, creates future. This future is virtual, general, not necessarily existent, and yet real. All selves partake of this 'living future'. Neotropical forests, such as those around Ávila, proliferate semiotic habits to a degree unprecedented in the biological world, and in the process they proliferate futures. (Kohn, 2013: 207)

For Kohn, 'to survive in the Anthropocene—this indeterminate epoch of ours in which the world beyond the human is being increasingly made over by the all-to-human—we will have to actively cultivate these ways of thinking' (that is, become indigenous) (2013: 227). Here, indigenous analytics enables the bringing into being of the pluriverse. The pluriverse is ontological in that the indigenous, as human agents, are merely part of a semiotic system of communicative interaction and are, in this regard, indistinguishable from any other form of 'life'.

This framing is speculative, in a similar way to that of Haraway's speculative narration of the Camille stories (see chapter 3), where indigenous communities are imagined to be vital constitutive agents in their becoming within multiple worlds. As Kohn states in an interview, published in 2017:

> I went to a particular place where certain qualities get amplified. There are many Runa, living elsewhere, who are no longer subsistence hunters; I just went with the ones that are so that I could see the forest in a particular way. . . . But, in the epilogue of the book I ask how we can continue to think like a forest even when we're not in the forest. This is a question that I think is addressed very eloquently at UC Santa Cruz—by Anna Tsing and Donna Haraway. (Kohn, 2017: 166)

The posthuman or speculative imagination of life in harmony with other forms of existence (unknowable and inaccessible in themselves) treats indigenous becoming no differently to that of any other object of its speculative gaze. This comes across unusually explicitly in Anna Tsing's contribution to a special issue of the journal *Theory, Culture & Society*, devoted to the work of influential anthropologist Marilyn Strathern (2014), where Tsing compares ethnographic work on indigenous people with that of work on fungal spores.

Tsing focuses on the speculative 'reification' of the ways of being and knowing of a fungal spore, which is used to bring into comparison and to deconstruct modernist ways of being and knowing. This counter-position, for the purpose of the edification of Western academic readers, highlights the speculative role played by critical Western constructions of indigeneity (a theme that has run right through this book on the transvaluation of indigenous life). For Tsing's purposes here, rather than a speculative framing of Amerindian being in a tropical rainforest, the role of the indigenous is played by 'introducing a fungal spore as an ethnographic subject' (Tsing, 2014: 223) and the space of performative pluriverse, of multi-species interaction, instead of a tropical rainforest is a village forest. The spore as speculatively imagined interlocutor tells us: 'Do you want to see species working together to build intricate but unintended designs? Do you want to observe the promise of interacting trajectories without central administration? Our village forest is a good place to look' (ibid.: 233).

Like the indigenous Amerindian communities of Viveiros de Castro and Kohn, the fungal spore has a lot to teach us about how to see and respond to the world and how to work with other forms of life. Fungi, we are told, do not make the binary cuts and separations that those brought up with the modernist episteme have and their ways of being challenge human-centred views of bodies, kinship, self and world. Where Strathern derived her critical perspectives from the indigenous societies of Melanesia, Tsing argues that travelling to the margins to find indigenous communities is not necessary and that any nonhumans could do just as well: 'Indeed, once we allow ourselves to cross (or flatten) the fence [cordoning off studies of humans from studies of all other species], the possibilities for making usefully shocking analogies multiply exponentially' (2014: 224):

> Just as Strathern relies on ethnographers of Melanesia for her thought experiments, I rely on mycologists and ecologists for mine. My goal, following Strathern, is to use what might otherwise be presented as merely 'scientific facts' to upset what we think we know—and thus what we can imagine. The radical potential of anthropology has always been this: other worlds are possible.

For the critical anthropologists who have done so much to establish pluriversal politics, such as Viveiros de Castro, Blaser, de la Cadena, Kohn and Tsing, 'the other world that is possible' is strikingly familiar and, of course, strikingly similar. It is the world of the Anthropocene, where humans are no longer possessive of special powers which might set them apart but, in fact, have to learn again to live as part of a multi-species pluriverse or more-than-human world. For Tsing:

> We become who we are through multispecies aggregations. We are more like mychorrhizal fungi than we imagine. This makes an enormous difference for

our theories of 'human' action in the world. How can humans act as an autonomous force if our 'we' includes other species that make us who we are? . . .
What might it mean for a multispecies aggregate to act upon the world? (Tsing,
2014: 230)

In the Anthropocene we are forced to become a 'multi-species aggregate'
as we become aware that we are not separate from or above the world. We
need to live like the fungal spore in nested relations with other forms of
life, in the village forest, living and becoming with others, 'adding our part
to a world in which pines, broadleafs, goats, humans, pigs, and matsutake
mushrooms live together' (Tsing, 2014: 233). We need to live like the
Amerindian indigenous communities in the tropical rainforest, living and
becoming with others: the forest spirits, the jaguar, the peccary, etc. (Kohn,
2013). In the Anthropocene, the world of 'heterogeneous worldings' is like a
tropical rainforest or a village forest, in that it thrusts the necessity of living
and becoming with other forms of life upon us and thus rather than becoming separate we need to learn to immerse ourselves in the swamps of mere
life, like a fungal spore or an Amerindian, responding and adapting to a new
shared, entangled way of being.

CONCLUSION

Pluriversal politics necessarily privileges indigenous analytics above any
other knowledge practices, but this should not be understood as having any
necessary connection to the political support for indigenous struggles or
rights claims. In fact, it doesn't. As we have argued here, indigenous communities are often merely mobilised as a speculative stage army in support of a
Western academic climate and resource advocacy born out of scientific trends
which themselves form part of the West's grand narrative of development
and security. In fact, as we highlight, the use of indigenous knowledge as an
analytical framing for speculative politics is potentially more essentialising
and exploitative than ever, offering overtly colonial appropriations of indigenous practices. The problem for those who wish to appropriate indigenous
practices, analytics and struggles in order to bolster their critical academic
claims, or to enable them to pluralise and decolonise academic disciplines, is
that it increasingly appears as unnecessary and perhaps a little too defensive
or disingenuous.
   We wonder whether those who wish to advocate for pluriversal politics
even need to risk the essentialising and romanticising moves implied in
discourses of 'becoming indigenous'. Despite the fact that theorists of pluriversal politics, from Walter Mignolo and Marilyn Strathern to Viveiros de

Castro, Donna Haraway, Bruno Latour and Timothy Morton, tend to root speculative approaches in anthropological or ethnographic framings which posit indigenous peoples as founders or leaders in bringing these new on-toethical practices into being, it would perhaps be less problematic if they were to take more self-responsibility for the advocacy of new speculative approaches to the political. Fungal spores could then perhaps enable speculative thought without comparison to anthropological work among the indigenous or, as Stefanie Fishel highlights, in her path-breaking work, *The Microbial State* (2017), the life sciences no less than anthropology could provide a lens for alternative political imaginaries emphasising vitality, connection and entangled responsibility (2017: 21).

Microbial and other entangled or relational metaphors (such as Michael Marder's 'plant thinking', 2013; Irigaray and Marder, 2016) equally enable the alternative ontologies of attentional being and becoming of pluriversal politics. As Fishel notes, following ecological activist Stewart Brand: if we are serious about tackling contemporary problems, perhaps the starting point should be to ask, 'What would a microbe do?' (Fishel, 2017: 56). Microscopic bacteria may seem 'small and simple' but they are what enable life to exist and highlight that living organisms are enmeshed in their environments, inside and out, enabling us 'to envision political community as an assemblage of multispecies groupings' (ibid.). Microbes speculatively enable us to go beyond binaries of self and other and to bring 'system-based understandings of complex processes' to the political realm, enabling 'different forms of practice for sustainable, ethical, global living with one another, and with other life forms, as a *bodies politic*' (ibid.: 61). Rather than fixed entities fighting for distinct interests, microbial imaginaries are ones of collective and sympoietic becoming where 'the world is a joint product between the human and the nonhuman . . . composing the world together' (ibid.: 105).

What we particularly appreciate about Fishel's project is that she foregrounds the fact that she is engaging metaphorically, figuratively, analogically and speculatively with her research subject rather than claiming some ontological or scientific truth. Working speculatively through the life sciences seems to us perhaps preferable to making claims based on anthropological or ethnographic research into alleged 'indigeneous' practices of 'worlding'. One reason why research grounding pluriversal politics in the life sciences might be encouraged is the fact that, as Fishel states, the dangers of taking literally biological metaphors are much more widely acknowledged. Whereas it is uncontroversial to state that 'any transfer from biology to politics should be carefully examined' (2017: 101), arguments that purport to draw upon indigenous thought and practices, to inform political and conceptual advocacy, are much more rarely put to the same level of examination.

NOTES

1. Cybernetics is a transdisciplinary science of how natural, social and mechanical systems govern or regulate themselves, popularised by Norbert Weiner after World War II in his book *Cybernetics, or Control and Communication in the Animal and the Machine* (1948; see also Hayles, 1999). It was heavily funded by the American military as well as inspired by American military-strategic needs during the Cold War (Kay, 2000). As Fred Turner notes, the appeal of cybernetics is to a 'nonhierarchical model of governance and power' (2006: 24). Yet its purpose was fundamentally to ensure the victory of the United States over the Soviet Union. Since the end of the Cold War it has become ever more fundamental to the strategic logics and rationalities of the liberal world order (See Dillon and Reid, 2009).

2. Randolph B. Persaud and R. B. J. Walker note the 'growing movement of global decoloniality' (2015: 83). Decolonial approaches broadly share the desire to question the Eurocentrism and hierarchical values at the heart of Western academia, calling for dialogue and research based upon 'pluri-versalism rather than uni-versalism' (Boidin et al., 2012: 2) and thus move away from the abstract Cartesian view of the subject toward the 'neo-cybernetic turn' emphasising knowledge as the product of 'embodiment and situatedness' (Ali, 2013: 42).

3. These approaches problematise modernist divides, such as those between culture and nature, human and nonhuman, mind and matter, and subject and object, through a focus on the material relationality of embodiment in an interactive, entangled world (see, for example, Coole and Frost, 2010; Gratton, 2014; Wolfendale, 2014). In this context, Syed Mustafa Ali correctly notes that 'decolonial thinking and actor-network theory (ANT) might be viewed as complementary endeavours' (Ali, 2013: 29).

4. A notable exception being the 'New Materialism & Decoloniality: A Conversation' workshop, organised by Pol Bargués-Pedreny and Olivia Rutazibwa at the Käte Hamburger Kolleg/Centre for Global Cooperation Research, Duisburg, Germany, in July 2016; a conversation that initiated the research for this chapter.

5. While pluriversal thinkers, like de Sousa Santos, make clear, that what he names as 'an epistemology of the South' can be conceived as a metaphor for the systemic and unjust human suffering caused by global capitalism and colonialism', it is important to note that this 'postabyssal thinking' implies no 'general theory of social emancipation', rather it aims to enable infinite differential becomings 'maximizing their emancipatory potential in loco (however defined)' (2016: 134–35).

6. There is thus a limit to the idea that ways of knowing can be reduced to or derived from discrete sets of practices, as suggested by Blaser's view that white middle-class women involved in Wicca could be seen to be practicing non-modern ways of being (2013: 553). We believe that cultural practices and symbols are far too globally cross-fertilised for any easy way of demarcating ways of worlding, without falling into the traps of essentialising or 'Sameing'.

7. We are not convinced that Shilliam's concluding provocation in *The Black Pacific*, that 'colonial science is a science that you can use or discard; decolonial science is another science' (2015: 185), adequately reflects the ontological commitments of 'deep relation' drawn out through the book itself. For a critique of instrumentalism, see Cuiscanqui (2012: 97–101); and in the field of international policy-making, Mac Ginty (2008: 139–63); Randazzo (2016).

Chapter 6

Resilience

Resilience has rapidly spread throughout the policy world over the last two decades, driven by the desire to use systems theories and process understandings to develop adaptive approaches to the world. However, this chapter argues that under the auspices of the Anthropocene, the assumptions and goals of resilience have become problematised. In modernity, supporting and enabling vulnerable communities and ecosystems can help resolve crises but in the Anthropocene resilience approaches can easily appear to be spreading rather than containing any problem. Attempts to resolve problems through focusing upon redistributing resources to enable capacity building can be seen to speed up the process of resource depletion and the arrival at the Earth's 'Planetary Boundaries' rather than slowing it down (Stockholm Resilience Centre, 2017). In the place of 'linear', infrastructural, engineering or 'top-down' approaches to resilience, alternative approaches have been advocated, based upon more responsive cybernetic framings of automated or 'algorithmic' real-time adaptation. This chapter highlights the limits of these two approaches to resilience so as to draw out the distinctive nature of the demand to 'become indigenous', often articulated as an agential and futural alternative relying upon speculative or indigenous analytics to enable or 'work with' so-called natural processes.

In the new context of global warming, extreme weather events, environmental disasters and the Anthropocene, indigenous ways of being and knowing are increasingly being integrated into governance (see, for example, the UN Educational, Scientific and Cultural Organization reports Hiwasaki et al. [2014], and Nakashima et al. [2012]). Indigenous knowledge as a set of speculative analytics is increasingly central to discourses of resilience because it is constructed as a different and better way of knowing and engaging with change. Modern knowledge focuses on causal understandings with a linear temporality, whereas indigenous analytics, we are told, lacks both the causal 'reductionism' and the linear temporality of modernity. In the past, when the world was seen as amenable to 'command-and-control', through the direction of modernist scientific and technical knowledge, indigenous modes of understanding were considered to be limiting. Today, as we have discussed (in chapter 1), Anthropocene discourses suggest that new approaches to adaptation and resilience are necessary.

This chapter is structured around the analysis of three differing approaches to resilience: the linear, the cybernetic and the speculative. The following section provides an overview of the problematic of resilience in the Anthropocene, where linear 'top-down' or 'engineering' approaches to resilience are considered to be artificial or 'coercive'. The second section considers alternative cybernetic or 'equilibrium' approaches that often rely on the rolling out of ubiquitous computational technologies, like the Internet of Things. The final section brings in a third resilience approach formulated around indigenous analytics and draws out the contradistinction between these futural imaginaries and attempts to modulate around equilibrium.

It can seem, today, that there is no alternative to indigenous approaches, focused not upon modernist imaginaries of perpetual progress and development but of futural sensitivity and care. Key to this chapter is the role of imaginaries of indigeneity as taking us beyond the limits of high-tech promises of resilience, reliant upon Big Data correlation and ubiquitous sensing technologies. As we considered in the previous chapter, discourses of indigenous, pluriversal, forms of knowing and responsivity drew largely on earlier cybernetic imaginaries of system feedback, now part of dominant resilience discourses. In contemporary framings, dominant appropriations of indigeneity have followed trends within cybernetic thought, moving from 'first order' understandings of homeostatic control to 'second order' or 'new' approaches which emphasise subjective agency, where feedback is much more mediated and speculative interpretations are key.

As we draw out in the final section, the shift toward the power and potential of speculative imaginaries can be seen to narrow rather than expand alternative possibilities. Subjective agency and imagination are no longer then to be directed toward future transformative goals but to making the present appear more intensely for us. Thus the world becomes richer and more present for us, suborning the subject to dwelling within it rather than seeking to instrumentalise it. Rather than projecting ourselves into a future, radically different from the present, the future is speculatively brought into the present itself through techniques alleged to be drawn from indigenous modes of being. For us, this is a radical foreclosing of the possibilities of transformative change, one that is particularly problematic as its promise of futural agency is one that traps us even further within the constraints of the present than earlier imaginaries of governance and resilience.

RETHINKING ADAPTATION
IN THE ANTHROPOCENE

Resilience approaches discursively frame policy problems, and their resolution, through the focus on enabling and capacity-building communities and systems—held to be 'vulnerable', 'at risk' or 'failing' (Chandler, 2014; Evans and Reid, 2014; Joseph, 2013; Walker and Cooper, 2011). These potential imaginaries of resilience—as a policy-making 'magic bullet' for problems as diverse as underdevelopment, conflict and environmental crises—have come under challenge in the Anthropocene. Anthropocene thinkers argue that the Anthropocene is not just another problem or crisis to be 'solved' or 'bounced-back' from or 'recouped' but rather a sign that modernity itself was a false promise of salvation, one that has brought us to the brink of destruction, and from which no recovery is possible (Latour, 2013; Stengers, 2015; Tsing, 2015). While resilience-thinking has recently achieved nearly universal success in the policy-making world—suggesting new sensitivities to problems and rejecting 'high-modernist' technocratic approaches, which depended upon universal 'one-size-fits-all' solutions from on high—resilience is still a 'modern' construction which assumes that problems are 'external' and that we need to develop 'internal' policy solutions to maintain and to enable our existing modes of being in the face of shocks and perturbations. 'We' need to be sensitive to minor changes and to 'tipping points'. In short, that 'we' are not the problem, but that 'we' need to develop new approaches of adaptive recovery to preserve our modernist imaginaries of development and progress.

The problems which the Anthropocene posits for resilience advocacy have been little recognised in contemporary academic discussions in the humanities and social sciences. In fact, for the Stockholm Resilience Alliance—which is, in the view of many commentators, the leading research and advisory body for resilience-thinking—the conceptualisations of resilience and of the Anthropocene are closely inter-connected. Particularly in the language of systems ecology, both concepts appear to share understandings of complex adaptive systems, 'tipping points' and 'phase transitions' and to be sensitive to the limits of 'top-down' or 'linear' approaches to problem-solving. A glance at the Resilience Alliance webpages[1] reveals the clear inter-connections between leading natural and social scientists, whose shared work in systems theory and adaptive systems has shaped thinking in both these areas, including Will Steffen, Paul Crutzen, Frank Biermann, Carl Folke, Johan Rockström and Jan Zalasiewicz, among others (see also Biermann et al., 2012; Steffen et al., 2011).

Yet even at the 'heart of the beast' not all is well. One example of the limits of resilience-thinking we'd like to highlight here comes from a group of Swedish ecology scientists linked with the Resilience Alliance (Stockholm Resilience Centre, 2014) and published in *Ecosphere*, the journal of the Ecological Society of America (Rist et al., 2014). These scientists argue that resilience-thinking has been slow to think through the implications of the Anthropocene and the hidden costs of 'anthropogenic impacts on the environment'. The problem of ignoring these hidden costs is highlighted in their conceptualisation of 'coerced resilience', which they define as:

> Resilience that is created as a result of anthropogenic inputs such as labour, energy and technology, rather than supplied by the ecological system itself. In the context of production systems, coercion of resilience enables the maintenance of high levels of production. (Rist et al., 2014: 3)

Rist et al. define 'anthropogenic inputs' as the external 'replacement of specific ecosystem processes by inputs of labor and manufactured capital (e.g., fossil fuel, technology, nutrients, pesticides and antibiotics)' (2014: 73). Thus sustaining or maintaining growth depends upon the taking of resources, technologies and materials from elsewhere, merely intensifying and redistributing or spreading the problems. This is first because the process is held to weaken and undermine 'natural processes' of resilience, and secondly because importing resources weakens other, external, ecosystems.

Anthropogenic inputs make the problem worse by weakening rather than strengthening natural ecosystem sources of resilience. For Rist et al., this can be clearly seen in the shift to anthropogenic dependencies: with the development of intensive agriculture techniques over a thousand years ago; in forestry, which has moved to the industrial scale over the last few hundred years; and in fisheries, which became industrial after the Second World War (2014: 4). In modernity, the problem was understood to be the ability to sustain these vulnerable systems, particularly with concerns over falling productivity. But in Anthropocene-thinking resilience itself becomes the enemy as the addition of anthropogenic inputs begins to shift the system regime state, moving further and further away from reliance on the natural ecological processes—and, in fact, causing permanent damage to them—until a new regime state is reached without the possibility of any return to 'nature' (Rist et al., 2014: 5). Thus vulnerabilities are cascaded through the larger system.

Rist et al. argue that one of the key problems with coerced resilience is that it 'masks' the real costs of production through the import of external capital, namely in the form of technology and fossil fuel–based energy (2014: 3). Thus the problem of modernist resilience policy interventions to enable sustainable development and human progress is thereby their 'artifice' or falsity. For some authors, this is akin to rearranging the deck chairs on a sinking ship as this merely takes materials from other ecosystems and contributes to spreading the problem rather than resolving it. In fact, coercive resilience is a kind of globalisation in reverse, where the ability to import goods from around the globe no longer adds to productivity but rather spreads the sickness of undermining natural processes by over-extraction in unsustainable ways. For Rist et al., this 'falsity' is itself a key problem of coercive resilience, as it undermines the very feedback processes that complex adaptive systems require. In order to be productive, these systems:

> rely on the maintenance of local ecological processes to retain a wider range of options for unforeseen future requirements, and thereby provide clearer feedbacks regarding proximity to ecological thresholds than do production systems . . . which require significant anthropogenic inputs. (Rist et al., 2014: 4)

Thus increasing resilience through 'coercion' merely enables tipping points to be reached sooner. The addition of anthropogenic inputs 'masks' the growing loss of natural ecological system resilience, maintaining systems in 'artificial' states, entirely dependent upon more and more external inputs:

> This raises an apparent paradox, whereby highly modified production systems can, through anthropogenic efforts rather than ecological processes, mimic the response of resilient natural systems to a specified disturbance, in their capacity to return to pre-disturbance system states. (Rist et al., 2014: 6)

This is a dangerous situation as 'coerced' resilience hides the capacities of these systems to draw upon natural ecological processes (highlighted in discussions of recent declines of wild and domestic pollinators and the plants and other species which rely upon them) (Rist et al., 2014: 6). A striking example of the limits of coerced resilience is provided by anthropologist Michael Taussig in his recent work, *Palma Africana*, on the mass production of palm oil in Colombia (2018). One of the unintended and ironic consequences of increasing reliance on anthropogenic inputs, for example, the development of mono-crops, such as the 'Hope of America' palm, is that although artificially designed to prevent the spread of insect predation it needs additional anthropogenic interventions to artificially inseminate it. Thus production becomes increasingly artificial, requiring more and more inputs, despite being sold as a wonderful technical solution for raising productivity:

> I see these women inseminators hard at it in the lustrous photographs provided by the Colombian Palm Growers Association. One woman is kneeling by an adult palm with a plastic tube in her mouth blowing sperm into the tiny flowers. In another photo a dark-skinned young woman wearing bright pink jeans and a coal black jacket and cap guides the inseminating tool in her right hand while with her left she pushes back the palm branches studded with fierce thorns. With a look of equally fierce concentration she guides her instrument into its target all because 'Hope of America' can't get it up. One would hope for more from 'Hope of America'. (Taussig, 2018: 74)

In language, which very much follows the lines of Rist et al., Taussig writes that:

> Once triggered, assemblages tend to proliferate and somersault, one leading to the next. . . . Another assemblage concerns the larger framework of relevant political cliché and self-awareness as to such—namely, third world women of color ministering to the sexual requirements of an impotent masculine 'Hope of America' designed to stall the plagues brought by the very act of mono-cropping. We could continue. Thus does the assemblage principle provoke movement, speed, and metamorphosis. This is the way of things as much as a way of thinking with things. (Taussig, 2018: 75)

Thus resilience, in traditional policy approaches, rather than halting or slowing down the process of environmental destruction and exhaustion, can in fact be seen as the very vector of its becoming. What is then to stop resilience from being retrospectively read into precisely the history of modernist developmentalism that it set out to produce an alternative to?

For Rist et al., coerced resilience cascades system effects of resource depletion through increasing 'cross-boundary interactions' spreading the problem globally. One example they provide is that of livestock production, initially dependent upon farm-based resources and recycling waste products. In today's globalised inter-dependent world there is a decoupling of these processes, farm waste leaches into the environment rather than being recycled and intensive food production elsewhere (like soybean or palm oil) depends on ever higher inputs of synthetic mineral fertilisers, while global transportation merely adds to the consumption and waste of resources (Rist et al., 2014: 6–7). Thus vulnerabilities cascade through systems of positive feedbacks, magnifying and extending the crisis of sustainability.

In the Anthropocene, it appears that any attempts to start from resilience 'problem-solving' assumptions merely make the initial problem worse.

Modernity—now recast as the development of anthropogenic forms of 'cheating' nature—reaches its closure at a global scale, making coercive resilience not just the last gasp of modernity but actually the driver for its demise: 'because continued inputs are largely dependent upon, and ultimately limited by globally finite resources, such as fossil-fuel energy and phosphorous' (Rist et al., 2014: 7). The Anthropocene thereby spells the death knell for 'coerced' resilience precisely through revealing the problem of 'masking' the environmental implications, which the distances of time and space had previously concealed. High levels of production and the speed of 'bounce-back' through resilience approaches were not enabling adaptation to new conditions but quite the opposite: merely working to 'mask or camouflage the ecological signals of resilience losses and thus the true underlying constraints to production' (ibid.: 8).

Resilience, understood in modernist ways, is thereby part of the problem, not part of the solution. You don't have to be a scientist of system ecology (the original home of resilience-thinking) to realise that the whole discourse of resilience is potentially put at risk. Resilience-thinking rather than being constructed as a challenge to modernist aspirations of 'command-and-control' is more likely to be seen as the last redoubt of eco-modernisers and of modernist dreams of technological and technocratic approaches which attempt to short-cut problems rather than to tackle them at source (for example, Schmidt, 2013; Tierney, 2015; Yarina, 2018). But what would non-coerced or non-anthropogenic approaches to resilience look like? The scientists linked to the Resilience Alliance do not make a very convincing case of what it would mean to 'attempt to use natural processes to enhance system resilience' and argue themselves that often 'techno-fixes' may be required in the short-term as part of the process of using and manipulating 'natural processes' (Rist et al., 2014: 8):

> In such cases where coerced resilience is desired, the impacts on supporting and recipient system resilience must be considered. We argue that the *ultimate goal* is to retain or enhance the provision of *global production system resilience* through *bolstering natural supporting processes* rather than an increased reliance on anthropogenic inputs. (Rist et al., 2014: 9; emphasis added)

The game is rather given away here. The problems vitiating this approach are clear in the preceding quote. First, there is a clearly instrumental approach to 'natural processes', which are to be harnessed to support the existing status quo, thus 'the ultimate goal' is to support 'global production system resilience'. This has come to the fore particularly in experiments in 'rewilding' and new forms of environmental conservation, seeking to enhance and expand 'ecosystem services', geo- and bioengineering nature to be more efficient (see, for example, Lorimer, 2015). As Anna Tsing notes, these resilience imaginaries are all part of an 'ecomodernist' fantasy of the 'good Anthropocene' (2017: 16). Even if this could be achieved, 'natural processes' would be further modified by anthropogenic manipulation: the mere need to intervene to 'bolster' these allegedly 'natural processes' would inevitably produce other unintended stresses and strains according to the logic of the authors' own arguments.

Thus the problems of 'coerced' resilience become clear, and we can see a growing consensus that resilience is far from unproblematic as a set of governing interventions. However, it is clear from the criticisms of resilience that there is hope for an alternative: resilience can be done better in other more responsive and less 'ecomodernist' ways. The first approach, considered immediately in the following, is that of applying new technological advances to sense and modulate feedback effects obscured by reductionist or modernist linear thinking. The second is the advocacy of indigenous analytics, which share the cybernetic imaginary but go beyond this to suggest that resilience can be seen as a way of bringing 'future worlds' into being rather than merely limiting responsivity to maintaining the status quo. We feel that the counter-position between homeostatic and the latter, autopoietic, more agential approaches informed by speculative appropriations of indigenous knowledge is key for grasping contemporary discussions and debates on resilience in the Anthropocene.

FEEDBACK THROUGH TECHNOLOGICAL RESILIENCE

One alternative to 'top-down' approaches to resilience focuses upon how new technological advances in algorithmic computation and distributive sensory capacities can enable local communities to be more self-sustaining. The use of technology, not as a 'techno-fix' that artificially hides feedback effects but rather as one that enables them to be seen and responded to, is now central to many internationally financed resilience imaginaries in the battle against the effects of climate change. The rolling out of Big Data and the Internet of Things approaches to local communities promises a level of responsiveness and sensitivity to environmental changes that was previously unimaginable. For its boosters, in the international development agencies and corporations, these approaches will transform small-scale agricultural production. Even palm oil production receives a critical makeover. Rather than environmentally destructive industrial mono-cropping, small plot alternatives can be made economically viable if farmers sign up to digitally enhanced 'cloud-based' management systems, where farmers enable large-scale data collection and sensory monitoring systems to be installed and so can monitor and minimise the use of chemicals and other anthropogenic resources as well as rapidly respond to drought, pests and disease—detecting problems even down to the level of specific trees and plots. Just as with Google and Amazon, sensitivities to feedbacks increases the more data is shared and drawn upon. As the founder of one agri-tech start-up states:

> We specifically use . . . cloud storage (to store raw and processed imagery), cloud compute (to process huge amounts of data and extract insights), database storage and to serve our applications . . . to help farmers grow healthier crops is a perfect example of the way in which technology transforms traditional industries, leading to better livelihood conditions. Africa can be a harsh environment for farming. Crops are constantly under threat from problems such as disease, pests, and drought. Using the . . . cloud, we are bringing computation, data analytics, and other advanced technologies to help farmers grow healthier crops, despite the harsh conditions. (Cline, 2018)

Thus there is a clear cybernetic dynamic behind some Big Data approaches. It is for this reason that Big Data discourses often concern patterns and correlations rather than knowledge of causal processes (Amoore and Piotukh, 2016; Chandler, 2015; Kitchin, 2014; Mayer-Schonberger and Cukier, 2013; McKenna, 2016; Morozov, 2013). Big Data approaches seek to derive data from variable sources, linked through coding or datafication, thus information no longer links to universal meaning in a modernist representational sense. Katherine Hayles, in her study of the development of informatics, notes that the ability to find patterns was key to moving beyond mechanical or reductionist approaches based on essence and enabled the field of cybernetics, merely concerned with effects not with the content of information (Hayles, 1999: 98).

The promise is that, with high levels of data generation and developments in computational analysis, the world (coded through datafication) can begin to speak for itself, moving beyond the limits of 'phenomenology-of' projections of fallible instrumental reason (Steadman, 2013). According to a much-cited article by former *Wired* editor Chris Anderson (2008), Big Data promises a world without the need for abstract theoretical models: 'Correlation supersedes causation, and science can advance even without coherent models, unified theories, or really any mechanistic explanation at all'. In these accounts, theories of causation can be dispensed with and massive and real-time data trials can stand in as reliable knowledge of the concrete relations on which policy and business decisions can be based.

According to the Rockefeller Foundation research group: 'Large data collection and analysis may support communities by providing them with timely

feedback loops on their immediate environment' (Crawford et al., 2013: 1).
Rather than centralising data produced through everyday interactions and
applying algorithms that produce linear and reductive understandings, the
aspiration of some Big Data approaches is that multiple data sources can enable individuals, households and societies to practice responsive and reflex-
ive self-management in ways which were considered impossible before (for
example, Halpern, 2014: 242–43; Marres, 2012). In fields such as disaster
risk reduction and disaster management the shift is already clear (de Coning,
2016; Ramalingam, 2013). Big Data is alleged to help empower precisely
those that are most marginal and vulnerable at the moments of highest risk.
Open information flows are thus held to contribute to the building of resilience by making communities aware of the risks and hazards they may encounter so that they can mobilise to protect themselves (Ahrens and Rudolph,
2006: 217). This process is captured well by Patrick Meier (2013):

> Thanks to [Information and Communication Technologies], social media and
> Big Data . . . we can better measure our own resilience. Think of it as the Quan-
> tified Self movement applied to an entirely different scale, that of societies and
> cities. The point is that Big Data can provide us with more real-time feedback
> loops than ever before. And as scholars of complex systems know, feedback
> loops are critical for adaptation and change.

On this basis, international agencies, such as the World Bank, argue that
it is possible for technological aids to enable us to be more attentive to feedback effects and for resilience to have more of a positive impact for the UN's
Sustainable Development Goals (Chandler, 2016; World Bank, 2018). One
thing is clear, however, in this increasingly dominant perspective for dealing
with risk: the world becomes much less amenable to transformative practices
and experimentation. This limitation of possible alternatives is highlighted in
Giorgio Agamben's (2014) critique of the cybernetic 'governance of effects'.
He argues that while the governing of causes is the essence of politics, the
governance of effects reverses the political process:

> We should not neglect the philosophical implications of this reversal. It means
> an epoch-making transformation in the very idea of government, which over-
> turns the traditional hierarchical relation between causes and effects. Since
> governing the causes is difficult and expensive, it is more safe and useful to try
> to govern the effects. (Agamben, 2014)

If societies or communities were able to govern effects, tackling problems
in their emergence through rapid or real-time adaptation, then, in the Big
Data imaginary, they would become resilient or effective complex adaptive
systems, able to cope autonomously with risks and threats without the need

for external support or assistance. Big Data thus becomes the 'Holy Grail' of neoliberal disaster management. This view of self-governing systems relies on cybernetic thinking on the basis of homeostatic feedback loops. The more responses are automatic, the more the detection of signs and signals are all that is required[2] no knowledge is necessary any more than a thermostat needs to know why temperature changes occur. The correlation between the sign or signal and the emergent problem is all that is necessary. The learning and adjustment of these correlations is the 'bouncing forward' aspect of society understood as a complex adaptive system; progress thus becomes reinterpreted as a process of managing stability better in the wake of additional potential risks and threats (for example, Rodin, 2015).

It is this cybernetic understanding of risk management that has driven the concern with information rather than with knowledge. Maurizio Lazzarato has usefully highlighted that governance through signs displaces modernist views of subjectivity founded on universal linguistic, communicational and cognitive models: he correctly (in our view) understands this as 'non-cognitive' capitalism:

> Instead of a rational subject who controls information and his choices, *homo economicus* is a mere terminal of asignifying, symbolic, and signifying semiotics and of non-linguistic constituents which for the most part escape his awareness. We are not only well beyond the individualism and rationality of *homo economicus*, we have moved beyond 'cognitive capitalism'. (Lazzarato, 2014: 99–100)

In attempting to remove the separation between being and the world, the knowing subject ceases to exist, replaced by the sensing, embedded, relational 'non-self' of the Quantified Self, responsive to minor changes and adapting to new information about the self or the environment. The removal of the knowing subject is key to the imaginary of the cybernetic world as one that is conflict-free, providing a cybernetic imaginary of a seamless interrelationship between the human, the machinic and the environment (Hayles, 1999: 288). This cybernetic desire to adaptively modulate around the equilibrium thereby erases the potential for human creativity. De Sousa Santos calls this 'epistemicide', 'the murder of knowledge' and the respect for difference (2016: 92–93).

It can also be argued that the cybernetic impulse behind Big Data, as prevalent in disaster risk management as in IBM's 'smart city' infrastructure experiments (Townsend, 2013: 65–69), is problematic in that 'non-cognitive' forms of responsivity to changes seek merely to modulate around the imaginary of a stable equilibrium. Machinic models of adaptation, even at high speeds or imagined as 'real time' forms of responsivity, in maintaining the world in its unsustainable state, can perversely only speed up the process of catastrophic collapse. The problematic is well drawn out in Bernard Stiegler's recent advocacy for a 'Neganthropocene' (2018). Drawing on the insights of Jacques Derrida, Alfred North Whitehead and Gilbert Simondon, Stiegler argues that these contemporary forms of automated 'algorithmic governance' speed up the processes of disintegration and entropy and limit the imaginary of any transformative alternatives.

Stiegler's reasoning is very important in terms of grasping the relationship between resilience and speculative 'indigenous' analytics. For Stiegler, the correlationist paradigm of Big Data is entropic: destructive of life in its plural and interactive development. It requires no new knowledge as the task of adaptation replaces human thinking with automated algorithmic processes (2018: 140–43). The key point that Stiegler makes is that living in the Anthropocene requires another alternative: neither modernist dreams of progress nor automated adaptive responsivity in the present but approaches to resilience that build speculative futures. As against the cybernetic or machinic destruction of 'living knowledge' (ibid.: 208) he counterposes a care for 'noetic différance' (ibid.: 221) which 'can be constituted only within a speculative cosmology, that is, only by conceiving the cosmos as a process within which localities are produced that give rise to various feedback loops or discontinuities' (ibid.: 239) productive of change, understood as a process of individuation or differentiation, multiplying forms of life rather than destroying or nullifying them. Thus resilience can be seen as the speculative struggle of life against entropy, the struggle of differences to make differences, to unfold and enable processes of becoming.

THE INDIGENOUS ALTERNATIVE

In new and alternative approaches to resilience, indigenous ways of knowing are valued for their speculative method (as discussed already in this book) understood as grounded, contextual and enabling or developmental and transformative practices, rather than as applications of abstract, fixed, deterministic or universal knowledge. The capacity that indigenous communities are imagined to have (and Western societies are imagined to lack) is the ability to speculatively experiment with and to anticipate and respond to feedback effects (for example, Lansing, 2006). Indigenous analytics have increasingly informed governance practices based on being attentive or sensitive to changes and alert to new possibilities or dangers: learning with or from an interactive or inter-agential environment and seeking to extend, to pluralise or to 'complexify' these 'becomings' rather than learning about nature as a fixed object of instrumental knowledge. According to First People's Worldwide, this speculative methodology revolves around the capacity to interpret 'signs', enabling indigenous approaches to develop a futural awareness or sensitivity:

> Indigenous science and knowledge are based largely on bioindicators, or natural signs. For instance, the timing of the onset of rains in Bolivia can be predicted by how high a certain species of bird builds its nests. Many animals can sense earthquakes and other natural disasters before humans can, and watching their behavior can give us time to get to safety if such an event occurs. Learning from nature in this way is an integral part of the Indigenous worldview that all things are connected, and that nature, when respected, can be a benevolent part of the whole community. (First People's Worldwide, n.d.)

It is thereby on the basis of the importance of alternative speculative ways of knowing and of adapting to change that indigenous knowledge has been brought to the forefront of international policy gatherings, as exemplified in the work of the Intergovernmental Panel on Climate Change (IPCC). Indigenous knowledge was acknowledged in the Fourth Assessment Report as 'an invaluable basis for developing adaptation and natural resource management strategies in response to environmental and other forms of change' (IPCC, 2007: 15.6.1). This recognition was reaffirmed at IPCC's 32nd Session (IPCC, 2010), and consideration of traditional and indigenous knowledge was included as a guiding principle for the Cancun Adaptation Framework adopted at the 2010 United Nations Framework Convention on Climate Change Conference (United Nations Framework Convention on Climate Change Conference, 2010). The IPCC's Working Group II contribution to the Fifth Assessment Report includes local and traditional knowledge as distinct topics within chapter 12 on human security (Adger et al., 2014). As a joint UN Educational, Scientific and Cultural Organization and UN report states:

> Indigenous [peoples] are not only potential victims of global climate change. Attentiveness to environmental variability, shifts and trends is an integral part of their ways of life. Community-based and local knowledge may offer valuable insights into environmental change due to climate change, and complement broader-scale scientific research with local precision and nuance. Indigenous societies have elaborated coping strategies to deal with unstable environments, and in some cases, are already actively adapting to early climate change impacts. While the transformations due to climate change are expected to be unprecedented, indigenous knowledge and coping strategies provide a crucial foundation for community-based adaptation measures. (Nakashima et al., 2012: 6)

The concern with seeing from the point of view of nonhuman actants and agents presupposes a close communal relationship of more-than-human be-

ing. Anthropologist Laura Rival provides the example of a project to reintro-
duce salmon to a polluted watershed which had failed when led by modernist science and technology but was a success when initiated by indigenous
knowledge: 'This was accomplished through observing the river, to know it
and experience it as a salmon would' not seeing the river as a straight line
but as a lively series of vortexes and branching fractals (Rival, 2009: 306;
see also Chandler and Reid, 2018). Thus indigenous ways of being are performatively constructed on the lines of speculative imaginaries of interactive
becoming within more-than-human communities. As Aboriginal research
anthropologist Deborah Bird Rose states:

> Rather than humans deciding autonomously to act in the world, humans are
> called into action by the world. The result is that country, or nature, far from
> being an object to be acted upon, is a self-organising system that brings people
> and other living things into being, into action, into sentience itself. (cited in
> Graham et al., 2010)

Julie Graham, Katherine Gibson and Gerda Roelvink thereby draw together indigenous, feminist and science and technology studies approaches,
in arguing that rather than the modernist ideal of human subjects acting upon
the world or responding automatically according to preset rules, we need to
let the world affect us through developing indigenous capacities of 'learning
to be affected' (2010). Allowing the country or the land to speak to us, thus
enabling the more-than-human communities necessary for life in the Anthropocene (see also Graham, 2008). Here, the speculative impulse is clear
in recognising that pluriversal and adaptive knowledge enables non-modern
ways of being and learning vis-à-vis universal and representative knowledge, which hubristically seeks to project its narrow self-interest upon the
external environment (see Bateson, 2000: 451). Here, it is clear that creative
and 'response-able' (Haraway, 2016: 2) human agency is at the forefront of
coping with change as there can be no assumptions of either preestablished
knowledge or of orientation toward a static equilibrium.

Thus resilience, in this 'indigenous' framing of policy interventions to
enable adaptive capacities, always necessitates the development of 'attentive' and 'responsive' sensitivities: natural or immanent processes cannot
be 'enabled' by being left alone. Similarly, the speculative processes of attunement and of differentiation require active agential engagement and cannot be left to automated algorithms. The starting assumption for resilience
discourses is that we are now 'after Nature' (Lorimer, 2015; Purdy, 2015)
or 'after ecology' (Latour, 2004; Morton, 2009, 2013). As Gleb Raygorodetsky argues, even if we set aside half the planet as nature, as the Harvard
biologist E. O. Wilson (2016) suggests:

This strict stance, however, does little to help get to the root of our destructive behaviour. Allowing development to destroy habitat in one area with a promise of 'offsetting' this destruction by conserving another place actually perpetuates humankind's assault on the environment. It creates an illusion that as long as a portion of nature is put away and locked up in some sort of a park, we can rape and pillage the rest of the planet. (Raygorodetsky, 2017: 180)

More importantly, as Paulo Tavares argues, the Western idea of a pristine 'nature' that can be preserved or kept away from human interaction has always been mythical (Tavares, 2013: 234). Even the Amazonian rainforests have been cultivated in sustainable ways by indigenous communities, thus 'Amazonia's deep history is not natural, but human' (ibid.): 'And this is perhaps the crucial paradox that the Anthropocene has brought to light: different regimes of power will produce different natures, for nature is not natural; it is the product of cultivation, and more frequently, of conflict' (ibid.: 236). Tavares argues that the biodiversity of the Amazonian rainforests is not a product of nature, they are 'cultural forests' (2017: 146) and cultured ones. Indigenous resilience is thereby not about letting nature guide understanding but drawing out the potential becomings immanent within it:

These biodiversity-enhancing designs are very much alive in the memory and everyday practices of forest peoples. The protection of their land rights thus also means the design of a more resilient planetary ecological system in face of ruinous anthropogenic climate change. (Tavares, 2017: 150)

This is very different to the adaptive responsiveness of equilibrium management. Rather than waiting for 'nature' to inform forms of adaptation, speculative approaches seek to creatively engage with new opportunities, 'becoming with' others rather than passively reacting to them. As Elizabeth Povinelli cautions, 'learning to be affected' or 'to listen to the land' should be understood as a different way of being responsive—quite unlike that of algorithmic or cybernetic forms of adaptation—in that the human agent is forced to do the work themselves (2016a: 142). In attempting to reduce emergent effects to signals for us to read-off and automatically respond to, the actual world is never really 'given its due', never appreciated in all its multiplicity and potentiality but instead flattened and reduced to networked relations. As Donna Haraway famously notes, there is no choice but to 'stay with the trouble' (2016). 'Nothing is connected to everything; [but] everything is connected to something' (ibid.: 31). Relations are concrete and fluid sets of shifting and contingent inter-connections, not amenable to easy intervention or datafication. Relational entanglements and inter-connections are not a ready-made or 'natural' solution: they do not provide new forms of problemsolving or an additional prop for acquiring more modernist ways of knowing.

Speculative approaches view our entanglement with nature and nonhuman beings as an invitation to explore alternative possibilities rather than to resolve problems of governance by maintaining the existing modes of being. As botanist Robin Wall Kimmerer argues, in her work *Braiding Sweetgrass* (2013), 'becoming indigenous' means 'to take care of the land as if our lives, both material and spiritual, depended upon it' through restoration as 're-story-ation' a process of speculative storytelling with the aid of nonhumans (2013: 9). Because 'the stories we choose to shape our behaviors have adaptive consequences' (ibid.: 30). Her emphasis is very much on the ethos of care as a reciprocal and speculative becoming with others, rather than a view that nature is separate. The real artifice is the tearing of modern society away from this reciprocity, creating a 'Potemkin village of an ecosystem where we perpetrate the illusion that the things we consume have just fallen off the back of Santa's sleigh, not been ripped from the earth' (ibid.: 199). In a world of liveliness, flux and change, speculative approaches affirm the entangled potentials, which the previous paradigms of resilience are held to close off from us. Anna Tsing captures the process well:

> Making worlds is not limited to humans. We know that beavers reshape streams as they make dams, canals and lodges; in fact, all organisms make ecological living places, altering earth, air, and water. . . . In the process, each organism changes everyone's world. Bacteria made our oxygen atmosphere, and plants help maintain it. Plants live on land because fungi made soil by digesting rocks. As these examples suggest, world-making projects can overlap, allowing room for more than one species. (Tsing, 2015: 22)

Anna Tsing calls this open-ended process, of collective and connective experimentation, 'ways of being', understood as 'emergent effects of encounters': the possibilities inherent in fluid assemblages with others (2015: 23). In life after modernist dreams of progress, disturbances and perturbations are not threats to the status quo but interactive invitations to creativity, seen as positive opportunities to make 'life in capitalist ruins'. Tsing, for example, tells the story of woodland revitalisation groups: 'who hope that small scale disturbances might draw both people and forests out of alienation, building a world of overlapping lifeways in which mutualistic transformation, the mode of mycorrhiza, might yet be possible' (2015: 258). She states: 'They hope their actions might stimulate a latent commons, that is, an eruption of shared assembly, even as they know they can't actually *make* a commons' (ibid.; emphasis in original). Here, we can see speculative analytics as a set of techniques not really 'making' something but rather acting as a stimulus, exploring, probing, facilitating, repurposing what already exists but which can only come into being 'with': the new potentialities thus do not lie latent within a preexisting entity but lie in the speculative creation of a new 'commons'.

Donna Haraway powerfully reinforces the importance of this approach, arguing that ongoing processes cannot be grasped through homeostatic or autopoietic frameworks, which assume too many separations between entities (that is, that relations are structured and limited). As she states:

> The earth . . . is sympoietic, not autopoietic. Mortal worlds . . . do not make themselves, no matter how complex and multileveled the systems. . . . Autopoietic systems are hugely interesting—witness the history of cybernetics and information sciences; but they are not good models for living and dying worlds. . . . Poesis is symchthonic, sympoietic, always partnered all the way down, with no starting and subsequently interacting 'units'. (Haraway, 2016: 33)

Instead of focusing on linear or cybernetic forms of adaptation, seeking to prevent or slow climate change, preserving the status quo, speculative approaches lead to a different set of (much more positive) assumptions and practices engaging with the present in ways which are creative rather than merely adaptively responsive:

> Staying with the trouble does not require such a relationship to times called the future. In fact, staying with the trouble requires learning to be truly present, not as a vanishing pivot between awful and edenic pasts and apocalyptic or salvific futures, but as mortal critters entwined in myriad unfinished configurations of places, times, matters, meanings. (Haraway, 2016: 1)

The indigenous imaginary constructed here is that of cultivation rather than extraction, an ethico-political duty of futural care that is situated fully in the present. This approach is theorised clearly by María Puig de la Bellacasa; drawing upon her experience of permaculture training, she states:

> Obligations of caring in naturecultures cannot be reduced to 'stewardship' or 'pastoral' care in which humans are *in charge* of natural worlds. Such conceptions continue to separate a human 'moral' subject from a naturalized 'object' of caring. Nor need we go to the other extreme: diluting the thinking of specific obligations of care in situational relations with nonhumans. . . . These are poor generalizations that avoid engaging with actual situated naturecultures and the speculative efforts demanded from ecological thought and practice. (Puig de la Bellacasa, 2017: 164)

For Puig de la Bellacasa this is speculative 'alterbiopolitics', creating different forces of world-making relationalities, capable of cultivating '"power with" and "power-from-within" rather than "power-over"' (2017: 165). Thus, in critical approaches to resilience, the alternative to mono-crop agriculture, industrialised fisheries, sea walls and river 'normalisation' is never to 'just let nature take its course'. In discursive framings that are little different to neo-liberal constructions of governance interventions that are 'for the market'— designed to enable or to 'free' the productive and organisational capacities of market forces, 'nature' (like market forces) is never assumed to be 'natural' (see Chandler, 2014; Chandler and Reid, 2016). Nature, no longer separate to human systems, requires wise and active stewardship, rather than instrumental control, like any other complex adaptive system. Speculative approaches to resilience are thereby not necessarily against technological applications and understandings but seek to apply them differently: unlike Big Data and 'algorithmic governance' approaches, to work 'with' rather than 'against' immanent productive processes, sensitive to feedbacks and unintended effects. Techniques such as 'bricolage, tinkering, the hack, the crack, the exploit' enable technology to be put to speculative use (Viveiros de Castro and Danowski, 2018: 187).

The indigenous are imagined as productive of resilient and self-sustaining communities, capable of coping, adapting to and 'bouncing back' from regular disturbances and disruptions but also, as importantly, of speculatively bringing into being alternative futures. As we discussed (in chapter 5) the speculative imaginary of indigenous peoples is centred on the empowering agency increasingly associated with the active and contextual interpretation of signs. This is a form of knowledge work said to be excluded from modernist attempts to capture the 'one world' world. As Pedro Neves Marques notes, this form of speculative interpretation goes beyond modernist distinctions of self and other as 'there is no illusion of transcendence or transparency' (2017: 34), in counter-position to a computerised or algorithmic reading of signs or images which constrains the world to what already exists, indigenous analytics enables us to:

> rupture the hegemonic gaze which sees objectivity everywhere. To think images as the embodiment of worlds means not only thinking the ontology of images but also thinking images ontologically, that is, not as representations but as *representatives*: . . . images through which we see other images. (Neves Marques, 2017: 37)

Thus signs or signals are held to enlarge the world of possibilities and of potentials rather than subtracting from or limiting it. Deborah Bird Rose uses the conceptualisation of 'shimmer', as aboriginal aesthetic, to discuss the ways that signs and signals 'appeal to the senses, things that evoke or capture feelings and responses . . . lures that both entice one's attention and offer rewards' (2017: G53). For de Sousa Santos, key to the power of indigenous knowledge as futural knowledge is the capacity to continually speculate with and upon the past, 'reinventing the past in such a way as to make it recapture the capacity for the fulguration, irruption and redemption . . . to construct new, powerful interrogations and passionate stands capable of inexhaustible meanings' (2016; 88–89; see also Sissons, 2005: 11). Rather than a universal, abstract or linear theory of progress, where the past was always a necessary moment, fixing the determination of the present, for speculative indigenous analytics, the past is an 'inexhaustible' resource for holding open transformative hope in the present.

De Sousa Santos draws upon the critical theorist Ernst Bloch to elaborate upon the speculative and futural analytics required in making the future an object of care as indigenous approaches 'to call attention to emergencies [processes of emergence] is by nature speculative and requires some philosophical elaboration' (2016: 182). He summarises the contemporary imaginary of indigenous thought well in terms of constructions of resilience that fit the catastrophic imaginary of the Anthropocene in the importance of paying attention to change to bring the future into the present:

> The Not Yet [Bloch's category of immanent potential] inscribes in the present a possibility that is uncertain but never neutral; it could be the possibility of utopia or salvation or the possibility of catastrophe or damnation. Such uncertainty brings an *element of chance or danger to every change*. Thus uncertainty is what, to my mind, *expands the present* while at the same time *contracting the future and rendering it an object of care*. At every moment, there is a limited horizon of possibilities, and that is why it is *important not to waste the unique opportunity of a specific change* offered by the present: carpe diem (seize the day). (de Sousa Santos, 2016: 183; emphasis added)

Unlike machinic real-time responses to adaptation which assume beforehand the correlations and changes to be modulated to maintain equilibrium, indigenous analytics makes no assumptions about the meaning or consequences of signs. Thus the process of attentivity, attunement or 'affectedness' is much greater and more intense. It is this process of speculative attention which 'expands the present' and cares for the future (as we discussed in chapter 5 on pluriversal politics), literally bringing the future into being through responding through speculative analytics. Every sign or signal or change in the state of being thus provides an 'opportunity' to bring new futures into being and demands to be 'seized' rather than 'wasted'.

De Sousa Santos provides an informative philosophical framing, to interpret or 'translate' indigenous analytics for Western consumption, with his two conceptions of a 'sociology of absences' and a 'sociology of emergences' which become a simple 'how-to-guide' for speculative thought. The 'sociology of absences' is designed to make the everyday unusual so that we can pay attention to it, thus 'expanding our available realm of experiences'. We can then see and speculate upon more 'signs or clues' as our world becomes stranger to us. The 'sociology of emergences' expands this speculative moment 'decelerating the present, giving it a denser, more substantive content', enabling 'ethical vigilance over the unfolding of possibilities' aided by such emotions as (negative) anxiety or (positive) hope. Together this speculative method provides what de Sousa Santos calls 'symbolic amplification' (2016: 186).

For speculative analytics the world is always necessarily more than its surface appearance. This is why 'symbolic amplification' is necessary to see beyond the limits of traditional modes of thought. What does not appear to exist or is not readily apparent is always more important and more rich in potential. This is what gives speculative analytics its agential and futural appeal. As Bird Rose argues: 'Part of what makes our common Earth condition so interesting is that which may yet be is infinitely more extravagant than that which already has been' (2011: 114). Uncertainty or unknowability do not close down our world but open it up as 'the possibilities of the living world always are greater than the mind or knowledge system that wants to understand' them (ibid.). The 'not yet' and the 'may yet be' are here and not here at the same time and thus the purpose is not to reproduce or conserve the present but 'to enable', 'to engender', 'to cultivate' or 'to care' futurally.

While linear modernist and homeostatic cybernetic approaches to resilience pay attention to systemic interaction, feedback effects and to tipping points, they are inevitably productionist, consumptionist and extractivist. They are always inevitably focused on saving or on prolonging or making more efficient what already exists. In the Anthropocene, these approaches stand accused of refusing to see that these contemporary forms of being are exactly the problem themselves. The only approach to resilience which promises change and transformation is the speculative approach which, we are told, can be learned from the coping strategies of indigenous peoples. This approach trains us in a quasi-paranoiac attentivity to the world around us, enabling us to develop speculative skills giving 'symbolic amplification' to the clues and signs all around us. This attentiveness, we are told, can be as transformatory for us as it has been for indigenous peoples, expanding our reality beyond modernist constrictions and making available infinitely more possible, concrete futures (de Sousa Santos, 2016: 186).

THE LIMITS OF THE SPECULATIVE

Speculative thought draws the future out of the present through attentiveness to changes, however momentary. It is not difficult to see how important speculation might be for a subsistence society, in which there is no choice but to seize every opportunity available. In societies where the vast proportion of resources is necessarily devoted to survival, attentivity or sensitivity to the world is vital, as is speculatively learning to interpret the actions and habits of other species, because a lack of attention can quickly lead to death. In this world of limited options, humans are not so clever or so distinct and clearly are forced to live in a relation of inter-dependency with plants and animal beings, which share in a condition of constant exposure to risk of death. Speculative thought is a vital aspect of being curious and interested in the world and something that should be valued and encouraged, regardless of the context of economic and social development.

Where we disagree with discursive framings of resilience and indigeneity is in the counter-positioning of speculative thought with instrumental applications of science and technology. We dispute the idea that speculative approaches of drawing out new futures from the present can address the challenges we face in the Anthropocene. Unlike earlier societies, dependent on their immediate environments and open to contingency, we think that attentiveness to our immediate relations takes away and obscures necessary concerns with the 'bigger picture' of political, social and economic relations, from which transformative political projects take their cue. The precondition for speculative approaches is the closure of time and space—the acceptance of the end of the world—making the present moment necessarily contain the entirety of the potentiality of the future. Everything has therefore to be always and already given as virtual potential to be actualised. This would constitute a fundamental closure for both thought and political practice.

It is precisely this closure that resilience advocates desire in their critique of the hubris of the productionism and consumerism of the modern world. As Robin Wall Kimmerer argues, it is possible for modern/colonial man to become indigenous but only by coming down to earth, by appreciating this closure, and accepting that its finitude is equal in measure to every other living system. To become indigenous modern/colonial man needs to understand: 'that all the knowledge he needed in order to live was present in the land. His role was not to control or change the world as a human, but to learn from the world how to be human' (2013: 208). To not appreciate that everything is always and already contained in the present time and space would be to act like our lives did not depend on the land, to take it for granted or exploit it for short-term gain. Thus, to become indigenous would not be understood as a limitation but as an affirmation of our entangled and radically endangered being. The reduction of the world and removal of modern extensions of being through material global time and space becomes affirmatively transvalued as a speculative immersion in plural becomings in a world of infinite dangers.

In which case, we may well be able to share romantic poet William Blake's vision of being able to see 'the world in a grain of sand' or 'heaven in a wild flower' and to have a sense of wonder and awe for a world so much richer and larger than our understandings. If we were to do so we would doubtless realise the power of speculative thought in taking us beyond our quotidian and everyday routines and experiences. For Leanne Betasamosake Simpson, the practice of indigenous freedom is a practice that enables the 'unfolding of a different present' (2017: 18); a way of being in the world that enables 'the present as an agent of change—a presencing of the present' (2017: 20). This form of speculative analytics enables the emergence of 'an elsewhere that is already here, if hidden from view' (2017: 213). This power of speculative sight enables a different seeing of the world, or rather the seeing of another world: 'The land itself is a coded representation of Nishnaabewin that is visible to those who live within Nishnaabewin but is opaque to those who do not' (2017: 215). Thus alternative worlds are already here once we can speculatively bring them into being. But there are limitations to the speculative bringing into being of infinite alternative worlds.

Speculative approaches promise infinite future possibilities but coerce us into a life which is lived only in the present, by being 'attentive' to the immediate present only and in exclusion of other possible temporalities: that is, they may be speculative but only in relation to what already exists in experience rather than enabling any speculation about the future itself. Any kind of thinking about, imagining or desire for experience of the future becomes diagnosed as dangerous in this indigenous governmentalisation of human time. As we have seen, to claim that outside or 'anthropogenic inputs' of non-indigenous or external resources and technology remove our resilience, rather than enhance it, is thus to posit dependency and humility as a goal in itself rather than as a means of survival. The problem is that the history of global human development and of cultural inter-connection makes this speculative restriction of the external potential in the world hard to accept. What if we want more? What if we decide that all we need is not immediately available to us? What if we do not feel gratitude for what we already have and think there is more out there to be had? What if we disagree with indigenous wisdom that tells us that: 'Scarcity and plenty are as much qualities of the mind and spirit as they are of the economy?' (Kimmerer, 2013: 376). What if even indigenous communities would refuse to 'become indigenous'? Jonathan Lear tells one such story in his well-cited book *Radical Hope* (2006).

Lear tells the story of Plenty Coups, the last great chief of the Crow Nation, confronting cultural catastrophe: the end of the Crow's traditional nomadic-hunting way of life and confinement to the reservation. For Lear, the comparison with the 'end of the world' of the Crow Nation and the current coming to terms with the Anthropocene is clear and prescient (2006: 7). What would it mean to witness the end of a way of life 'from inside that way of life' and yet still to take responsibility for a responsible and ethical way of being in the world (ibid.)? Survival, in this case, meant to live a life where, in Plenty Coups's words 'nothing happened': nothing that was meaningful in terms of the Crow's 'reality', shaped through their traditional cultural practices (2006: 2–3). According to Lear, the devastation of the Crow was ontological (2006: 50), leaving them without a world in which they could have a point of view, 'having lost the concepts with which they could construct a narrative' of self (2006: 32). Left with nothing to orient around to create a new framework of meaning, Plenty Coups practiced resilience through radical hope, which enabled the Crow's survival. Radical hope, for Lear, is the speculative belief that beyond the limits of our understanding radically different futures are possible (2006: 93–94). Rather than speculatively thinking about 'the world in a grain of sand', Plenty Coups speculated about the world through the eyes of the chickadee in order to see 'great power in little things' (2006: 81) and to speculate about adaptation.

The key message of Lear's work of 'philosophical anthropology' (2006: 7) is that radical hope requires a leap of faith in the rejection of a former subjectivity (2006: 104). Plenty Coups survived through accepting 'the end of the world' without despair, understanding that new frameworks of meaning needed to be speculatively generated (2006: 152). Lear counterposes Plenty Coup's speculative pragmatism with Sitting Bull, the last great chief of the Sioux Nation, who is held to have lacked resilience in his refusal to cooperate with the US government and to adapt to changing conditions even without any assurance as to what the future might bring (ibid.: 106). Sitting Bull refused the speculative pragmatism of resilience approaches and instead favoured religious messianism in the ungrounded or 'wishful' hope that the whites would be wiped out and the previous way of life revived (2006: 135). Sitting Bull, it turns out, chose not to 'become indigenous', whereas Plenty Coups opted to use speculative analytics to enable his tribe to survive and to adapt while still keeping their traditional heritage. Lear's lesson for 'ontologically vulnerable' humanity is clear: that we need to 'become indigenous'. Our catastrophic times call neither for rejection nor passive resignation but for affirmation and a speculative faith in the world beyond our understanding.

We summarise Lear's story here to illustrate the dangers of Western academics and commentators imposing the benefits of speculative analytics for resilience with little regard for the real suffering or the real moral choices of indigenous peoples whose indigeneity does not fit Western preconceptions. Although often well intentioned, it is difficult for Western advocates and activists to escape accusations that they are essentialising and romanticising the lifestyles and coping strategies of the marginalised communities they are offering up as role models for adaptive approaches. Speculative imaginaries, through the Western gaze, always become adaptive to change in ways that are accepting, open and affirmative, neither resigned nor resisting. To 'become indigenous' is to refuse the subject position of separation or autonomy: rather than starting from the self, starting from the new context, the trouble, or entanglement. Thus indigeneity is increasingly seen as a mode of being rather than a fixed ethnic identity. As Jeffrey Sissons states, the imbrication of indigenous peoples within a certain policy imaginary has had deleterious effects:

> Over the last decade or so, as marginalized Third World peoples have joined the UN Working Group on Indigenous Populations, there has been a broadening of the definition of indigenous at the United Nations, so that it has now become widely equated with having subsistence economies and being close to 'Mother Earth'. This is eco-indigenism and . . . primitivizes indigenous peoples living in settler states who have adopted urban lifestyles or it calls into question their authenticity; [and] opens up the possibility for almost any people with a subsistence-based culture to claim membership in international indigenous forums. (Sissons, 2005: 16–17)

The imagining of indigeneity as a mode of being has rapidly expanded those included under the classifications of the United Nations to around 370 million people (larger than the combined population of the United States and Canada) but also fed into the binary construction of 'indigenous' and 'modern' that we have so far problematised in this book. For many Western theorists and policy-makers the climate catastrophe of the Anthropocene posits the political choice of either keeping modernist subjectivities, based upon the divide between culture and nature, or choosing to put the needs of the environment first, learning to become resilient or to 'become indigenous'. Thus the 'Gaia War' constructs a binary (Viveiros de Castro and Danowski, 2018), neither based on traditional colonial tropes of race or ethnicity nor modernist ones of class or nation, but the choice of two alternative modes of being in the world.

The enrolling of indigenous peoples into Western critical projects and their feting as 'saviours' of the world and bearers of specific forms of knowledge (Altamirano-Jiménez and Kermoal, 2016: 6) creates a gap between the Western construction of indigeneity and the struggles of real peoples. This gap regularly undermines some of the claims made by critical theorists and environmental campaigners, who insist that indigenous communities be enrolled as 'traditional custodians' in support of the latest IPCC reports (for example, Forest Peoples Programme, 2018). It is also apparent in the degrading imaginaries of environmentalists wherein indigenous communities are pictured as "testing grounds" and "laboratories" (Raygorodestsky, 2017: 258) for climate change. These essentialist and exploitative framings, which seek to 'support' indigenous communities in maintaining biodiversity on 'our' behalf, often lead to oppressive forms of regulation and categorisation where indigenous rights become dependent on community members pledging to maintain their ancestral beliefs and practices (Andersen, 2014; Simpson, 2014; Sissons, 2005; Tallbear, 2013). As Sissons suggests, 'indigenous authenticity is racism and primitivism in disguise' (2005: 37). These views are merely a Western revaluation of 'primitivism and tribalism in relation to destructive western rationality and individualism'. Rather than a discourse of indigeneity, Sissons suggests these views be understood as 'eco-ethnicity', where ecological threats are 'ethnicized' and ethnic subordination 'ecologized' (ibid.: 23).

Apart from being romanticising and essentialising, a lot of the claims made on behalf of these marginalised communities do not stand up to close examination. In many ways it is ironic that although the interlocutors from indigenous and subsistence communities that Western advocates draw upon repeatedly state that they can no longer adapt in traditional ways—for example, to changes in a river's path and momentum (Chandler, 2017: 121; Yarina, 2018)—or that the climactic and seasonal signs that used to provide a guide to everyday life are now much more erratic and unreliable (Raygorodestsky, 2017: 59)—the 'voices' of the people themselves are rarely heard in the rush to instrumentalise these survival strategies as 'critical' and futuristic alternatives.

What is being drawn from these communities would appear to say much more about the desires of Western advocates and activists than about these communities themselves, many of which are adapting to change (including the impacts of climate change) in ways which have increasingly less and less relation to traditional or local knowledge-based practices (Raygorodestsky, 2017: 52, 193, 243). Even reparations or indigenous repossession cannot return speculative analytics to real indigenous peoples, where the return of lands is often synonymous with capitalist development and the growth of tribal corporations or a resource for tourist ventures, forestry and other capitalist enterprises (Sissons, 2005: 146). It seems clear that the imaginaries of speculative indigenous modes of resilience are for Western audiences rather than oriented to assisting indigenous communities themselves. As Arun Agrawal argues, it would appear that the crisis of Western modernity means that we are faced with a paradox of speculative thought being wrenched from any meaningful context: 'Indigenous knowledge is here to stay, even if what it represents is forever and always disappearing' (2009: 158).

CONCLUSION

Resilience has certainly been problematised in the Anthropocene. Few contemporary advocates of resilience would forward eco-modernising claims of problem-solving, seeking to increase productivity as an end in itself. Similarly, many commentators critique the homeostatic imaginaries of Big Data and algorithmic governance, seeking to enable resilience through warding off change and modulating around equilibrium. However, there are few critiques of indigenous imaginaries of resilience, and the speculative or futural analytics, claimed to be derived from indigenous peoples, appear to escape many of the problems of modernist framings of resilience. In speculatively entangling human agency with the appearances of the world, these approaches no longer assume that problems are somehow 'external' and that existing modes of being, producing and consuming need to be defended.

Where indigenous approaches diverge from a Big Data or algorithmic imaginary is in no longer imaging the world as a harmonious cybernetic system. Homeostasis is no longer an option in the Anthropocene. However, the fact that ways of knowing are pluralised rather than universalised does little to open up 'alternative worlds', but merely enforces the reification or essentialisation of what exists as the horizon of the possible, determined by forces beyond human direction and control. The 'pluriversalisation' of knowledge is correctly understood in pluriversal discourses as neither modernist universalism nor postmodernist relativism (Rojas, 2016: 380). The imaginary of speculative forms of resilience is neither that of a liberal telos of universal progress nor that of incapacity in the face of uncertainty but precisely the pluriversal one of a process of permanent adaptation, whereby being is a process of knowing required by life itself.

Taken to its extreme, in the cognate ontology of speculative realism, we would aspire to enable plural worlds to 'knowledge' us rather than we as autonomous subjects aspire to know an 'objective' or universal world (for example, Morton, 2013: 48). The fact that in these speculative approaches there can only be flux and flows, which actors are always and already within, does not mean that alternative worlds can be speculatively brought into being. As Druscilla Cornell and Stephen Seely note in their recent book, the irony of these speculative perspectives, which problematise representational or instrumental knowledge, is that 'everything must ultimately remain exactly as it is' (2016: 12). The postcybernetic promise of knowing as pluriversal being, without ontological or epistemological hierarchies, reifies reality or 'life itself' as the normative horizon of being, making existence itself the only possible goal.

NOTES

1. https://www.resalliance.org.
2. As Orit Halpern notes, thus what is lacking in contemporary cybernetic imaginary is 'any sense of historical contingency or possibility' (2014: 244).

Chapter 7

Governing Imaginaries

We saw in the previous chapters how indigenous modes of being are interpellated into neoliberal regimes of subjectification which hail them for their supposed resilience to crisis, their perseverance in the face of suffering, and their dispossessed conditions of existence. Making sense of the subjectification of people and communities as being or becoming indigenous, along these lines, means understanding the power which neoliberalism holds over the images of indigenous modes of being, the governance of images of indigeneity, and the vast scope today of the neoliberal imaginary, which constructs both indigenous and non-indigenous people alike as resilient to crisis, perseverant in the face of present and future suffering, and appreciative of their conditions of dispossession. To be fully understood, neoliberalism has to be grasped as a form of power which works through the imaginations of its subjects, convincing us of the naturalness of the image of the human with which it presents us, and which it presents itself as merely enabling and seeking to protect (Fisher, 2018).

How could it be that imaginaries of indigeneity are so amenable to this neoliberal imaginary without the powers pushing this mode of being having access to our imaginations? How could the vast plurality of indigenous modes of being come to be represented in very specific forms of relationship to this world, as a space of endless disaster, without having our imaginations worked upon, such that we come to picture indigenous worlds thus? How else could our conceptions of time have been shaped so dramatically such that our visions of the future are ones of further misery and endless struggles for survival, without our imaginations being employed? How could it increasingly become central to policy governance and critical academic belief, that we can cope with living in a world of endless disasters, in the ways the ideologues of resilience preach, without our self-images, also, being employed? Of course, neoliberalism, like most if not all regimes of power, also involves reason. We have to be convinced that what it says about the world and about ourselves really is true and reasonable. But the arguments by which it convinces us don't work unless they are able to call upon our imaginations too.

For those who wish to resist the demand to become indigenous, the task today is to find a way out of the discursive traps laid by neoliberal regimes of power. Which is why we are calling in this book for a suspicion towards these new discourses of indigenous resilience, perseverance and dispossession, and the development of a political intelligence capable of resisting the traps now being set by powers seeking to govern us with these discursive strategies. The image of the indigenous subject as the resilient, perseverant, endlessly adaptive being, capable of coping with serial disasters, and bouncing back is precisely such a trap (Reid, 2018a, 2019). Images are traps into which we sometimes fall, and often are led to in order that we may do so (Reid, 2017). Which is why we need to be wary of how our imaginations can deceive us, as well as invest in the powers of our imaginations to create images capable of leading us onto different and better paths.

Intriguingly, in the language of the Sámi, one indigenous people of the Arctic region, the word for trap (giela) is the same as the word for language (giela) itself (Gaski, 1997: 11). Perhaps there are things in the cultures of indigenous peoples that might, by their very own natures, lend themselves to this problematic of discursive interpellation? Perhaps indigenous modes of being are not simply those of resilient, wilfully dispossessed, perseverant subjects of neoliberal lore, but also those of power-savvy hunters of power, who know both how to trap and hunt power, as well as the risks of being trapped and hunted by power themselves. Indeed the language of the Sámi would indicate as much. The Sámi writer Harald Gaski has already detailed how the history of Sámi resistance to colonisation has been defined by the basic idea of the need to hide messages of resistance in imaginative forms such as the yoik, the original song and music of the Sámi (Gaski, 2011: 36). Colonisation of the Sámi, like every other indigenous people, took the form of cultural suppression, and thus Sámi people have had to struggle not only to maintain these cultural traditions, but to use their traditions in imaginative ways, to hide and convey resistance through a clever deployment of images. How might indigenous peoples' imaginations be deployed in ways that contest and subvert the colonisation of indigenous imaginaries, which we have detailed in this book? How, indeed, do indigenous imaginations often appear to disregard the framings of indigenous imaginaries by Western governance?

Engaging with indigenous imaginations and images strategically is important today because the representation of indigenous imaginaries remains so heavily policed by colonial powers. Of course, there are plenty of settler-states and powers only too happy to talk about the need to revive and protect indigenous cultures today, and promote the indigenous imagination, as long as the images it produces and the work which indigenous cultures perform remains complicit with a neoliberal agenda. 'Language, cultural expression, and even spirituality don't pose an unmanageable threat to settler colonialism, because cultural resurgence can rather effortlessly be co-opted by liberal recognition', as Leanne Betasamosake Simpson, herself of the Nishinaabeg people, which has long suffered the colonisation of the Canadian state, argues (2017: 50). Colonising the imaginations of indigenous peoples was a direct strategy of the Jesuits who, as the anthropologist Hans Belting recounts, 'set out to colonize the imaginary world of the natives . . . not only by placing pictures before their eyes, but also by attempting actually to imprint the pictures bodily, so that they would take possession of their viewers' imaginations and dreams' (Belting, 2011: 40). Today this strategy is still in place, as indigenous peoples across the world are asserting. The National Indigenous Corporation of Chile, in protest at the appropriation and manipulation of a photographic image of a Mapuche woman by a Congress on mental health, alcohol and drugs in Santiago in 1998, described the situation well:

> We were stripped of our land. We were deprived of our gods and language. We were brought alcohol and venereal diseases. And after all the plunder, now they want to appropriate our images, and treat us like drunks, criminals, and drug addicts. Our faces and ways of seeing have been taken away. Besides negating our images and usurping our archives of dreams, they have colonized our imagination through the mass media. (quoted in Salazar and Cordova, 2008: 39)

The colonisation of the indigenous imagination and the policing of indigenous imaginaries take many forms. Projects arising out of well-intended desires to heal indigenous peoples, by engaging their arts of imaginations, to reduce their suffering, to enable and empower them, or develop indigenous knowledge systems, are often equally as problematic (Rathwell and Armitage, 2016). Similarly, some projects aim simply at giving the power to indigenous peoples to 'reimagine' themselves, by making and circulating their own images—as if doing this would validate the results as authentic and free from the dangers of repeating colonialism. In this chapter we are particularly interested in the ways in which indigeneity is represented, politically, in images, to underscore the 'resilience' of indigenous peoples. In contrast with the circulation of images of indigenous resilience, and as a way of cracking open that one particular and dominant image, we will excavate the alternatives which indigenous imaginations avail for us, of themselves, their cultures and ways of being. There are vast differences between indigenous imaginaries, and they always require the work of interpretation. Indigenous imaginaries and the imaginations from which they derive are always political, but as we will explore, in radically different ways.

INDIGENOUS POETICS

One of the most well-known Sámi poets of all time was a man called Paulus Utsi (1918–1975). Hailing from Jokkmokk, a small town in Swedish Lapland, Utsi became well known in the Sámi community in the 1960s and early 1970s as a pioneer of the poem as a form of political expression (Svensson, 1978: 229–30). Before his death, Utsi penned a collection titled *Giela giela*, which translates as 'Ensnare the Language' (Gaski, 1997). In other words, it was language itself that Utsi urged his fellow Sámi to hunt and trap. Never, we believe, was that injunction of Utsi more urgent than it is today. Indigenous imaginaries can be seen to be far in excess of the compliant and accepting modes of being engendered in dominant Western discourses. They can also be seen as challenging these strategies, in which indigeneity is made into an homogenous mode of being, through Western discourses which prey on their lives, practices and ways of being, rendering them functional to the aims and ambitions of the West in this new era of the Anthropocene.

Utsi's poetry still remains, despite the global attention commanded by elements of Sámi culture today, largely obscure to Western readers. His work was always written in Sámi, and sometimes translated into Swedish. English language translations of his poems are still hard to find and access, and where they do appear have often been translated from the Swedish rather than directly from Sámi. Their translation and the wider interest in Sámi poetry that developed in the 1970s and 1980s occurred in the context of the development of eco-political and eco-poetic movements, which often took inspiration from indigenous voices. Utsi's poems often contain descriptions of nonhuman nature. For example, 'Snowstorm' and 'The Hut's Smoke', which were translated into English for the Canadian eco-philosophical journal *The Trumpeter* in the 1980s, contain descriptions of reindeer, animals the herding of which is integral to Sámi ways of life, and birch trees, which are poetic emblems of the landscapes of the homelands of the Sámi people (Utsi, 1987). Yet other poems, for example, 'Thought Work', describe the distinctively human world of thinking and doing.

> Tool in, tool your thoughts
> in silver, wood and bone

The poem begins by inciting the reader (Utsi, 1987: 18). Clearly Utsi is referencing the traditional materials from which Sámi handicrafts are made, but in a way that is celebrative of the distinctly human capacity to work nature into tools and through which humans are enabled to shape their worlds. The poem continues:

> Spin, spin your reflections
> into rope and threads of skin.
> Weave, weave fast your fate
> in shoe-laces and wagon straps

Art itself, in Sámi culture, as Gaski tells us, has a distinctly functional value (Gaski, 2011: 33). *Duodji*, as it is called, is a tradition in which value derives from utility, and the arts of which depend on the abilities of the maker to subject nonhuman nature to instrumentalisation. When Western theorists like Timothy Morton reduce 'indigenous people' to a subject-position of alliance with nonhuman nature (2017: x), they do so by ignoring these foundations of many indigenous cultures and practices, which, in many senses are yet more instrumentalising of nonhuman nature than the Western cultures, supposedly defined and made ill by that propensity.

Another widely regarded Sámi poet, Nils-Aslak Valkeapää, himself a relative of Utsi, once condemned 'the self-righteous grandeur' of the colonisers of the Arctic tundra, and sought to give counter-representation to 'indigenous peoples' values and philosophy', including those of the Sámi, but also of all other indigenous peoples with whom Valkeapää identified (Gaski, 2010: 301–5). What would Valkeapää say today, were he still alive, in observation of the importance now given to indigenous knowledge, by the Arctic Council that governs his own land, Sápmi, as well as by so many other states and powers? Would he simply affirm the embrace of indigenous knowledge, welcome the interests of anthropologists and other Western thinkers and scientists in indigenous ways of being, as steps forward in the advancement of indigenous freedoms, or would he display the same cynicism with which he condemned the colonialisms of his own time?

Poetry itself can be a powerful resource for equipping peoples with the intelligence and necessary cynicism with which to avoid discursive traps and make language and concepts work for and not against peoples. Not least because poetry incites the imaginations of peoples by deploying images in ways that open up the possibility of new worlds, rather than simply governing worlds in the ways that states and international institutions seek to (Chandler and Reid, 2016). The poetry of Valkeapää contains many different ideas, images and thoughts but, like that of Utsi before him, is well known for the importance and beauty it attaches to the image of reindeer. The reindeer herd is a central motif in many of Valkeapää's works (Gaski, 2010: 312).

On the one hand this motif might seem simply to embody the poet's defence of Sámi traditions and as yet another example of their appreciation of nonhuman nature and life forms over and against the hubristic humanism of the coloniser (Gaski, 2010: 306–7). Reindeer are revered in Sámi culture, it is said, because as 'perfectly adapted Arctic survivors' they provide meat; milk; hides for clothing, shoes and tents; bones and antlers for tools, handicrafts and weapons; and their sinews are used for clothing (Wall, 2019). This is also attested to in the language of the Sámi, which is said to have over one thousand words for describing reindeer (Magga, 2006: 31). The reasons for this are not necessarily poetic nor owing to any sense of reverence, but due to the basic need of reindeer herders to be able to describe individual reindeer as exactly as possible, as a means of identification. It is a highly advanced taxonomic system that works to classify reindeer on the basis of age, size, colour and appearance (Magga, 2006: 25). Identification and classification are necessary for Sámi reindeer herders in order to determine which reindeer belongs to whom, because reindeer from one herd are liable to get mixed up with another (Magga, 2006: 25). In other words, it owes to the insistence of property—that institution and practice which so many contemporary theorists of indigeneity have claimed has no place in indigenous cultures (see chapter 2). It owes also to the needs of the Sámi to decide which of the reindeer are ready for slaughter (Magga, 2006: 25). In other words, the complexities and refinements of Sámi language, when it comes to reindeer, owes much not to any simple love, care and interests in nonhuman nature, but to their objectification and instrumentalisation of it for their own peculiarly human ends; ends which they have in common with many other non-indigenous peoples, and which conveniently get left out of the ethnographic descriptions of indigenous peoples by their colonial observers.

The Sámi poet Valkeapää had no interest himself in continuing the tradition of herding reindeer (Gaski, 2010: 316). The reindeer he owned were of a distinctly 'private' nature, existing in his head, the property of his imagination, shared with others by way of his poetry (Gaski, 2010: 316). Within the poetics through which Valkeapää constructs his images of reindeer, through the deployment of Sámi language, the reader can encounter ideas that conjoin also with the interests of indigenous peoples, including the Sámi, in maintaining their autonomy from Western powers. Here the reader, whether indigenous or non-indigenous, can encounter anthropomorphised images of reindeer through the redeployment of the taxonomic vocabulary by which the Sámi propertify reindeer into a poetic language and aestheticised form that also evokes a political sensibility of a distinctly human kind. Property, too, has its own aesthetics, and it is not simply a liberal Western one.

In a poem published in his book *The Sun, My Father*, for example, the words of the poem, which themselves are drawn from the taxonomic vocabulary of reindeer, spread out, gradually, across the pages in a manner that, to the eye of the reader, directly evokes the image of a herd of reindeer moving from right to left in the opposite direction of the reader. The first reindeer the reader encounters is named *Menodahkes* (Gaski, 2010: 320). *Menodahkes* represents not just any reindeer but the reindeer who 'thrives best by itself', and which 'is in the habit of trying to avoid being taken hold of' and 'prefers to keep to itself' (ibid.). It relates to the verb, *eaidat*, 'to become a stranger to something or someone, to keep apart by itself, without having anything to do with others' (ibid.).

While in ordinary Sámi language *Menodahkes* might be used to designate a reindeer of that nature for purposes merely of distinguishing ownership, in the poetry of Valkeapää this feature of the behaviour of the animal takes on an aesthetic form. The resistance of the reindeer to its indigenous master becomes itself a poetic substance. Becoming a stranger, maintaining distance, avoiding being taken hold of—these are fundamentally political practices, the poetics of which are integral to Valkeapää's work and ethics, and to Sámi poetics and practices as a whole. In chapter 2 we already encountered the importance of concepts of autonomy and self-mastery to forms of indigenous thought and practice marginalised by neoliberal discourses on indigeneity. The Yaqui shaman, Don Juan, whose life and teachings were detailed in the anthropology of Carlos Castaneda and which we invoked in chapter 2, described a set of practices that come close to *eaidat*, and a way of being *Menodahkes* as it were. Like Valkeapää, Don Juan taught respect for the earth and for species of life other than humans, while at the same time being immensely concerned with the arts by which we humans can best live (ibid.). He taught the arts by which the indigenous subject can 'build a fog' around itself and cultivate the 'ultimate freedom of being unknown' (Castaneda, 1972: 31). Don Juan emphasises the importance of disconnection as life practice and as the basis of ethics. 'Your friends, those who have known you for a long time, you must leave them quickly,' he advised Castaneda (ibid.: 42).

In her analysis, Kathleen Osgood Dana has argued that Valkeapää is best understood as a 'shaman-poet' whose vision penetrates time itself, employing poetry as a power to look into the past, future and reality itself (Dana, 2004: 9). *The Sun, My Father* is itself, she argues, a kind of shamanic drum, 'capable of seeing into other worlds, into the past, and into the future' (ibid.: 9). Like Don Juan, what Valkeapää is really concerned with is truth: the search for it, and the ability of the subject to align itself with its own truths, to act without doubt or remorse. 'I have no doubts or remorse,' as Don Juan said, 'everything I do is my decision and my responsibility,' because in this world 'there is no time for regrets or doubts. There is only time for decisions' (Castaneda, 1972: 56). Like Don Juan, Valkeapää's shamanism seeks to free the self from doubt and attain the power of decision that is the hallmark of sovereign subjectivity.

In much of the literature on indigeneity today we encounter the claim that indigenous subjectivity is defined by a sense of the inter-connectedness of the self to others. The life histories of indigenous peoples are said to show 'a moral ordering of sociality that emphasises mutual support and concern' (Moreton-Robinson, 2015: 15). Doubtless these are important aspects of many indigenous cultures and life practices as they are, probably, of most cultures. Indigenous cultures, however, are also rich in ideas about how the self cannot just support but achieve power over others, hunt and trap, deceive and outwit the other. The recent case of the attempts of a Christian missionary, John Allen Chau, to connect with an indigenous people known as the Sentinelese who inhabit an island in the Indian Ocean quite well illustrates the point. Chau is believed to have been speared to death by the Sentinelese, a people with deft archery skills, who have been killing anyone who attempts to land on their island and make contact since records of their existence began (Wallace, 2018). These are not cultures defined, simply, if at all, by 'mutual support and concern' but by a will to defend their autonomy, to the death. Which is every bit as admirable, and possibly even more so, than the moral capacities for care and concern by which scholars today package indigenous peoples to make them more appetizing to liberal sensibilities.

Imagination is perhaps the greatest weapon that the human has. In the West, the power to deceive, hunt and trap the other has, since Plato at least, been understood to owe to the power which some humans hold over the imaginations of other humans: the ability to deploy images, and make the illusory appear true (Plato, 1993). In the Western tradition it has been seen to be at the root of many human problems, from madness to political fanaticism to illegitimate government. In indigenous cultures too, though, writers state that we can encounter the same ideas, involving power and imagination, perhaps even in a more affirmative way. Valkeapää writes, in *The Sun, My Father*, much of images, employing the Sámi words *govva*, to evoke a world which, in Osgood Dana's descriptions of it, is itself *govvás máilbmi*, a 'world full of images', or world-as-image (Dana, 2004: 9). The word *govva* evokes, in Northern Sámi language as much as in its Finnish language equivalent *kuva* (picture/image), Osgood Dana also argues, the particular image of a drum, and the drum of the shaman himself especially, an instrument for the making of images (ibid.). At the same time, it also evokes the power of the hunter, for both *govva* in Northern Sámi and *kuva* in Finnish were originally terms for decoys used by hunters to lure birds (Dana, 2004: 9). The image in Valkeapää's poetry is unambiguously powerful, as a means with which to hunt and trap, empower the self, and live more. As Dana expresses it, images are, for Valkeapää, 'potent emblems of life itself, written both on the drum and on the land' (Dana, 2004: 13).

The suppression of Sámi culture in the Arctic proceeded through the confiscation and destruction of Sámi drums; the *govadasat*, with which they conjured images (ibid.: 19). The war on indigenous peoples in the Arctic, as conducted more or less worldwide by Western colonial regimes, was a war upon their image-making powers, a war to either extinguish or control their imaginations. As it was for those indigenous peoples unfortunate enough to have encountered the Jesuits who colonised their imaginations, not just by placing pictures before their eyes but by imprinting pictures upon the bodies of natives, 'so that they would take possession of their viewers' imaginations and dreams' (Belting, 2011: 40). The struggle against the imposition of a particular imaginary of an indigenous mode of being can only happen through the restitution of the powers of imagination. Today, however, indigenous peoples are facing a new and different, more subtle and clever regime of power relations, which seeks to imagine for them what their imaginations can do. Colonial images of indigenous peoples as exemplars of resilience are more difficult to reject and destroy because, as we will see in the next section, they offer a new form of legitimacy, iconising indigenous resistance to Western colonialism.

THE IMAGE OF INDIGENOUS RESILIENCE

How does the production of the image of indigenous resilience work? Today the colonisation of indigenous imaginaries takes different and subtler forms when compared with the past. One example, which we trace here, is that of one of the most iconic recent images of indigenous resilience: Ernesto Yerena Montejano's image, developed for the 'We the People' mobilisation of indigenous peoples and their settler allies against the election of Donald Trump as president of the United States in 2016. Following Trump's racist and xenophobic electoral campaign, and in the wake of his election to become the forty-fifth president of the United States in November 2016, Montejano teamed up with fellow artists Jessica Sabogal and Shepard Fairey, and the non-profit Amplifier Foundation, a self-described 'art machine for social change', to produce works for the foundation's campaign. The campaign's objective was, as described to its Kickstarter funders, to resist Trump, by flooding Washington, DC, with symbols of hope on 20 January 2017, the date of Trump's inauguration. And indeed, pictures and video footage of the marches and demonstrations that took place that day, in Washington, as well as throughout much of America, indicate the efficacy of the campaign. To look at those pictures is to see people marching in their numbers carrying the images created by Fairey, one of an African American woman, another of a Muslim woman, and one of a Latino woman, each titled, 'We The People'. We can also see Sabogal's image being displayed, depicting two women, looking at each other tenderly, one above the other, whose neck she cradles, and whose hat reads 'Women Are perfect'. The image itself is titled underneath, 'We The Indivisible'.

Yerena's contribution was a stencilled image, featuring Lakota elder Helen 'Granny' Redfeather, a frontline warrior fighting against the Dakota Access Pipeline at Standing Rock, where Yerena himself also spent time in the November of Trump's election. Yerena's work situates the Lakota elder underneath its title 'We the Resilient: Have Been Here Before'. Giving background to his work, reasons for making it, and thinking behind it, Yerena explained:

> My relationship with the US is very complicated. . . . I was born here, I live here, but the government is like an occupying force on this land. The colonisation process was so violent. It outlawed people from being able to practice Indigenous traditions and languages. How, through all that, have people been able to survive? Considering how hostile the attempted erasure was toward everything to do with our people, Indigenous people, it's incredible. That's resilience. (Gursoz, 2017)

The image Yerena created soon became ubiquitous, a symbol of hope and defiance for peoples protesting the xenophobia and white supremacist racism which Trump's election represented. On 21 January 2017, Yerena could be seen distributing four thousand of his 'We The Resilient' posters within fifteen minutes at the Women's March in Los Angeles. Yerena himself was born in California, close to the Mexican border, and identifies as a 'straight cis-gender Mexican American Chicano male'. Although identifying as Chicano, he also strongly identifies as indigenous. As such his work is dedicated to exposing 'the weight of colonization and the effects of Westernization of Indigenous cultures'. 'Trump is the Chernobyl of colonialism', he explains, 'but I don't want to make artwork that's against him; it gets too dark. I want to make artwork that's for something. I'm for dignity. I'm for resilience. I'm for Mother Earth. I'm for honoring elders. I'm for working with my friends. I'm for making positive messages' (Gursoz, 2017).

The power of Yerena's image of the resilient indigenous grandmother, Helen Redfeather, to have not only made the protests at Standing Rock of indigenous peoples fighting against the construction of the Dakota Access Pipeline more visible and known, but to connect indigenous struggles and subjectivities to the wider struggles and protests against Trump, 'the Chernobyl of colonialism', as well as global resistances to continuing forms of colonialism worldwide, is significant. Yet at the same time the underscoring of the image of this indigenous warrior as a figure defined by her and their collective resilience is problematic, for all the reasons we have already given in previous chapters throughout this book.

What then to make of that particular image of indigenous resilience? And what to make of the many people carrying the 'We The Resilient' banners on the marches and protests against Trump? Is that image, and the people spreading it, on the streets of American cities, as well as virtually by dissemination on websites and via social media accounts, also to be condemned, along with the discourse and concept of resilience itself, as we have already argued, as part of the problem of colonialism today? Is resilience universally subjugating, or does it leave itself open to different usages when it comes to the indigenous? Are there different ways of imagining indigenous resilience? And how do indigenous imaginaries avail themselves of such differences?

We recognise the salience of critiques of the critique of resilience that have appeared in recent years. We have read with interest the work of colleagues, such as Peter Rogers, who have argued that we must avoid the cynicism of a blanket dismissal of resilience and seek to distinguish between its positive and negative aspects, and recognise instead its potential—a potential for more open and inclusive democratic political orders, as he has claimed (Rogers, 2015: 66). The geographer Ben Anderson has made similar kinds of points when asking 'What kind of thing is resilience?' and by imploring that 'we make the connections between resilience and neoliberalism into a question to be explored rather than a presumption from which analysis begins' (Anderson, 2015: 60). These are useful interventions, the basis for which we think echoes throughout this phenomenon of the power of indigenous resilience to mobilise and symbolise popular resistances of indigenous peoples and their allies to extractive industries and the states which support them. The resilience at stake in strategy documents of states and international organisations is not simply the same as that which was enunciated on the streets of Washington, Los Angeles and other American cities as indigenous people and their allies took to those streets to fight the election of Donald Trump.

There is a difference likewise between indigenous peoples imagining themselves as 'we the resilient' and intergovernmental forums made up of the representatives of colonial states, such as the Arctic Council, saying that indigenous peoples are resilient. For one thing, the resilience which indigenous peoples claim for themselves refers fundamentally to their having survived a centuries-old project of colonial extermination, while the resilience which colonial states now identify with indigenous peoples more often refers to their abilities to cope with environmental disasters and pays little heed to their own history of colonial violence against indigenous peoples. Perhaps we need more imagination when it comes to the political theorisation of resilience, and recognition of the multiplicity of possible worlds which indigenous resilience makes possible.

Nevertheless, there is a surface of contact between these different usages of resilience and, while their points of articulation are indeed different and to some extent opposed, they are related by the concept itself. In each case, the indigenous subject which resilience refers to is defined by its capacity to survive. But is there anything problematic in that? Ernesto Yerena Montejano, like everybody else, and every other entity with a stake in the future, has also to survive. An artist has to make a living, and art, for the most part and for the majority of artists, pays badly. In Yerena's case, survival requires once in a while taking a job that entails a relative sacrifice of principle. Which is why Yerena has sold his images to the manufacturer of the energy drink, Red Bull. Some of their cans are decorated with his signature rose symbolising dignity and a calavera (Mexican sugar skull). As he candidly explains, 'sometimes corporations will hire me because they want to tap into the "Latino" market. I take some of the jobs because I need to keep paying rent, but it's a fine line. What I really want is to make critical, challenging work. A lot of times I have to self-fund [these pieces] or work with a small stipend. Unfortunately, the people with the best ideas don't have a lot of money' (Gursoz, 2017).

Many of us know this conflict between good intention and its sacrifice to political and economic power. Images, ideas, concepts and arguments are all eminently open to manipulation, appropriation and commodification by agencies whose intentions and effects are malign, or simply self-interested, as is the case with the profit-maximising Red Bull, an Austrian company with the highest market share of any energy drink in the world, selling five billion cans a year; a market share that owes in no small part to the distinctiveness and recognisability of the blue silver design of the cans in which its drink is sold and on which Yerena's designs appear.

There is no direct connection between Yerena's work for Red Bull and the 'We Are Resilient' poster that he made for the campaign against Trump and in defence of indigenous rights. In effect, the former served the latter. Selling to Red Bull meant Yerena could pay the rent and paying the rent meant Yerena could design for the nonprofit Amplifier Foundation and its political campaign against the particular formation of white racist neoliberal capital that Trump's presidency exists to defend. We have no reason to believe Red Bull saw any capital in hiring an artist with his politics or with his links to indigenous peoples and political struggles. As Yerena is aware and states clearly, Red Bull were interested in tapping into the Latino market, and it is the resonance of his designs with Chicano culture that attracted them. But there is some sense of a connection, vague and difficult to see, but there somewhere nevertheless, in this collaboration, between Yerena and Red Bull on the one hand, and the 'collaborations' taking place between resilience and neoliberalism on the other.

Red Bull, as the most iconic energy drink of its generation, epitomises resilience culture. It is what you drink when you are struggling to cope, stay awake or persevere amid stress, physical or psychic. If you need resilience in a liquid form, you need Red Bull. It is also the drink that, besides giving you resilience, gives you stereotypes. On the website, Native Appropriations, a forum for discussing representations of native peoples, including stereotypes and cultural appropriation, a commercial campaign of Red Bull, beginning in 2009, is described as reading like a 'check list of native stereotypes' (Adrienne, 2010). Amid tipis, smoke signals, war whoops and "tom-tom" drumming, two natives, Brown Bear and White Dove, express in third person broken English their frustrated sexual desire for each other.

'Greetings White Dove, my heart is heavy', says Brown Bear. 'Mine too, Brown Bear', replies White Dove. 'The end of the year is near, and we still can't get together. Brown bear can't jump that far!' complains Brown Bear. 'And White Dove can't fly! We are only united in mind', concludes White Dove. 'Yes, but my body longs for you too', confirms Brown Bear. White Dove sighs. 'No Red Bull, no happy ending', warns the narrator. Red Bull is not only the drink that gives you resilience—it's the drink that gets you laid. Or it's the drink that gives you the necessary resilience to get laid. And, in sexualising resilience, indigeneity is also sexualised, making a commercial stereotype out of indigenous perseverance and stoking colonial myths.

Red Bull is responsible for mythic representations of indigenous peoples, but what about resilience itself? In March of 2017 the *Journal of Multidisciplinary Healthcare* published an article titled 'Mental Resilience, Perceived Immune Functioning, and Health'. The article is a generic representative of its kind, describing resilience as the 'trait that enables an individual to recover from stress and to face the next stressor with optimism' (Lantman et al., 2017: 107). People with resilience, it argues, 'have a better mental and physical health' (Lantman et al., 2017: 107). The conclusion the article comes to, on the basis of a large empirical study, is that people with reduced immune functioning tend to be those who are less resilient, whereas people with resilience tend to have better functioning immune systems (Lantman et al., 2017: 112). Like a lot of medical research, the article had as many as eight authors, among who is named a Dr Joris Verster from the University of Utrecht in the Netherlands. In the disclosure section of the article the authors list the sources of financial support that have funded their research. Verster, an advocate of resilience, lists, among the many different funders he is in the patronage of, Red Bull, which is interesting. In fact Verster is also the author of another study, in the *Journal of Human Psychopharmacology*, titled 'Mixing Alcohol with Energy Drink: A Systematic Review and Meta-Analysis' (2016).

The article addresses the popular social belief that people who mix energy drinks such as Red Bull with alcohol end up drinking more alcohol than they ordinarily would. Reassuringly, Verster and his colleagues conclude that their research proves that mixing energy drinks with alcohol does not increase the total amount of alcohol consumed, which is also interesting. What to make of these connections between the science of resilience, so assured in its conclusions concerning the reality of resilience as a property of healthy people everywhere, and an energy drink manufacturer which funds the science of resilience, and which employs the same science to defend itself from mythic representations of the properties of the product as a source of alcoholism and ill health? A corporation and icon of the neoliberal economy, furthermore, which sells its products on the basis of colonial representations of indigenous people, as well as by decorating its cans with the designs of an artist who, unwittingly no doubt, is himself a proponent of indigenous resilience, and the creator of what is one of the most iconic images of indigenous resilience: the picture of Lakota elder Helen 'Granny' Redfeather, carried on banners by the many people who showed up to protest the election of Donald Trump, in Washington, DC, and other American cities in January of 2017.

REIMAGINING INDIGENEITY

Given the complexity of these power relations, how, if at all, might indigenous images of resilience be reclaimed? When and where does indigenous art and image-making become political and how to recognise when it expresses a politics which is no longer neoliberal? How might we all 'create networks of reciprocal resurgent movements with humans and other humans' and radically imagine our way 'out of domination', as Leanne Simpson urges us (Simpson, 2017: 10)? Which among us is 'not afraid to let those imaginings destroy the pillars of settler colonialism' (Simpson, 2017: 10)?

Regardless of the many complex, as well as unwitting, ways in which images of indigeneity serve a neoliberal imaginary, indigenous peoples and indigenous art does no doubt offer alternatives to the stultifying image of indigenous resilience generated by this nexus of relations between science, art and corporate capital that, in turn, governs discourses of 'becoming indigenous'. Judith Bessant and Rob Watts have usefully detailed the ways in which community development projects aimed at the neoliberal governance of indigenous youth, in Western Australia, and operating through the making of video art and digital media, contain the basis for politicisation, because they entail the possibility for indigenous peoples to reclaim images of indigenous peoples for themselves (Bessant and Watts, 2016: 1). Are there ways in which indigenous propaganda art, of which Yerena's 'We the Resilient' poster is an obvious example, breaks with a neoliberal strategy of interpellation?

In the Arctic an interesting and potentially political example exists in the form of Suohpanterror, a largely anonymous group of Sámi 'artivists', whose propaganda art made in the form of posters has achieved wide popularity in Finnish Lapland and beyond. All of the images which we discuss here are available to see on their website.[1] What they do is to appropriate iconic images drawn often from Western traditions of art and image-making and subject them to their own defacement such that they function to politicise the governance of Sámi identity and draw attention to the continued colonisation of their homelands in Finnish Lapland and the wider Arctic region (Junka-Aikio, 2018).

Rather than attempt to stay true to Sámi aesthetic traditions, Suohpanterror have deliberately embraced and subverted Western techniques, symbols and images (Hautala-Hirvioja, 2015). For example, Edvard Munch's *The Scream* is repurposed such that the figure is dressed in the traditional clothing of the Sámi people and screaming in horror at the exploitation of the land. Wind turbines appear in the background of the defaced image of the painting and a sign warns in Finnish language, 'Mining Area: Trespassing Forbidden'. Their use of *The Scream* is interesting not least insofar as it is an iconic image of Western expressionism in art, a movement which drew deliberately on insights derived from medical and psychological sciences to depict the human unconscious, deconstruct and explore human emotions, moods and psychiatric disorders of depression and anxiety of which the artist Munch himself was a victim (Kandel, 2012). The image has been claimed to depict the distortion of the human by the subjectivising force and flows of nature.

In its appropriation by Suohpanterror, the figure suffers the distortions of the natural landscape marked by an industrialisation, which it feels itself powerless to do anything about. In that sense, it appropriates an image that aestheticises the human/nature divide and depicts the fear and anxiety, which flows from modern man's encounter with its sublimity and reverses the power relations involved, such that it is nature which is threatened by human encroachment. But the image, of course, does more than that, for it also appropriates the aesthetics of neurosis, which underpin modern psychiatric discourses and images of selfhood. In so much of the Western anthropological literature on indigeneity we encounter the claim that indigenous peoples are above and beyond any sense of self, that they do not possess a self, and that their concept of otherness is ontologically inaccessible for self-minded cultures such as those that define the West. Here, in the iconography of Suohpanterror, by way of contrast, the indigenous self is asserted, and in every bit as neurotic a modality as the psychiatrised versions of the self, which Munch's art depicted.

Indeed, while drawing attention to the kinds of land-related issues for which indigenous politics is well known, the images Suohpanterror make tend mostly to leave nature to the background while foregrounding, like Munch and other modernists, distinctly human figures. Nature figures as backdrop in the political aesthetics of Suohpanterror while the human is foregrounded. Often the images celebrate a violent militancy. For example, an image of a Sámi offering a handshake to a businessman carrying a briefcase is juxtaposed with an image of the same Sámi delivering a karate-style kick to his head. Again, we are a far cry from the image of the indigenous suffering the instrumental and structural violence of the colonial state and not being equipped to fight back other than through strategies of queering and performativity.

Reindeer, that motif of the Sámi poets who came before Suohpanterror, also appear in the images, but in radically different ways. In one image a military checkpoint on a road into Lapland is depicted. The politics of the checkpoint depicted is ambiguous. Is it a checkpoint manned by the state and an expression of colonial power? The combat fatigues and guns of the soldiers in the image manning it would indicate as much. Or is it a Sámi checkpoint designed to keep the colonisers out from their lands? 'Area of reindeer husbandry' reads the text in the familiar language that does indeed appear in signs around Lapland. A smaller sign appears in the foreground of the image in which a drawing of a reindeer is depicted as is the case of many signs around Lapland. 'Stop! Halt!' the sign in the foreground of the image reads. 'Checkpoint Sapmi No. 169'.

The reference is to International Labour Organization Convention 169, which binds states to consult with indigenous peoples about the uses of natural resources on their lands, and which Finland has so far refused to ratify; a refusal which is denounced in the Sámi Manifesto, endorsed by the principal artist behind Suohpanterror, Jenni Laiti, and her collaborators (Holmberg and Laiti, 2015). In another image, a group of Sámi and their reindeer are depicted standing before a wall, which recalls the wall erected in Israel, which functions to divide Palestinians from each other and which for many symbolises colonial occupation. The wall, in the image of Suohpanterror, likewise divides one group of Sámi from another, depicted on the other side, as well as from the fells that appear in the distance on the other side of the wall. In another image reindeer are depicted crossing the fells marked in text as *Gallok*, the Sámi name for Kallak, an area close to Jokkmokk, the town where the poet

Paulus Utsi was born, and where the Sámi are now mobilising to prevent the proposals of the British mining company Beowulf to build an iron ore mine.

All of these images express a very different imaginary of indigeneity to that which enables the image of indigenous resilience, perseverance and dispossession critiqued in the preceding chapters of this book. In many ways what we see happening here is an indigenous people doing a cultural appropriation of a political modernity denied to them by the Western guardians of the image of indigenous peoples as existing outside of and in antagonism to that of modernity. An appropriation that shifts the image of indigeneity out of its colonial grounding in the capacities that the coloniser has sought to pin indigenous people down to, and asserts the radical equality of indigenous people to the access of distinctly political capacities for emancipation from the imagination of the other.

CONCLUSION

Imagination is integral to the political strategies by which colonial powers have sought control over indigenous populations and the image of their indigeneity, as well as to the strategies of radical resistance of indigenous peoples to colonialism historically as much as today. The policing of the indigenous imagination and the image of indigeneity it avails to us permeates Western discourses on indigenous peoples as much as it does the reception of the political aesthetics of indigeneity. When we examine, more closely, the actuality of indigenous aesthetics, and the development of indigenous poetics, we get a very different picture, literally, to that told and represented to us of how indigenous peoples see themselves in art and political aesthetics. Far from the image of indigenous peoples celebrating their subjugation to a natural world which is beyond their control, the analysis of indigenous poetics we have made here reveals all the tropes of the political modernity which indigenous peoples are represented as existing outside of and against. Corporate-sponsored artists, as well as corporate capital itself, may still possess the power to control some of the images of indigeneity that circulate, as resilient, perseverant and dispossessed, but there arc plenty of other images available which project alternative and more empowering visions of what indigeneity entails and can, in the future, become.

NOTE

1. https://suohpanterror.com/.

Chapter 8

Conclusion

In the introductory chapter we explained that this book is an engagement with Western discourses, emanating from the Western academy and across the sciences, as well as from the policy worlds of colonial states and their governments, and international organisations, advocating the need for everybody, everywhere, to 'become indigenous'. As we have seen, this is a discourse in which many others are engaged too. Political activists, including environmentalist movements, as well as anti-capitalist groups, are at the centre of the struggle to transform the human along 'indigenous' lines, to make us all think and feel ourselves indigenous, and for those of us from the West, to recover that indigeneity we once lost, whenever the moment of that loss might be dated. Indigenous people too, wherever they self-identify as indigenous, often repeat this Western mantra, and Indigenous Studies, that discipline set up to think about, study and theorise indigeneity within the Western academy, has its fair share of advocates who assert the imperative that it's time for the world to indigenise.

We are troubled by this demand, but not simply because of the obvious convergences of the discourse of the representatives of indigenous peoples with the discourses of their oppressors. As we emphasised, there is something strangely reassuring and unchallenging about not just the powerful and oppressive sources of this discourse, but the ways in which this call to become indigenous is being expressed as well as in what it leaves out and makes impossible to say. We highlighted that, in the past, Western academic and political advocacy offered very different discourses of indigeneity: discourses of concern and of care, discourses of the need to redress historic injustices, to overcome colonial dependencies, to demand opportunities for fuller participation and better social outcomes for indigenous peoples. These discourses were unsettling for Western readers: restitutions would pose a fundamental challenge to settler-colonial ways of life (Tuck and Yang, 2012). Also unsettling and controversial were discourses on the need for different research methods when dealing with indigenous concerns and for respect for alternative approaches to epistemology. Today, however, rather than taking indigenous concerns and approaches seriously, in order to address histories of marginalisation, exclusion and subjugation (Jung, 2008), it would appear that indigenous research methods, approaches, epistemologies and ontologies are seen as resources to be mined to solve distinctly Western problems, specifically the crises foregrounded by what a wide range of Western theorists, scientists, philosophers, policy-makers and activist groups identify as the Anthropocene.

The interests of the West in indigeneity today appears to us to have arisen less out of any genuine concern for appreciating the diverse realities and powers of indigenous ways of being and more about the crisis that is afflicting the West's confidence in its own future and survivability. This crisis in Western ways of being and becoming is increasingly negotiated (as we have noted) through the terminology of the Anthropocene. Ostensibly named as a new geological era in which humans have substantially impacted the strata of the Earth, the Anthropocene is seen to herald climate and environmental crises of unpredictable proportions and also to call into question modernist knowledge assumptions of a 'One World World' (Law, 2015)—propped up by the binaries of culture/nature, mind/matter, subject/object, human/non-human—reducing difference to the problem of representation and subjective belief (Rojas, 2016). It is this double crisis of Western ways of being and becoming—the Anthropocene—that is the starting point for understanding the demand to 'become indigenous'. Arturo Escobar neatly captures this in stating 'that the contemporary conjecture is best characterised by the fact that *we are facing modern problems for which there are no modern solutions*' (2016: 15; emphasis in original).

In the apparent exhaustion of the modern, where 'progress' appears to meet unsurpassable environmental limits, the 'gains' of modernity easily seem to be not worth the sacrifices they took to achieve. What might have appeared to be 'collateral damage' while the moderns were victorious, now, in their defeat, can only be crimes for which the moderns must be held to account. It seems clear to us that much of the dynamic behind the call to 'become indigenous' is an attempt to evade this accounting. This is not attempted through 'redeeming' or 'salvaging' indigenous knowledge, justifying alternative ways of knowing and preserving them (Agrawal, 2005: 71–72). Today, discourses of 'becoming indigenous' are not about 'alternative' or other ways of being but new ways of constructing the Western self as adaptive and resilient in the face of unknowable adversities. There can be no accounting with modernity because it seems that the moderns were never really 'modern' (Latour, 1993). The imaginary of 'becoming indigenous' thus becomes a settler-colonial 'move to innocence', as noted by Eve Tuck and K. Wayne Yang (2012: 3). This move to innocence depends on the rearticulation of indigeneity as the universally immanent mode of being in the Anthropocene. For us, this is best expressed in the imaginary presented by Deborah Danowski and Eduardo Viveiros de Castro, cited in this book's introductory chapter:

> Let the reader imagine herself watching—or rather, acting in—a sci-fi B movie in which the Earth is taken over by an alien race pretending to be humans, whose goal is to dominate the planet and to extract all its resources, after having used its home planet to the full. . . . And now let the reader imagine that this *has already happened*, and that the alien race is, in fact 'we ourselves'. . . . suppose a small shift in sensibility has suddenly made that self-colonization visible to us. We would thus all be indigenous, that is Terrans, invaded by Europeans, that is Humans; all of us, of course, including Europeans, who were after all the first Terrans to be invaded. (Danowski and Viveiros de Castro, 2017: 108)

In this imaginary narrative, the fault lies not so much with colonial and capitalist practices of genocide, slavery, oppression, extraction and exploitation but with the prior 'colonisation' of the European mind by Platonic, Christian and Enlightenment ideas which were to cohere in the modernist paradigm of the separation of culture and nature—of a hierarchy of knowing subjects in a universal 'one world world'. We are all victims of this alien race, so the narrative goes. Thus the undoing or 'recalling' of modernity and the call to become 'indigenous', 'Earthbound' or 'Terran' in a pluriversal 'world of many worlds' (de la Cadena and Blaser, 2018) aspires to 'reset modernity' (Latour and Leclercq, 2016). While calls to 'become indigenous' may differ in their finer details and conceptual framings, they concur on the generalisability of speculative analytics as a tool to enable adaptation and resilience. For us, this strategy evades any accounting with the past and denies the political and practical tools of resistance in the present. Of course, this does not mean that we are not happy to learn from indigenous struggles, only that learning from is very different from the ontopolitical requirement to 'become indigenous'. Indeed, in contesting what is meant by 'becoming indigenous', we have also stressed the values of indigenous cultures and systems of knowledge which militate against the rationalities shaping the call to 'become indigenous'.

'Becoming indigenous' keeps far too much of what exists in place and puts the burdens of our contemporary crisis on those least able to withstand them. The binary divides of the 'Gaia war', that pit 'moderns' or 'humans' against 'indigenous' or 'Terran' modes of being, smack of disingenuity and false radicalism (Viveiros de Castro and Danowski, 2018). We do not agree that, in facing the Anthropocene, 'the invaders are invaded, the colonized are the colonizers' (ibid.: 194). If only it was true that 'becoming indigenous' was a call to hold power to account and to transform political possibilities. This book has attempted to question this consensus and to argue that contemporary approaches to indigenous modes of being, which see them as a solution to very Western problems, are patronising and oppressive not just to indigenous peoples but everyone else as well.

In place of heeding the call to become indigenous, it is important that non-indigenous scholars like ourselves treat the growing discourse on indigeneity in the Western academy with the same scepticism which many indigenous scholars already do. We know much less about indigeneity than any indige-nous person, whether a scholar or not, but it's obvious to us from our engage-ments with Western and neoliberal discourses of resilience and adaptation that much of what is said today about indigeneity is falsely instrumentalising. For this reason indigeneity is too important an issue today to be confined to indigenous studies. Whether indigenous or not, our task is the same, we be-lieve: the need to reclaim the capacities for political subjectivity and struggles denied to us by the ideologues of the Anthropocene. We need, likewise, to emancipate ourselves from the imaginaries of those agencies projecting false images of indigenous peoples as resilient shock absorbers of endemic crises and disasters, and see what lies latent, hidden and disguised in indigenous cultures and practices by their would-be representatives. For it seems to us that underneath these fake imaginaries lies another set of capacities abso-lutely opposed to images of indigenous resilience and mere adaptation.

Instead of looking at the Anthropocene as a distinct time in which 'the human becomes thinkable in a non-teleological, non-metaphysical sense' (Morton, 2017: 42), we have to grasp and confront it as a trap into which the human has been led, with the precise purpose of robbing it of its very capaci-ties for thought and political agency. 'Formula of our happiness: a Yes, a No, a straight line, a goal' (Nietzsche, 1990: 125). No Oxbridge-educated white European is going to convince us otherwise. The task is not one of losing the remnants of our human hubris to embrace our co-implications with the non-linear circuitry of other resilient, adaptive living systems; it is to recover the image we once had of ourselves and are now in danger of losing—as a being with capacities different to other merely adaptive creatures, capable of saying no to mere nature, yes to human empowerment, existing free from the neces-sities of a mere life of endless toil, struggle and survival, which the blackmail of the Anthropocene would so happily reduce us to.

Imagination is a paradox. It is, as we have known since the Socratic revo-lution in thought, what traps and deceives us, and the sources of deceptions which can lead us into subjection, but it is also what potentially liberates us, taking us onto better and alternative paths toward existences we couldn't dream of without its deployment. The journeys we have taken in writing and researching this book have only affirmed our sense that it is also the capacity which we have most in common with every other human, whether from colonial cultures and societies like ourselves, or from colonised, indigenous ones like so many of the authors whose works we have read to write this book. Indigenous cultures are not, as far as we are concerned, resources for the equipping of a global world of resilient peoples, but resources for the political imaginations of peoples everywhere, much in need of support and encouragement, in evading the traps being set for them by a form of neoliberalism which only ever seems to reach deeper into the human soul in order to subjectify it.

We have approached indigeneity from the outside, sceptical about what we have been taught to believe about indigenous ways of being, while open and interested to learn more about indigenous ways of living. Everything we have learned has reaffirmed our belief that indigenous peoples are as interested in acting upon the world, utilising it, instrumentalising it, subjecting it to human needs and interests as we are. These cultures and their peoples speak to us about issues of common concern, such as how to hunt power, evade and outwit the strategies of others, and emancipate ourselves from the images and illusions which others project onto us. We take inspirations from indigenous peoples who continue to defend their autonomy to the death, refuse the invites of the international organisations, the researchers, the scientists, the art therapists and the full range of neoliberal missionaries who seek to connect with them. We support their cultural appropriation of the political modernity denied to them by the Western guardians of the image of indigenous peoples as existing outside of and in antagonism to Western modernity.

It has become obvious to us that there is a vast and troubling contradiction between the image of indigeneity as it is projected onto indigenous peoples— as well as how it is utilised in the incitation of demands that everybody everywhere 'become indigenous'—and the actual imaginations of indigenous peoples. 'Becoming indigenous' is, as we have demonstrated, not about exiting modernity, but ensuring that liberal modernity keeps its shape, in displacement of whatever other expression modernity might take. No discourse on modernity, however attuned to the violence, suffering and suppression which we moderns have done in and to the world, should fail to arouse admiration and wonder at the immensity of the achievements, progression and breakthroughs made possible by the human guile, ingenuity and labour which the term evokes. If it does not arouse such then it is a bad and false discourse of little worth. It's time to say no to becoming indigenous and yes to the recovery of the hubris on which modernity was built and from which other worlds are yet to come, in destruction of the old, and in welcome of the new.

References

Acharya, A. (2014). *Rethinking Power, Institutions and Ideas in World Politics: Whose IR?* Abingdon: Routledge.

Adese, J. (2014). 'Spirit Gifting: Ecological Knowing in Metis Life Narratives', *Decolonization: Indigeneity, Education & Society* 3(3): 48–66.

Adger, W. N., Pulhin, J. M., Barnett, J., Dabelko, G. D., Hovelsrud, G. K., Levy, M., Spring, U. O., and Vogel, C. H. (2014). 'Human Security', in *Climate Change 2014: Impacts, Adaptation, and Vulnerability. Part A: Global and Sectoral Aspects. Contribution of Working Group II to the Fifth Assessment Report of the Intergovernmental Panel on Climate Change.* Cambridge: Cambridge University Press, 755–91.

Adorno, T., and Horkheimer, M. (1997). *Dialectic of Enlightenment.* London: Verso.

Adrienne, K. (2010). 'Red Bull Gives You Stereotypes', *Native Appropriations*, 22 July. Available at: http://nativeappropriations.com/2010/07/red-bull-gives-you-stereotypes.html.

Agamben, G. (2014). 'For a Theory of Destituent Power: Public Lecture in Athens, 16.11.2013', *Chronos*, February. Available at: http://www.chronosmag.eu/index.php/g-agamben-for-a-theory-of-destituent-power.html.

Agrawal, A. (1995). 'Indigenous and Scientific Knowledge: Some Critical Comments', *IK Monitor* 3(3): 3–6.

Agrawal, A. (2002). 'Indigenous Knowledge and the Politics of Classification', *International Social Science Journal* 54(173): 287–97.

Agrawal, A. (2005). 'The Politics of Indigenous Knowledge', *Australian Indigenous Knowledge and Libraries* 36(2): 71–78.

Agrawal, A. (2009). 'Why "Indigenous" Knowledge?', *Journal of the Royal Society of New Zealand* 39(4): 157–58.

Ahmed, S. (2007). 'A Phenomenology of Whiteness', *Feminist Theory* 8(2): 149–68.

Ahrens, J., and Rudolph, P. M. (2006). 'The Importance of Governance in Risk Reduction and Disaster Management', *Journal of Contingencies and Crisis Management* 14(4): 207–20.

Ali, M. (2013). 'Towards a Decolonial Computing', in *Ambiguous Technologies: Philosophical Issues, Practical Solutions, Human Nature*. Lisbon: International Society of Ethics and Information Technology, Universidade Autonoma de Lisboa, pp. 28–35.

Altamirano-Jiménez, I., and Kermoal, N. (2016). 'Introduction: Indigenous Women and Knowledge', in N. Kermoal and I. Altamirano-Jiménez (eds.), *Living on the Land: Indigenous Women's Understanding of Place*. Edmonton: Athabasca University Press, 3–17.

Amoore, L., and Piotukh, V. (eds.). (2016). *Algorithmic Life: Calculative Devices in the Age of Big Data*. London: Routledge.

Andersen, C. (2014). *Métis: Race, Recognition, and the Struggle for Indigenous Peoplehood*. Vancouver: UBC Press.

Anderson, B. (2015). 'What Kind of Thing Is Resilience?' *Politics* 35(1): 60–66.

Anderson, C. (2008). 'The End of Theory: The Data Deluge Makes the Scientific Method Obsolete', *Wired Magazine* 16(7), 23 June. Available at: http://archive.wired.com/science/discoveries/magazine/16-07/pb_theory.

Arctic Human Development Report. (2004). *Societies and Cultures: Change and Persistence*. Borgir: Stefansson Arctic Institute.

Badiou, A. (2003). *Saint Paul: The Foundation of Universalism*. Stanford: Stanford University Press.

Barad, K. (2007). *Meeting the Universe Halfway: Quantum Physics and the Entanglement of Matter and Meaning*. London: Duke University Press.

Bargués-Pedreny, P. (2019). 'From Critique to Affirmation in International Relations', *Global Society* 33(1): 1–11.

Barker, A. (2012). 'Already Occupied: Indigenous Peoples, Settler Colonialism and the Occupy Movements in North America', *Social Movement Studies: Journal of Social, Cultural and Political Protest* 11(3-4): 327–34.

Barker, J. (2015). 'The Corporation and the Tribe', *The American Indian Quarterly* 39(3): 243–70.

Bateson, G. (2000). *Steps to an Ecology of Mind*. Chicago: University of Chicago Press.

Battiste, M. (ed.). (2000). *Reclaiming Indigenous Voice and Vision*. Vancouver: UBC Press.

Beier, M. J. (2005). *International Relations in Uncommon Places: Indigeneity, Cosmology, and the Limits of International Theory*. New York: Palgrave.

Belting, H. (2011) *An Anthropology of Images*. Princeton: Princeton University Press.

Benjamin, R. (2018). 'Black Afterlives Matter: Cultivating Kinfulness as Reproductive Justice', in A. E. Clarke and D. Haraway (eds.), *Making Kin Not Population*. Chicago: Prickly Paradigm Press, 41–65.

Bennett, J. (2010) *Vibrant Matter: A Political Ecology of Things*. London: Duke University Press.

Berardi, F. 'Bifo'. (2015). *AND: Phenomenology of the Mind*. South Pasadena: Semiotext(e).

Berkouwer, C. G. (1958). *Faith and Perseverance*. Michigan: Eerdmans.

Bessant, J., and Watts, R. (2016). 'Indigenous Digital Art as Politics in Australia', *Culture, Theory & Critique* 58(3): 306–19.

Bessire, L., and Bond, D. (2014). 'Ontological Anthropology and the Deferral of Critique', *American Ethnologist* 41(3): 440–56.

Biermann, F., Abbott, K., Andresen, S., Bäckstrand, K., Bernstein, S., Betsill, M. M., Bulkeley, H., Cashore, B., Clapp, J., Folke, C., Gupta, A., Gupta, J., Haas, P. M., Jordan, A., Kanie, N., Kluvánková-Oravská, T., Lebel, L., Liverman, D., Meadowcroft, J., Mitchell, R. B., Newell, P., Oberthür, S., Olsson, L., Pattberg, P., Sánchez-Rodríguez, R., Schroeder, H., Underdal, A., Camargo Vieira, S., Vogel, C., Young, O. R., Brock, A., and Zondervan, R. (2012). 'Navigating the Anthropocene: Improving Earth System Governance', *Science* 335(6074): 1306–7.

Bird Rose, D. (2011). *Wild Dog Dreaming: Love and Extinction.* Charlottesville: University of Virginia Press.

Bird Rose, D. (2017). 'Shimmer: When All You Love Is Being Trashed', in A. Tsing, H. Swanson, E. Gan, and N. Bubandt (eds.), *Arts of Living on a Damaged Planet.* Minneapolis: University of Minnesota Press, G51–63.

Blaney, D., and Tickner, A. (2017). 'Worlding, Ontological Politics and the Possibility of a Decolonial IR', *Millennium: Journal of International Studies* 45(3): 293–311.

Blasdel, A. (2017). '"A Reckoning for our Species": The Philosopher Prophet of the Anthropocene', *Guardian*, 15 June. Available at: https://www.theguardian.com/world/2017/jun/15/timothy-morton-anthropocene-philosopher.

Blaser, M. (2013). 'Ontological Conflicts and the Stories of Peoples in Spite of Europe: Toward a Conversation on Political Ontology', *Current Anthropology* 54(5): 547–68.

Blaser, M. (2014). 'Ontology and Indigeneity: on the Political Ontology of Heterogeneous Assemblages', *Cultural Geographies* 21(1): 49–58.

Blaser, M., and de la Cadena, M. (2018). 'Introduction, Pluriverse: A World of Many Worlds', in M. de la Cadena and M. Blaser (eds.), *A World of Many Worlds.* London: Duke University Press, 1–22.

Boidin, C., Cohen, J., and Grosfoguel, R. (2012). 'Introduction: From University to Pluriversity: A Decolonial Approach to the Present Crisis of Western Universities', *Human Architecture: Journal of the Sociology of Self-Knowledge* 10(1): Article 2.

Bonneuil, C., and Fressoz, J.-B. (2016). *The Shock of the Anthropocene.* London: Verso.

Braidotti, R. (2013). *The Posthuman.* Cambridge: Polity Press.

Brassier, R. (2007). *Nihil Unbound: Enlightenment and Extinction.* Basingstoke: Palgrave Macmillan.

Brigg, M. (2008). *The New Politics of Conflict Resolution: Responding to Difference.* New York: Palgrave Macmillan.

Bryant, L. (2011). *The Democracy of Objects.* Ann Arbor: Open Humanities Press.

Bryant, L. (2012). 'Thoughts on Posthumanism', *Larval Subjects*, 10 November. Available at: https://larvalsubjects.wordpress.com/2012/11/10/thoughts-on-posthumanism/.

Butler, J., and Athanasiou, A. (2013). *Dispossession: The Performance in the Political.* Cambridge: Polity.

Carrithers, M., Candea, M., Sykes, K., Holbraad, M., and Venkatesan, S. (2010). 'Ontology Is Just another Word for Culture: Motion Tabled at the 2008 Meeting of the Group for Debates in Anthropological Theory, University of Manchester', *Critique of Anthropology* 30(2): 152–200.

Castaneda, C. (1972). *Journey to Ixtlan: The Lessons of Don Juan*. London: Penguin.

Chakrabarty, D. (2000). *Provincializing Europe: Postcolonial Thought and Historical Difference*. Princeton: Princeton University Press.

Chakrabarty, D. (2015). 'The Anthropocene and the Convergence of Histories', in C. Hamilton, C. Bonneuil, and F. Gemenne (eds.), *The Anthropocene and the Global Environmental Crisis: Rethinking Modernity in a New Epoch*. Abingdon: Routledge, 44–56.

Chakrabarty, D. (2018). 'Planetary Crises and the Difficulty of Being Modern', *Millennium: Journal of International Studies* 46(3) 259–82.

Chandler, D. (2014). *Resilience: The Governance of Complexity*. Abingdon: Routledge.

Chandler, D. (2015). 'A World without Causation: Big Data and the Coming of Age of Posthumanism', *Millennium: Journal of International Studies* 43(3): 833–51.

Chandler, D. (2016). 'How the World Learned to Stop Worrying and Love Failure: Big Data, Resilience and Emergent Causality', *Millennium: Journal of International Studies*, 44(3): 391–410.

Chandler, D. (2017). 'Securing the Anthropocene? International Policy Experiments in Digital Hacktivism: A Case Study of Jakarta', *Security Dialogue* 48(2): 113–30.

Chandler, D., and Reid, J. (2016). *The Neoliberal Subject: Resilience, Adaptation and Vulnerability*. London: Rowman & Littlefield.

Chandler, D., and Reid, J. (2018). '"Being in Being": Contesting the Ontopolitics of Indigeneity Today', *European Legacy* 23(3): 251–68.

Chandler, M. J., Lalonde, C. E., Sokol, B. W., and Hallett, D. (2003). 'Personal Persistence, Identity Development, and Suicide: A Study of Native and Non-Native North American Adolescents', *Monographs of the Society for Research in Child Development* 68(2): vii–138.

Chen, K.-H. (2010). *Asia as Method: Toward Deimperialization*. Durham: Duke University Press.

Clark, N. (2010). *Inhuman Nature: Sociable Life on a Dynamic Planet*. Washington, DC: Sage Publications, Kindle Edition.

Clark, N. (2012). 'Perseverance, Determination, and Resistance: An Indigenous Intersectional-Based Policy Analysis of Violence in the Lives of Indigenous Girls', in O. Hankivsky (ed.), *An Intersectionality-Based Policy Analysis Framework*. Vancouver, BC: Institute for Intersectionality Research and Policy, Simon Fraser University, 133–58.

Clay, K. (2019). '"Despite the Odds": Unpacking the Politics of Black Resilience Neoliberalism', *American Educational Research Journal* 56(1): 75–110.

Cline, T. (2018). 'Big Data and Smart Farmers for Africa's Agricultural Transformation', *Forbes Africa*, 30 October. Available at: https://www.forbesafrica.com/focus/2018/10/30/big-data-and-smart-farmers-for-africas-agricultural-transformation/.

Colebrook, C. (2014). *Death of the Posthuman: Essays on Extinction*, volume 1. Ann Arbor: University of Michigan.

Colebrook, C. (2017). 'We Have Always Been Post-Anthropocene: The Anthropocene Counterfactual', in R. Grusin (ed.), *Anthropocene Feminism*. Minneapolis: University of Minnesota Press, 1–20.

Connolly, W. E. (2011). *A World of Becoming*. London: Duke University Press.

Connolly, W. E. (2013). *The Fragility of Things: Self-Organizing Processes, Neoliberal Fantasies, and Democratic Activism*. London: Duke University Press.

Coole, D., and Frost, S. (2010). *New Materialisms: Ontology, Agency, and Politics*. London: Duke University Press.

Cornell, D., and Seely, S. (2016). *The Spirit of Revolution: Beyond the Dead Ends of Man*. Cambridge: Polity Press.

Coulthard, G. (2007). 'Subjects of Empire: Indigenous Peoples and the "Politics of Recognition" in Canada', *Contemporary Political Theory* 6(4): 437–60.

Coulthard, G. (2014). *Red Skins, White Masks: Rejecting the Colonial Politics of Recognition*. Minneapolis: University of Minnesota Press.

Crawford, K., Faleiros, G., Luers, A., Meier, P., Perlich, C., and Thorp, J. (2013). *Big Data, Communities and Ethical Resilience: A Framework for Action*, 24 October. Available at: http://poptech.org/sys- tem/uploaded_files/66/original/BellagioFramework.pdf.

Crowdy, J. (2017). 'Queer Undergrowth: Weeds and Sexuality in the Architecture of the Garden', *Architecture and Culture* 5(3): 423–33.

Crutzen, P. J. (2002). 'Geology of Mankind', *Nature* 415: 23.

Crutzen, P. J., and Steffen, W. (2003). 'How Long Have We Been in the Anthropocene Era?' *Climatic Change* 61: 251–57.

Crutzen, P. J., and Stoermer, E. (2000). 'The "Anthropocene"', *Global Change News* 41: 17–18.

Cuiscanqui, S. R. (2012). 'Ch'ixinakax utxiwa: A Reflection on the Practices and Discourses of Decolonization', *The South Atlantic Quarterly* 111(1): 95–109.

Dalby, S. (2017). 'Autistic Geopolitics/Anthropocene Therapy', *Public Imagination* 10(42), 22 June. Available at: www.21global.ucsb.edu/global-e/june-2017/autistic-geopolitics-anthropocene-therapy.

Dallmayr, F. (2010). *The Promise of Democracy: Political Agency and Transformation*. New York: State University of New York Press.

Dana, K. O. (2004). 'Áillohaš and His Image Drum: The Native Poet as Shaman', *Nordlit* 15(1): 7–33.

Danowski, D., and Viveiros de Castro, E. (2017). *The Ends of the World*. Cambridge: Polity.

Davies, J. (2016). *The Birth of the Anthropocene*. Oakland, CA: University of California Press.

Davis, H., and Todd, Z. (2017). 'On the Importance of a Date, or, Decolonizing the Anthropocene', *ACME: An International Journal for Critical Geographies* 16(4): 761–80.

de Coning, C. (2016). 'From Peacebuilding to Sustaining Peace: Implications of Complexity for Resilience and Sustainability', *Resilience: International Policies, Practices and Discourses* 4(3): 166–81.

de la Cadena, M. (2010). 'Indigenous Cosmopolitics in the Andes: Conceptual Reflections beyond "Politics"', *Cultural Anthropology* 25(2): 334–70.

de la Cadena, M. (2015). 'Uncommoning Nature', *e-Flux journal 56th Biennale*, 22 August. Available at: http://supercommunity.e-flux.com/texts/uncommoning-nature/.

de la Cadena, M., and Blaser, M. (eds). (2018). *A World of Many Worlds*. London: Duke University Press.

de la Cadena, M., Lien, M. E., Blaser, M., Jensen, C. B., Lea, T., Morita, A., Swanson, H., Ween, G. B., West, P., and Wiener, M. (2015). 'Anthropology and STS Generative Interfaces, Multiple Locations', *Hau: Journal of Ethnographic Theory* 5(1): 437–75.

DeLanda, M. (2006). *A New Philosophy of Society: Assemblage Theory and Social Complexity*. London: Continuum.

Demos, T. J. (2017). *Against the Anthropocene: Visual Culture and Environment Today*. Berlin: Sternberg Press.

Denby, D. (2016). 'The Limits of "Grit"', *The New Yorker*, 21 June. Available at: https://www.newyorker.com/culture/culture-desk/the-limits-of-grit.

Descola, P. (2013a). *Beyond Nature and Culture*. Chicago: University of Chicago Press.

Descola, P. (2013b). *The Ecology of Others*. Chicago: Prickly Paradigm Press.

de Sousa Santos, B. (2016). *Epistemologies of the South: Justice against Epistemicide*. Abingdon: Routledge.

Dillon, M., and Reid, J. (2009). *The Liberal Way of War: Killing to Make Life Live*. London and New York: Routledge.

Duckworth, A. L. (2016). *Grit: The Power of Passion and Perseverance*. New York: Scribner.

Dupuy, J-P. (1999). 'Philosophy and Cognition: Historical Roots', in J. Petitot, F. J. Varela, B. Pachoud, and J.-M. Roy (eds.), *Naturalizing Phenomenology: Issues in Contemporary Phenomenology and Cognitive Science*. Stanford, CA: Stanford University Press.

Ebron, P., and Tsing, A. (2017). 'Feminism and the Anthropocene: Assessing the Field through Recent Books', *Feminist Studies* 43(3): 658–83.

Escobar, A. (2016). 'Thinking-Feeling with the Earth: Territorial Struggles and the Ontological Dimension of the Epistemologies of the South', *Revista de Antropología Iberoamericana* 11(1): 11–32.

Evans, B., and Reid, J. (2014). *Resilient Life: The Art of Living Dangerously*. Cambridge, UK: Polity Press.

Federici, S. (2012). *Revolution at Point Zero: Housework, Reproduction and Feminist Struggle*. Oakland, CA: PM Press.

First People's Worldwide. (n.d.). 'Who Are Indigenous Peoples: How Our Societies Work', *First People's Worldwide*. Available at: http://firstpeoples.org/who-are-indigenous-peoples/how-our-societies-work.

Fishel, S. R. (2017). *The Microbial State: Global Thriving and the Body Politic*. Minneapolis: University of Minnesota Press.

Fisher, M. (2018). 'Foreword', in W. Davies (ed.), *Economic Science Fictions*. London: Goldsmiths Press, xi–xiv.

Forest Peoples Programme. (2018). November Newsletter, *Forest Peoples Programme*, 1 November. Email communication.

Gabay, C. (2018). *Imagining Africa: Whiteness and the Western Gaze*. Cambridge: Cambridge University Press.

Gaski, H. (1997). 'Introduction: Sami Culture in a New Era', in H. Gaski (ed.), *Sami Culture in a New Era: The Norwegian Sami Experience*. Karasjok: Davvi Girji, 9–28.

Gaski, H. (2010). 'Nils-Aslak Valkeapaa: Indigenous Voice and Multimedia Artist', in A. Ryall, J. Schimanski, and H. H. Waerp (eds.). *Arctic Discourses*. Newcastle Upon Tyne: Cambridge Scholars Publishing, 301–28.

Gaski, H. (2011). 'Song, Poetry and Images in Writing: Sami Literature', *Nordlit* 27: 33–54.

Ghosh, A. (2016). *The Great Derangement: Climate Change and the Unthinkable*. Chicago: University of Chicago Press.

Graham, J., Gibson, K., and Roelvink G. (2010). 'An Economic Ethics for the Anthropocene', *Antipode* 41, s1: 320–46.

Graham, M. (2008). 'Some Thoughts about the Philosophical Underpinnings of Aboriginal Worldviews', *Australian Humanities Review* 45. Available at: http://www.australianhumanitiesreview.org/archive/Issue-November-2008/graham.html.

Granville Miller, B. (2003). *Invisible Indigenes: The Politics of Nonrecognition*. Lincoln and London: University of Nebraska Press.

Gratton, P. (2014). *Speculative Realism: Problems and Prospects*. London: Bloosmbury.

Grosz, E. (2011). *Becoming Undone: Darwinian Reflections on Life, Politics, and Art*. London: Duke University Press.

Grosz, E. (2017). *The Incorporeal: Ontology, Ethics, and the Limits of Materialism*. New York: Columbia University Press.

Grusin, R. (2017). 'Introduction: Anthropocene Feminism: An Experiment in Collaborative Theorizing', in R. Grusin (ed.), *Anthropocene Feminism*. Minneapolis: University of Minnesota Press, xii–xix.

Gursoz, A. (2017). 'Meet Ernesto Yerena Montejano: Artist Behind Ubiquitous "We Are Resilient" Poster', *ColourLines*, 13 February. Available at: https://www.colorlines.com/content/meet-ernesto-yerena-montejano-artist-behind-ubiquitous-we-resilient-protest-poster.

Halpern, O. (2014). *Beautiful Data: A History of Vision and Reason since 1945*. Durham: Duke University Press.

Hamilton, C. (2013). *Earthmasters: The Dawn of the Age of Climate Engineering*. London: Yale University Press.

Hamilton, C. (2015). 'Human Destiny in the Anthropocene', in C. Hamilton, C. Bonneuil, and F. Gemenne (eds.), *The Anthropocene and the Global Environmental Crisis: Rethinking Modernity in a New Epoch*. Abingdon: Routledge, 32–43.

Hamilton, S. (2017). 'Securing Ourselves from Ourselves? The Paradox of "Entanglement" in the Anthropocene', *Crime, Law and Social Change*, 29 July.

Haraway, D. (1988). 'Situated Knowledges: The Science Question in Feminism and the Privilege of Partial Perspective', *Feminist Studies* 14(3): 575–99.

Haraway, D. (1989). *Primate Visions: Gender, Race, and Nature in the World of Modern Science*. New York: Routledge.

Haraway, D. (2015). 'Anthropocene, Capitalocene, Plantationocene, Chthulucene: Making Kin', *Environmental Humanities* 6: 159–65.

Haraway, D. (2016). *Staying with the Trouble: Making Kin in the Chthulucene*. Durham: Duke University Press.

Haraway, D. (2018). 'Making Kin in the Chthulucene: Reproducing Multispecies Justice', in A. E. Clarke and D. Haraway (eds.), *Making Kin Not Population*. Chicago: Prickly Paradigm Press, 67–99.

Harman, G. (2005). *Guerrilla Metaphysics: Phenomenology and the Carpentry of Things*. Chicago: Open Court.

Harman, G. (2010). *Towards Speculative Realism: Essays and Lectures*. Winchester: Zero Books.

Harvey, D. (2005). *A Brief History of Neoliberalism*. Oxford: Oxford University Press.

Harvey, D. (2013). *The New Imperialism*. Oxford: Oxford University Press.

Hautala-Hirvioja, T. (2015). 'Reflections of the Past: A Meeting between Sámi Cultural Heritage and Contemporary Finnish Sámi', in T. Jokela and G. Coutts (eds.), *Relate North: Art, Heritage and Identity*. Rovaniemi: University of Lapland Press, 78–97.

Hayles, K. (1999). *How We Became Posthuman: Virtual Bodies in Cybernetics, Literature, and Informatics*. Chicago: University of Chicago Press.

Head, L., Atchison, J., Phillips, C., and Buckingham, K. (2014). 'Vegetal Politics: Belonging, Practices, and Places', *Social & Cultural Geography* 15(8): 861–70.

Hiwasaki, L., Luna, E., Syamsidik, and Shaw, R. (2014). *Local & Indigenous Knowledge for Community Resilience: Hydro-meteorological Disaster Risk Reduction and Climate Change Adaptation in Coastal and Small Island Communities*. Jakarta: UNESCO.

Holbraad, M. and Pedersen, M. (2017). *The Ontological Turn: An Anthropological Exposition*. Cambridge: Cambridge University Press.

Holmberg, N., and Laiti, J. (2015). 'The Saami Manifesto 15: Reconnecting Through Resistance', *IdleNoMore*, 23 March. Available at: http://www.idlenomore.ca/the_ saami_manifesto_15_reconnecting_through_resistance_the_saami_manifesto_15_ reconnecting_through_resistance.

Hunt, S., and Holmes, C. (2015) 'Everyday Decolonization: Living a Decolonizing Queer Politics', *Journal of Lesbian Studies* 19(2): 154–72.

Inayatullah, N., and Blaney, D. L. (2004). *International Relations and the Problem of Difference*. New York: Routledge.

Intergovernmental Panel on Climate Change (IPCC). (2007). *Contribution of Working Groups I, II and III to the Fourth Assessment Report of the Intergovernmental Panel on Climate Change*. Geneva: IPCC.

Intergovernmental Panel on Climate Change (IPCC). (2010). *Review of the IPCC Processes and Procedures, Report by the InterAcademy Council (IPCC–XXXII/ Doc. 7), 32nd Session, Busan, Seoul, 11–14 October 2010*. Geneva: IPCC.

Irigaray, L., and Marder, M. (2016). *Through Vegetal Being: Two Philosophical Perspectives*. New York: Columbia University Press.

Jackson, M. (2014). 'Composing Postcolonial Geographies: Postconstructivism, Ecology and Overcoming Ontologies of Critique', *Singapore Journal of Tropical Geography* 35(1): 72–87.

Joseph, J. (2013). 'Resilience as Embedded Neoliberalism: A Governmentality Approach', *Resilience: International Policies, Practices and Discourses* 1(1): 38–52.

Jung, C. (2008). *The Moral Force of Indigenous Politics: Critical Liberalism and the Zapatistas*. Cambridge: Cambridge University Press.

Junka-Aikio, L. (2018). 'Indigenous Culture Jamming: Suohpanterror and the Articulation of Sami Political Community', *Journal of Aesthetics & Culture* 10: 1–14.

Kandel, E. R. (2012). *The Age of Insight: The Quest to Understand the Unconscious in Art, Mind and Brain, From Vienna 1900 to the Present*. New York: Random House.

Kauanui, J. K. (2016). '"A Structure, Not an Event": Settler Colonialism and Enduring Indigeneity', *Lateral: Journal of the Cultural Studies Association* 5(1). Available at: http://csalateral.org/issue/5-1/forum-alt-humanities-settler-colonialism-enduring-indigeneity-kauanui/.

Kay, L. E. (2000). *Who Wrote the Book of Life? A History of the Genetic Code*. Stanford: Stanford University Press.

Kilibarda, K. (2012). 'Lessons from #Occupy in Canada: Contesting Space, Settler Consciousness and Erasures within the 99%', *Journal of Critical Globalisation Studies* (5): 24–41.

Kimmerer, R. W. (2013). *Braiding Sweetgrass: Indigenous Wisdom, Scientific Knowledge and the Teachings of Plants*. Minneapolis: Milkweed Editions.

Kitchin, R. (2014). *The Data Revolution: Big Data, Open Data, Data Infrastructures & Their Consequences*. London: Sage.

Kohn, E. (2013). *How Forests Think: Toward an Anthropology beyond the Human*. Berkley, CA: University of California Press.

Kohn, E. (2017). 'Leaving the Forest', in A.-S. Springer and E. Turpin (eds.), *The Word for World Is Still Forest*. Berlin: K. Verlag & Haus der Kulturen der Welt, 158–68.

Kuokkanen, R. (2007). *Reshaping the University: Responsibility, Indigenous Epistemes, and the Logic of the Gift*. Vancouver: UBC Press.

Lansing, J. S. (2006). *Perfect Order: Recognizing Complexity in Bali*. Princeton: Princeton University Press.

Lantman, M. V. S., Mackus, M., Otten, L. S., de Kruijff, D., van de Loo, A. J. A. E., Kraneveld, A. D., et al. (2017). 'Mental Resilience, Perceived Immune Functioning, and Health', *Journal of Multidisciplinary Healthcare* 10: 107–11.

Larkey, M. (2017). 'From Occupy to Standing Rock: Paths Forward', *LA Review of Books*, 2 April. Available at: https://lareviewofbooks.org/article/from-occupy-to-standing-rock-paths-forward/#!

Latour, B. (1993). *We Have Never Been Modern*. Cambridge, MA: Harvard University Press.

Latour, B. (1996). 'Not the Question', *Anthropology Newsletter* 37(3): 1–6.

Latour, B. (2004). *Politics of Nature: How to Bring the Sciences into Democracy.* Cambridge, MA: Harvard University Press.

Latour, B. (2009). 'Perspectivism: "Type" or "Bomb"', *Anthropology Today* 25(2): 1–2.

Latour, B. (2010). *On the Modern Cult of the Factish Gods.* Durham, NC: Duke University Press.

Latour, B. (2013). *Facing Gaia, Six Lectures on the Political Theology of Nature: Being the Gifford Lectures on Natural Religion, Edinburgh, 18th–28th of February 2013* (draft version 1–3–13).

Latour, B. (2014). 'Agency at the time of the Anthropocene', *New Literary History* 45: 1–18.

Latour, B. (2018a). *Down to Earth: Politics in a New Climatic Regime.* Cambridge: Polity Press.

Latour, B. (2018b). 'Down to Earth Social Movements: An Interview with Bruno Latour', *Social Movement Studies* 17(3): 353–61.

Latour, B., Harman, G., and Erdélyi, P. (2011). *The Prince and the Wolf: Latour and Harman at the LSE.* Winchester: Zero Books.

Latour, B., and Leclercq, C. (eds.). (2016). *Reset Modernity!* New York: MIT Press.

Latour, B., and Woolgar, S. (1986). *Laboratory Life: The Construction of Scientific Facts.* Princeton, NJ: Princeton University Press.

Law, J. (2015). 'What's Wrong with a One-World World?' *Distinktion: Scandinavian Journal of Social Theory* 16(1): 126–39.

Lazzarato, M. (2014). *Signs and Machines: Capitalism and the Production of Subjectivity.* South Pasadena, CA: Semiotext(e).

Lea, T. (2012). 'Contemporary Anthropologies of Indigenous Australia', *Annual Review of Anthropology* 41: 187–202.

Lear, J. (2006). *Radical Hope: Ethics in the Face of Cultural Devastation.* Cambridge, MA: Harvard University Press.

Lederman, S. (2016). 'Making the Desert Bloom: Hannah Arendt and Zionist Discourse', *The European Legacy* 21(4): 1–15.

Lee, D. (1950). 'Notes on the Conception of the Self among the Wintu Indians', *The Journal of Abnormal and Social Psychology* 45(3): 538–43.

Lindroth, M., and Sinevaara-Niskanen, H. (2018). *Global Politics and its Violent Care for Indigeneity.* Cham, Switzerland: Palgrave.

Ling, L. H. M. (2002). *Postcolonial International Relations: Conquest and Desire between Asia and the West.* London: Palgrave.

Locke, J. (2005). *Second Treatise of Government.* Oxford: Oxford University Press.

Lorimer, J. (2015). *Wildlife in the Anthropocene: Conservation after Nature.* Minneapolis: University of Minnesota Press.

Losurdo, D. (2016). *Liberalism: A Counter-History.* London and New York: Verso Press.

Macfarlane, R. (2016). 'Generation Anthropocene: How Humans Have Altered the Planet for Ever', *Guardian*, 1 April. Available at: www.theguardian.com/books/2016/apr/01/generation-anthropocene-altered-planet-for-ever.

Mac Ginty, R. (2008). 'Indigenous Peace-Making Versus the Liberal Peace', *Cooperation and Conflict* 43(2): 139–63.

Magga, O. H. (2006). 'Diversity in Saami Terminology for Reindeer, Snow and Ice', *International Social Science Journal* 58(187): 25–34.

Marder, M. (2012). 'Resist Like a Plant! On the Vegetal Life of Political Movements', *Peace Studies Journal* 5(1): 24–32.

Marder, M. (2013). *Plant-Thinking: A Philosophy of Vegetal Life*. New York: Columbia University Press.

Marres, N. (2012). *Material Participation: Technology, the Environment and Everyday Politics*. Basingstoke: Palgrave Macmillan.

Marx, K. (1976). *Capital: Volume One*. London: Penguin.

Mayer-Schonberger, V., and Cukier, K. (2013). *Big Data: A Revolution That Will Transform How We Live, Work and Think*. London: John Murray.

McKenna, B. (2016). 'Analytics Is Not Just about Patterns in Big Data', *Computer Weekly.com*, 11 November. Available at: http://www.computerweekly.com/blog/Data-Matters/Analytics-is-not-just-about-patterns-in-big-data.

Meier, P. (2013). 'How to Create Resilience Through Big Data', *iRevolutions*, 11 January. Available at: https://irevolutions.org/2013/01/11/disaster-resilience-2-0/.

Meillassoux, Q. (2008). *After Finitude: An Essay on the Necessity of Contingency*. London: Continuum.

Mignolo, W. (2011) *The Darker Side of Western Modernity: Global Futures, Decolonial Options*. Durham: Duke University Press.

Mignolo, W. (2013). 'On Plurversality', *waltermignolo.com*. Available at: http://waltermignolo.com/on-pluriversality/.

Mignolo, W. (2015). 'Foreword: Yes, We Can', in Hamid Dabashi, *Can Non-Europeans Think*. London: Zed Books, viii–xlii.

Mol, A. (2002). *The Body Multiple: Ontology in Medical Practice*. Durham, NC: Duke University Press.

Moore, J. W. (2015). *Capitalism in the Web of Life: Ecology and the Accumulation of Capital*. London: Verso.

Moreton-Robinson, A. (2015). *The White Possessive: Property, Power and Indigenous Sovereignty*. Minneapolis: University of Minnesota Press.

Morozov, E. (2013). *To Save Everything Click Here: Technology, Solutionism and the Urge to Fix Problems That Don't Exist*. London: Allen Lane/Penguin.

Morton, T. (2009). *Ecology without Nature: Rethinking Environmental Aesthetics*. Cambridge, MA: Harvard University Press.

Morton, T. (2013). *Hyperobjects: Philosophy and Ecology after the End of the World*. Minneapolis: Univerity of Minnesota Press.

Morton, T. (2017). *Humankind: Solidarity with Nonhuman People*. London: Verso.

Murphy, M. (2018). 'Against Population, Towards Alterlife', in A. E. Clarke and D. Haraway (eds.), *Making Kin Not Population*. Chicago: Prickly Paradigm Press, 101–24.

Myers, N. (2015). 'Conversations on Plant Sensing: Notes from the Field', *Nature-Culture* 3: 35–66.

Myers, N. (2017a). 'From the Anthropocene to the Planthroposcene: Designing Gardens for Plant/People Involution', *History and Anthropology* 28(3): 297–301.

Myers, N. (2017b). 'Ungrid-able Ecologies: Decolonizing the Ecological Sensorium in a 10,000-Year-Old NaturalCultural Happening', *Catalyst: Feminism, Theory, Technoscience* 3(2): 1–24.

Nakashima, D., McLean, K. G., Thulstrup, H., Castillo, A. R., and Rubis, J. (2012). *Weathering Uncertainty: Traditional Knowledge for Climate Change Assessment and Adaptation*. Paris: UNESCO.

Native Council of Nova Scotia. (2018). 'Our Perseverance'. Available at: https://ncns.ca/our-perseverance/.

Needham, R. (1978). *Primordial Characters*. Charlottesville: University Press of Virginia.

Nelson, S., and Braun, B. (2017). 'Autonomia in the Anthropocene: New Challenges to Radical Politics', *South Atlantic Quarterly* 116(2): 223–35.

Neves Marques, P. (2017). 'Mimetic Traps: Forest, Images, World', in A.-S. Springer and E. Turpin (eds.), *The Word for World Is Still Forest*. Berlin: K. Verlag & Haus der Kulturen der Welt, 21–38.

Nietzsche, F. (1990). *The Anti-Christ*. London: Penguin.

Nichols, R. (2017). 'Theft Is Property! The Recursive Logic of Dispossession', *Political Theory* 46(1): 3–28.

Palecek, M., and Risjord, M. (2013). 'Relativism and the Ontological Turn within Anthropology', *Philosophy of the Social Sciences* 43(1): 3–23.

Pasternak, S. (2015). 'How Capitalism Will Save Colonialism: The Privatization of Reserve Lands in Canada', *Antipode* 47(1): 179–96.

Pechenkina, E. (2017). 'Persevering, Educating and Influencing a Change: A Case Study of Australian Aboriginal and Torres Strait Islander Narratives of Academic Success', *Critical Studies in Education*, 1–17.

Pedri-Spade, C. (2014). 'Nametoo: Evidence That He/She Is/Was Present', *Decolonization: Indigeneity, Education & Society* 3(1): 73–100.

Persaud, R. B., and Walker, R. B. J. (2015). 'Introduction: Race, De-Coloniality and International Relations', *Alternatives: Global, Local, Political* 40(2): 83–84.

Pickering, A. (2010). *The Cybernetic Brain: Sketches of Another Future*. Chicago: University of Chicago Press.

Plato. (1993). *Sophist*. Indianapolis: Hackett.

Polanyi, K. (2001). *The Great Transformation: The Political and Economic Origins of Our Time*. Boston: Beacon Press.

Povinelli, E. (2011). *Economies of Abandonment: Social Belonging and Endurance in Late Liberalism*. Durham: Duke University Press.

Povinelli, E. (2012). 'The Will to Be Otherwise/The Effort of Endurance', *South Atlantic Quarterly* 111(3): 453–75.

Povinelli, E. (2015). 'The Rhetorics of Recognition in Geontopower', *Philosophy & Rhetoric* 48(4): 428–42.

Povinelli, E. (2016a). *Geontologies: A Requiem to Late Liberalism*. Durham: Duke University Press.

Povinelli, E. (2016b). 'The World Is Flat and Other Super Weird Ideas', in K. Behar (ed.), *Object-Oriented Feminism*. Minneapolis: University of Minnesota Press, 107–21.

Proctor, J. D. (2013). 'Saving Nature in the Anthropocene', *Journal of Environmental Studies and Sciences* 3: 83–92.

Prosper, K., McMillan, L. J., Davis, A. A., and Moffitt, M. (2011). 'Returning to Netukulimk: Mi'kmaq Cultural and Spiritual Connections with Resource Stewardship and Self Governance', *The International Indigenous Policy Journal* 2(4): 1–16.

Puig de la Bellacasa, M. (2017). *Matters of Care: Speculative Ethics in More Than Human Worlds*. Minneapolis: University of Minnesota Press.

Purdy, J. (2015). *After Nature: A Politics for the Anthropocene*. Cambridge, MA: Harvard University Press.

Quijano, A. (2000). 'Coloniality of Power, Eurocentrism, and Latin America', *Nepantla: Views from South* 1(3): 533–80.

Ramalingam, B. (2013). *Aid on the Edge of Chaos*. Oxford: Oxford University Press.

Ramos, A. R. (2012). 'The Politics of Perspectivism', *Annual Review of Anthropology* 41: 481–94.

Randazzo, E. (2016). 'The Paradoxes of the Everyday: Scrutinizing the Local Turn in Peace Building', *Third World Quarterly* 37(8): 1351–70.

Rathwell, K., and Armitage, D. (2016). 'Art and Artistic Processes Bridge Knowledge Systems about Social-Ecological Change: An Empirical Examination with Inuit Artists from Nunavut, Canada', *Ecology and Society* 21(2): 21.

Raygorodetsky, G. (2017). *The Archipelago of Hope: Wisdom and Resilience form the Edge of Climate Change*. New York: Pegasus Books.

Read, J. (2017). 'Anthropocene and Anthropogenesis: Philosophical Anthropology and the Ends of Man', *South Atlantic Quarterly* 116(2): 257–73.

Reid, J. (2006). 'Life Struggles: War, Discipline and Biopolitics in the Thought of Michel Foucault', *Social Text* 86(1): 127–52.

Reid, J. (2017). 'Cunning and Strategy', *Unbag* 1. Available at: http://unbag.net/issue-1-metis/cunning-strategy/.

Reid, J. (2018a). 'The Cliché of Resilience: Governing Indigeneity in the Arctic', *Arena Journal* 51/52: 10–17.

Reid, J. (2018b). 'Reclaiming Possession: A Critique of the Discourse of Dispossession in Indigenous Studies', *On Culture* 5. https://www.on-culture.org/journal/issue-5/reid-reclaiming-possession/.

Reid, J. (2019). 'Narrating Indigeneity in the Arctic: The Script of Disaster Resilience versus The Poetics of Autonomy', in N. Selheim, Y. Zaika, and I. Kelman (eds.), *Arctic Triumph: Northern Innovation and Persistence*. Cham, Switzerland: Springer.

Revkin, A. C. (2014). 'Exploring Academia's Role in Charting Paths to a "Good" Anthropocene', *New York Times*, 16 June. Available at: https://dotearth.blogs.nytimes.com/2014/06/16/exploring-academias-role-in-charting-paths-to-a-good-anthropocene/.

Rickards, L., Neale, T., and Kearnes, M. (2017). 'Australia's National Climate: Learning to Adapt?', *Geographical Research* 55(4): 469–76.

Rist, L., Felton, A., Nystrom, M., Troell, M., Sponseller, R. A., Bengtsson, J., et al. (2014). 'Applying Resilience Thinking to Production Ecosystems', *Ecosphere*, 5(6), article 73.

Rival, L. (2009). 'The Resilience of Indigenous Intelligence', in Kirsten Hastrup (ed.), *The Question of Resilience: Social Responses to Climate Change*. Copenhagen: The Royal Danish Academy of Sciences and Letters, 293–313.

Rodin, J. (2015). *The Resilience Dividend: Managing Disruption, Avoiding Disaster, and Growing Stronger in an Unpredictable World*. London: Profile Books.

Rogers, P. (2015). 'Researching Resilience: An Agenda for Change', *Resilience: International Policies, Practices and Discourses* 3(1): 55–71.

Rojas, C. (2016). 'Contesting the Colonial Logics of the International: Toward a Relational Politics for the Pluriverse', *International Political Sociology* 10(4): 369–82.

Rosenow, D. (2018). *Un-Making Environmental Activism: Beyond Modern/Colonial Binaries in the GMO Controversy*. Abingdon: Routledge.

Ross, A. (1855). *The Fur Hunters of the Far West: A Narrative of Adventures in the Oregon and Rocky Mountains*. London: Smith Elder and Co.

Rousseau, J.-J. (1997). 'Discourse on the Origin and the Foundations of Inequality among Men', in J.-J. Rousseau, *The Discourses and Other Early Political Writings*. Cambridge: Cambridge University Press, 111–88.

Rubis, J. M., and Theriault, N. (2019). 'Concealing Protocols: Conservation, Indigenous Survivance, and the Dilemmas of Visibility', *Social & Cultural Geography* 4 February).

Sahlins, M. (1999). 'What Is Anthropological Enlightenment? Some Lessons of the Twentieth Century', *Annual Review of Anthropology* 28: i–xxiii.

Salazar, J.-F., and Cordova, A. (2008). 'Imperfect Media and the Poetics of Indigenous Video in South America', in P. Wilson and M. Stewart (eds.), *Global Indigenous Media: Cultures, Poetics and Politics*. Durham: Duke University Press.

Sandilands, C. (2017). 'Fear of a Queer Plant?', *Journal of Lesbian and Gay Studies* 23(3): 419–29.

Schmidt, J. (2013). 'The Empirical Falsity of the Human Subject: New Materialism, Climate Change and the Shared Critique of Artifice', *Resilience: International Policies, Practices and Discourses* 1(3): 174–92.

Sedgwick, E. K. (1996). 'Introduction: Queerer Than Fiction', *Studies in the Novel* 28(3): 277–80.

Serres, M. (1995). *The Natural Contract*. Ann Arbor: University of Michigan Press.

Sharp, H. (2011). *Spinoza and the Politics of Renaturalization*. Chicago, IL: Chicago University Press

Shilliam, R. (2015). *The Black Pacific: Anti-Colonial Struggles and Oceanic Connections*. London: Bloomsbury.

Simpson, A. (2014). *Mohawk Interruptus: Political Life across the Borders of Settler States*. Durham: Duke University Press.

Simpson, L. B. (2017). *As We Have Always Done: Indigenous Freedom through Radical Resistance*. Minneapolis: University of Minnesota Press.

Sissons, J. (2005). *First Peoples: Indigenous Cultures and their Futures*. London: Reaktion Books.

Skafish, P. (2014). 'Introduction', in E Viveiros de Castro, *Cannibal Metaphysics: For a Post-Structural Anthropology*. Minneapolis: Univocal Publishing, 9–33.

Sloterdijk, P. (2013). *In the World Interior of Capital*. Cambridge: Polity Press.

Smith, A. (2010). 'Queer Theory and Native Studies: The Heteronormativity of Settler Colonialism', *GLQ: A Journal of Lesbian and Gay Studies* 16(1): 44.

Smith, L. T. (2012). *Decolonizing Methodologies: Research and Indigenous Peoples*. London: Zed Books.

Solnit, R. (2017). *A Field Guide to Getting Lost*. Edinburgh: Canongate.

Spinoza, B. (1972). *Ethics*. London: Heron Books.

Spivak, G. C. (1993). 'Can the Subaltern Speak?' in Laura Chrisman and Patrick Williams (eds.), *Colonial Discourse and Postcolonial Theory: A Reader*. New York: Harvester Wheatsheaf, 66–111.

Steadman, I. (2013). 'Big Data and the Death of the Theorist', *Wired Magazine*, 25 January. Available at: http://www.wired.co.uk/news/archive/2013-01/25/big-data-end-of-theory.

Steffen, W., Å. Persson, L. Deutsch, J. Zalasiewicz, M. Williams, K. Richardson, C. Crumley, P. Crutzen, C. Folke, L. Gordon, M. Molina, V. Ramanathan, J. Rockström, M. Scheffer, H. Joachim Schellnhuber, and U. Svedin (2011). 'The Anthropocene: From Global Change to Planetary Stewardship', *Ambio* 40(7): 739–61.

Stiegler, B. (2018). *The Neganthropocene*. London: Open Humanities Press.

Stengers, I. (2015). *In Catastrophic Times: Resisting the Coming Barbarism*. Paris: Open Humanities Press.

Stengers, I. (2017). 'Autonomy and the Intrusion of Gaia', *South Atlantic Quarterly* 116(2): 381–400.

Stockholm Resilience Centre. (2014). 'The Hidden Cost of Coerced Resilience: Centre Researchers Look into Forced Resilience of Intensive Agriculture, Forestry, Fisheries and Aquaculture Systems', *Stockholm Resilience Centre*, 29 November. Available at: https://www.stockholmresilience.org/research/research-news/2014-11-29-the-hidden-cost-of-coerced-resilience.html.

Stockholm Resilience Centre. (2017). 'The Nine Planetary Boundaries', *Stockholm Resilience Centre*. Available at: www.stockholmresilience.org/research/planetary-boundaries/planetary-boundaries/about-the-research/the-nine-planetary-boundaries.html.

Svensson, T. G. (1978). 'Culture Communication and Sami Ethnic Awareness', *Ethnos: Journal of Anthropology* 43(3-4): 213–35.

Swyngedouw, E. (2011). 'Whose Environment? The End of Nature, Climate Change and the Process of Post-Politicization', *Ambiente & Sociedade* 14(2). Available at: www.scielo.br/scielo.php?script=sci_arttext&pid=S1414-753X2011000200006.

Tallbear, K. (2013). *Native American DNA: Tribal Belonging and the False Promise of Genetic Science*. Minneapolis: University of Minnesota Press.

Tallbear, K. (2018). 'Making Love and Relations: Beyond Settler Sex and Family', in A. E. Clarke and D. Haraway (eds.), *Making Kin Not Population*. Chicago: Prickly Paradigm Press, 145–64.

Taussing, M. (2018). *Palma Africana*. Chicago: University of Chicago Press.

Tavares, P. (2013). 'The Geological Imperative: On the Political Ecology of the Amazonia's Deep History', in E. Turpin (ed.), *Architecture in the Anthropocene: Encounters among Design, Deep Time, Science and Philosophy*. Ann Arbor: Open Humanities Press, 207–39.

Tavares, P. (2017). 'The Political Nature of the Forest: A Botanic Archaeology of Genocide', in A.-S. Springer and E. Turpin (eds.), *The Word for World Is Still Forest*. Berlin: K. Verlag & Haus der Kulturen der Welt, 125–57.

Tierney, K. (2015). 'Resilience and the Neoliberal Project: Discourses, Critiques, Practices-And Katrina', *American Behavioural Scientist* 59(10): 1327–42.

Todd, Z. (2015). 'Indigenizing the Anthropocene', in H. Davies and E. Turpin (eds.), *Art in the Anthropocene: Encounters among Aesthetics, Politics, Environments and Epistemologies*. London: Open Humanities Press, 241–54.

Todd, Z. (2016). 'An Indigenous Feminist's Take on the Ontological Turn: "Ontology" Is Just Another Word for Colonialism', *Journal of Historical Sociology* 29(1): 4–22.

Toulmin, S. (1990). *Cosmopolis: The Hidden Agenda of Modernity*. Chicago: University of Chicago Press.

Townsend, A. M. (2013). *Smart Cities: Big Data, Civic Hackers, and the Quest for a New Utopia*. New York: W. W. Norton & Co.

Tsing, A. L. (2014). 'Strathern beyond the Human: Testimony to the Spore', *Theory, Culture & Society* 31(2/3): 221–41.

Tsing, A. L. (2015). *The Mushroom at the End of the World: On the Possibility of Life in Capitalist Ruins*. Princeton: Princeton University Press.

Tsing, A. L. (2017). 'The Buck, the Bull, and the Dream of the Stag: Some Unexpected Weeds of the Anthropocene', *Suomen Anthropologi* 42(1): 3–21.

Tuck, E., and Yang, K. W. (2012). 'Decolonization Is Not a Metaphor', *Decolonization: Indigeneity, Education and Society* 1(1): 1–40.

Tully, J. (1995). *Strange Multiplicity: Constitutionalism in an Age of Diversity*. Cambridge: Cambridge University Press.

Turner, F. (2006). *From Counterculture to Cyberculture: Stewart Brand, the Whole Earth Network, and the Rise of Digital Utopianism*. Chicago: University of Chicago Press.

United Nations Educational, Scientific and Cultural Organization (UNESCO). (2017). *Local Knowledge, Global Goals*. Paris: UNESCO. Available at: http://www.unesco.org/new/fileadmin/MULTIMEDIA/HQ/SC/pdf/ILK_ex_publication_E.pdf.

United Nations Framework Convention on Climate Change (UNFCCC). (2010). *Report of the United Nations Framework Convention on Climate Change Conference of the Parties on Its 16th Session, Cancun, Mexico 29 November–10 December 2010*, Bonn: UNFCCC.

Utsi, P. (1987). '"Snowstorm", "The Hut's Smoke" and "Thought Work"', *The Trumpeter: Voices from the Canadian Eco Philosophical Net Work* 4(3): 17–19.

Verster, J. C., Benson, S., Johnson, S. J., Scholey, A., and Alford, C. (2016). 'Mixing Alcohol with Energy Drink (AMED) and Total Alcohol Consumption: A Systematic Review and Meta-analysis', *Journal of Human Psychopharmacology* 31(1): 2–10.

Viveiros de Castro, E. (2014). *Cannibal Metaphysics: For a Post-Structural Anthropology*. Minneapolis: Univocal Publishing.

Viveiros de Castro, E., and Danowski, D. (2018). 'Humans and Terrans in the Gaia War', in M. de la Cadena and M. Blaser (eds.), *A World of Many Worlds*. London: Duke University Press, 172–203.

Vrasti, W. (2008). 'The Strange Case of Ethnography and International Relations', *Millennium: Journal of International Studies* 37(2): 279–301.

Walker, J., and Cooper, M. (2011). 'Genealogies of Resilience: From Systems Ecology to the Political Economy of Crisis Adaptation', *Security Dialogue* 42(2): 143–60.

Wall, T. (2019). 'The Battle to Save Lapland: 'First, They Took the Religion, Now They Want to Build a Railroad', *Guardian*, 23 February.

Wallace, S. (2018). 'Death of American Missionary Could Put This Indigenous Tribe's Survival at Risk', *National Geographic*. Available at: https://www.nation algeographic.com/culture/2018/11/andaman-islands-tribes/.

Wark, M. (2015). *Molecular Red: Theory for the Anthropocene*. London: Verso.

Weiner, N. (1948). *Cybernetics, or Control and Communication in the Animal and the Machine*. New York: MIT.

White, R. (1995). *The Organic Machine: The Remaking of the Columbia River*. New York: Hill & Wang.

White, R. (2011). *The Middle Ground: Indians, Empires, and Republics in the Great Lakes Region, 1650–1815* (twentieth anniversary edition). New York: Cambridge University Press.

Whitehead, A. N. (1978). *Process and Reality* (corrected edition). New York: The Free Press.

Wiebe, S. M. (2017). 'Emergency Life and Indigenous Resistance: Seeing Indigenous Resistance Through the Prism of Political Ecology', in J. Lawrence and S. M. Wiebe (eds.), *Biopolitical Disaster*. London and New York: Routledge, 139–57.

Wiegman, R. (2014). 'The Times We're In: Queer Feminist Criticism and the Reparative "Turn"', *Feminist Theory* 15(1): 4–25.

Wildcat, M., McDonald, M., Irlbacher-Fox, S., and Coulthard, G. (2014). 'Learning from the Land: Indigenous Land Based Pedagogy and Decolonization', *Decolonization: Indigeneity, Education & Society* 3(3): I–XV.

Williams, C. (2016). 'Unravelling the Subject with Spinoza: Towards a Morphological Analysis of the Scene of Subjectivity', *Contemporary Political Theory* 16(3): 342–62.

Wilson, E. O. (2016). *Half-Earth: Our Planet's Fight for Life*. New York: Liverlight Publishing Corporation.

Wolfendale, P. (2014). *Object-Oriented Philosophy: The Noumenon's New Clothes*. Falmouth: Urbanomic Media.

Working Group on the Anthropocene. (2017). 'What Is the "Anthropocene"?—Current Definition and Status', *Quaternary Stratigraphy*. Available at: https://quaternary.stratigraphy.org/workinggroups/anthropocene/.

World Bank. (2018). *Machine Learning for Disaster Risk Management: A Guidance Note on How Machine Learning Can Be Used for Disaster Risk Management,*

Including Key Definitions, Case Studies, and Practical Considerations for Implementation. Washington, DC: World Bank.

Wynter, S. (2003). 'Unsettling the Coloniality of Being/Power/Truth/Freedom: Towards the Human, After Man, Its Overrepresentation—An Argument', *CR: The New Centennial Review* 3(3): 257–337.

Yarina, L. (2018). 'Your Sea Wall Won't Save You', *Places Journal*, March. Available at: https://placesjournal.org/your-sea-wall-wont-save-you/.

Zentner, A., Gutierrez, R., Bell, E., and Pham, P. (2016). 'Exploring Asian-American/Pacific Islander Student Grit within the Two-Year College System', 2 October. Available at: https://papers.ssrn.com/sol3/papers.cfm?abstract_id=2846623.

Zigon, J. (2014). 'An Ethics of Dwelling and a Politics of World-Building: A Critical Response to Ordinary Ethics', *Journal of the Royal Anthropological Institute* 20(4): 746–64.

Index

actor network theory, 3–5, 45–46, 86, 90–91, 102n3

adaptation: Anthropocene needing, 104; data feedback for, 112; for future, 82; human control and natural, 3, 14; indigenous knowledge and, 4, 115; as no longer possible, 127; ontopolitics for, 17; from resilience, 103; resilience not enabling, 109; speculate about, 125; speculative analytics for, 83, 94–95, 151; Western thought constructed as, 150

Adese, Jennifer, 31

Agamben, Giorgio, 112

Ahmed, Sara, 90, 93

Amerindian perspectivism, 47, 51, 62n3, 68

animals, 116–18, 137

Anthropocene: adaptation and resilience for, 104; 'becoming indigenous' from, 126; from civilization as barbarism, 22n3; coloniser, colonised in, 4; control lost in, 13; ecomodernist theory of "good," 110; as ethnicized, 127; false salvation and, 105; forward thought enabled by, 11–12; geoengineering for good, 10–11; Holocene differentiation from, 5–6, 22nn5–6; human freedom disappearing in, 15; humans and multi-species pluriverse in, 99–100; indigeneity for solving, 1–2, 150–51; indigenous knowledge integrated for, 103; indigenous 'paying attention' for, 97, 121; indigenous people challenging, 134; indigenous speculation from, 13; as leveler, 47; life without modernity in, 9; loss tropes and, 7, 49; microbes and, 101; modernity failure as, 46–47; Morton and philosopher prophet of, 8; multiple resistance forms on, 24–25; nature and culture divide ended with, 61; 'Neganthropocene' and, 7, 114; new ontopolitics and, 13–14, 41; nonhuman agency revival for, 84; no technical fixes for, 10; 'one way of thinking' for, 94; perseverance for supporting, 67; Planthropocene and, 69; posthuman theorists on, 11, 22n9; power regimes governing, 19; precarity embraced in, 12–13, 36; progress and, 10–12, 22n3; resilience needed by, 104; resilience worsening, 103, 106, 108–9, 128; speculative thought not addressing, 123; struggle and blackmail by, 132, 152; Western thought and, 4, 49

About the Authors

David Chandler is Professor of International Relations at the University of Westminster, UK. He was the founding editor of the *Journal of Intervention and Statebuilding* and currently edits the journal *Resilience: International Policies, Practices and Discourses*. His research interests focus on analysis of policy interventions in the international arena, including humanitarianism, statebuilding and the promotion of resilience. He is also interested in contemporary theories challenging the anthropocentrism of modernist thought, particularly in relation to the Anthropocene, the ontopolitics of critique and new technologies, including algorithmic governance, sensorial assemblages and Big Data. He is a major authority in his field and has published around twenty books (authored and edited) and around 200 chapters and journal articles.

Julian Reid is Chair and Professor of International Relations at the University of Lapland, Finland. He is renowned for his advance of the theory of biopolitics, contributions to cultural theory, postcolonial and post-structural thought, critique of liberalism, and seminal deconstruction of resilience. He is co-editor of the journal *Resilience: Policies, Practices and Discourses* (with David Chandler, Melinda Cooper and Bruce Braun). He is a member of the RELATE Center of Excellence, based at the University of Oulu, Finland, and a member of the Advisory Board to the Histories of Violence project.